Antique Trader®

JEWELRY

PRICE GUIDE

2nd Edition

Edited by

Kyle Husfloen

Contributing Editor

Marion Cohen

©2007 Krause Publications

Published by

kp krause publications
A subsidiary of F+W Media, Inc.

700 East State Street • Iola, WI 54990-0001
715-445-2214 • 888-457-2873
www.krausebooks.com

Our toll-free number to place an order or obtain
a free catalog is (800) 258-0929.

Library of Congress Control Number: 2006935580
ISBN 13: 978-0-89689-451-8
ISBN 10: 0-89689-451-7

Designed by Wendy Wendt
Edited by Kyle Husfloen

Printed in China

TABLE OF CONTENTS

INTRODUCTION

Jewelry has held a special place for humankind since prehistoric times, both as an emblem of personal status and as a decorative adornment worn for its sheer beauty. This tradition continues today. We should keep in mind, however, that it was only with the growth of the Industrial Revolution that jewelry first became cheap enough so that even the person of modest means could win a piece or two.

Only since around the mid-19th century did certain forms of jewelry, especially pins and brooches, begin to appear on the general market as a mass-produced commodity and the Victorians took to it immediately. Major production centers for the finest pieces of jewelry remained in Europe, especially Italy and England, but less expensive pieces were also exported to the booming American market and soon some American manufacturers also joined in the trade. Especially during the Civil War era, when silver and gold supplies grew tremendously in the U.S., did jewelry in silver or with silver, brass or gold-filled (i.e. gold-plated or goldplate) mounts begin to flood the market here. By the turn of the 20th century all the major mail-order companies and small town jewelry shops could offer a huge variety of inexpensive jewelry pieces aimed at not only the feminine buyer but also her male counterpart.

As with all types of collectibles, yesterday's trinket can become today's treasure and so it is with jewelry. Today jewelry collecting ranks as one of the most popular areas of collecting and with millions of pieces on the market any collector, no matter what their budget, can find fascinating and attractive jewelry to collect. Of course the finest and rarest examples of antique or "preowned" estate jewelry can run into the many thousands of dollars, but thanks to the mass-production of jewelry over the last century and a half, there is lots for the less well-heeled to enjoy.

Inexpensive jewelry of the late 19th and early 20th century is still widely available and often at modest prices. Even more in demand today is what is called "costume jewelry," that is, well-designed jewelry produced of inexpensive materials and meant to carefully accent a lady's ensemble. The idea was launched in the 1920s by the famous French clothing designer Coco Chanel and her inspiration immediately took root. From that time forward any lady of taste would afford well-designed and attractive pieces which mirrored the glitziest bijoux but were available at a fraction of the cost. Today costume jewelry of the 20th century has become one of the most active areas in the field of collecting and some of the finest pieces, signed by noted designers and manufacturers, can reach price levels nearly equal to much earlier and scarcer examples.

Whether you prefer the glittering and gaudy or the subtle and elegant, jewelry offers the collector a vast realm to choose from. In addition to being an investment the owner also has the opportunity to wear and shade the beauty or whimsy of a piece of our past.

I hope you will enjoy the selection of jewelry pieces we have brought together in this new edition of the *Antique Trader Jewelry Price Guide*. We have divided our listings into several chapters: Antique Jewelry (1800-1920), including a section on American Painted Porcelain Jewelry; Costume Jewelry (19th & 20th Century); Mod Jewelry (1960s-1980s); Modern Jewelry (1920-1960s+), and Twentieth Century Designer & Fine Estate Jewelry. This last chapter is sub-divided into several further sections: Designers; Fine Jewelry Retailers and Miscellaneous Pieces of Estate Jewelry. Included in both the Antique and Modern sections are also listed a selection of both pocket watches and wristwatches.

For the detailed listings and photographs in the Costume Jewelry section I owe a great debt of thanks to Contributing Editor Marion Cohen. Marion has collected and dealt in fine Costume Jewelry for many years and has also other several books on the subject. My sincere thanks to Marion for her major contribution to this updated reference.

In addition to Marion Cohen's contributions, I'd like to thank Dorothy Kamm, author and authority on American Hand-painted Porcelain, who shares a selection of antique painted porcelain pieces here. Also, Dana Cain, expert on all things Mid-Century Modern, has also provided me with a variety of "Mod" style jewelry pieces, the colorful and unique pieces so popular with the "in crowd" of the 1960s and 1970s. I also need to offer my special thanks to the people of the noted auction house, Skinner, Inc., of Bolton and Boston, Massachusetts. They graciously shared their extensive photo archives of fine jewelry of various periods based on many of their recent specialty jewelry auctions. Finally, thanks also to my part-time assistant, Torsten Kerr, who worked very hard to help coordinate the wealth of material that came in for this project.

In preparing our listings I have done my best to provide detailed and accurate descriptions of pieces included but as always the reader should use the prices listed only as a **guide.** Jewelry prices, as in every other major collecting field, are influenced by a number of factors including local demand, quality, condition and rarity. As market prices have risen in recent years it has become even more important for the collector to shop and buy with care. Learn as much as you can about your favorite area of jewelry and keep abreast of market trends and stay alert to warnings about alterations, repairs or reproductions that can be found on the market. Use this book as a reference and general guide to broaden your understanding and appreciation of the wonderful world of jewelry collecting and it can serve you well.

Good luck and happy collecting!

Kyle Husfloen, Editor

<u>Special Note from Marion Cohen</u>

My thankful appreciation to those who so generously allowed their costume jewelry collections to be catalogued and photographed for this book: Davida Baron, Paula Beck, Mary Ann Bosshart, Doris Skarka and Shirley Dreyer.

A special thank you to my photographer Robert Cohen for his beautiful costume jewelry photographs and my editor Kyle Husfloen for his excellent suggestions.

Please note: Though listings have been double checked and every effort has been made to ensure the accuracy, neither the compilers, editors nor publisher can assume responsibility for any losses that might be incurred as a result of consulting this guide, or of errors, typographical or otherwise.

Collecting Costume Jewelry

Costume jewelry…what is it? To say that it's jewelry made of inexpensive materials is only part of the story. It's a personal adornment old as mankind. In early historic times shells, animal bones teeth and feathers were used as personal ornaments. Ancient civilizations produced jewelry made of glass, ceramics, iron, copper and bronze.

During the mid to late 19th century, mass production made it possible for the average woman to purchase inexpensive jewelry. Daytime jewelry of the 19th century was the forerunner of 20th century costume jewelry. Hair jewelry, jet, gutta percha, bog oak, black glass jewelry, pinchbeck as well as gold-filled and sterling silver jewelry were popular. Shell cameos were available in gold-filled and silver mountings as well as in precious 14k and 18k gold. Garnet jewelry set in gold-plated brass, copper, gunmetal, silverplate on copper, celluloid and enamel on sterling were some of the materials used in daytime jewelry.

Sears Roebuck catalogs enabled almost every woman to afford at least one piece of finely made inexpensive jewelry. Amber and coral beads, gold-filled and sterling lockets and gold-filled festoon necklaces set with "fine imitation diamonds" could be purchased for less than $3. Gold-filled and rolled gold-plated bangle bracelets, expansion bracelets and chain link bracelets were also available at these low prices. Daytime jewelry imitated the designs of precious jewelry and the more "real" it looked, the better.

During this time it became stylish for some women to show off their wealth with precious jewelry. The more precious jewelry someone wore, the richer she was and rich women, and those who aspired to be, looked down at inexpensive jewelry as "sham jewelry" or "imitation jewelry."

Two art movements of the late 19th and early 20th century helped make non-precious jewelry more acceptable to fashionable women. The Arts and Crafts and Art Nouveau artisans felt that their art was an expression of the design and the materials used weren't as important as the design itself. Their work showed that beauty and craftsmanship were not limited to expensive metals and precious stones. Jewelry was made of glass, ivory, enamels tortoiseshell and freshwater pearls.

Rene Lalique, a jewelry craftsman of the time, used glass and a variety of semi-precioius gemstones in his designs. These art designs made jewelry of inexpensive materials more acceptable to the public, but it wasn't until after World War I that costume jewelry was created and became widely accepted.

After the grim reality of a world war, to show off one's wealth became socially inappropriate. Dress designer Coco Chanel saw costume jewelry as the mark of the post-ware liberated woman who dressed to please herself and not to display her wealth. She designed original and conspicuously fake costume jewelry to complement her clothing collection. She did not try to disguise the fact that these art forms were made of inexpensive materials and that they did not imitate precious jewelry. She also went against the conventions of the time by mixing precious and costume jewelry as accessories for her clothing collections.

Art Deco became the major art and design movement of the 1920s. Geometric forms and bright colors replaced the snake-like gale-swept curves and pastel colors of Art Nouveau. Art Deco motifs emphasized speed and movement and were influenced by Native American, African, Egyptian, Chinese, Japanese art.

Elsa Schiaparelli and other dress designers also began designing their own jewelry for their costume designs and, by 1933, the term "Costume Jewelry" came into use. During the 1930s costume jewelry, originally a fun fashion accessory, became a fashion necessity for the Depression-poor public. An inexpensive clip or pin could extend the wardrobe for a woman who couldn't afford new clothing and many makers of costume jewelry helped to meet this need. Coro, founded in the first decade of the 20th century, produced thousands of different designs each month. Its production ranged from higher end fashion jewelry to very inexpensive jewelry marketed in 5 and 10 cents store. The United States division of Coro discontinued production in the 1970s and the Candadian division in 1996.

Trifari was founded in 1918 as a maker of hair ornaments. In the 1920s women bobbed their hair and when combs became passé, Trifari turned to making costume jewelry. By 1930 designer Alfred Philippe joined the company. His designs made costume jewelry become totally acceptable to fashion conscious women when First Lady Mami Eisenhower, commissioned him to design sets of costume jewelry for both of her inaugural balls in 1953 and 1957. In doing so, she became the first wife of a president to wear costume jewelry to her inaugural ball. Trifari continues making lovely costume jewelry designs today.

Eisenberg originally started as a women's clothing firm in 1880. An attractive piece of jewelry made with Swarovski crystals was attached to each dress to appeal to customers and increase sales. By the 1930s theft of the pins from the dresses became so great that Eisenberg made a separate line of costume jewelry to sell to the public. Eisenberg is still in business today and continues making fine rhinestone jewelry.

Miriam Haskell founded her own jewelry company in 1924 in New York City. Her designs were not mass produced but each one was made by hand. Many designs featured beads, seed pearls and rhinestones put together with tiny wires on an openwork metal background. Her very pretty, detailed style was continued by her assistant Frank Hess in 1953 when she fell ill. Miriam Haskell jewelry is still being made today.

Wartime restrictions of metals affected the costume jewelry industry during the 1940s. Metals such as brass, copper, chrome and nickel were commandeered by the government for the war effort. Sterling silver, which was not needed for the war, became a base metal for costume jewelry and was also plated with gold. Other materials including plastic, glass, leather, fabric and straw were used to meet the increased public demand for costume jewelry.

The 1950s and 1960s were prosperous decades for the nation and for the costume jewelry industry as well. People were very fashion conscious and had money to spend and woman looked for designer names as indicative of good quality costume jewelry.

By the 1970s, women no longer followed the fashion trends and many costume jewelry makers went out of business, but some survived and are still in business today.

During the 1980s celebrities such as Princess Diana of England, Madonna and Michael Jackson helped revive an interest in costume jewelry. Collecting vintage costume jewelry became the hot new hobby and continues into the 21st century.

Originally not meant to last any longer than the clothing is accessorized, costume jewelry did survive as many woman saved it for its beauty and continued to wear it. More than merely jewelry made of inexpensive materials it is art, design and fine craftsmanship. It is a reflection of its time and representative of art and design movements of those times. It's a wonderful 20th century accessory which continues to be made in the 21st. But best of all, costume jewelry is not only meant to be collected, but to be worn and enjoyed!

Marion Cohen

Special Contributors

Marion Cohen
14 Croyden Ct.
Albertson, NY 11507
(516) 294-0055

Dorothy Kamm
10786 Grey Heron Ct.
Port St. Lucie, FL 34986
e-mail: dorothykann@adelphia.net

Dana Cain
5061 s. Stuart Ct.
Littleton, CO 80123
e-mail: dana.cain@att.net

  For other photographs and data we sincerely express appreciation to the following auctioneers and galleries: Alderfers, Hatfield, Pennsylvania; Charlton Hall Galleries, Columbia, South Carolina; William Doyle Galleries, New York, New York; Jackson's International Auctioneers, Cedar Falls, Iowa; James D. Julia, Fairfield, Maine and New Orleans Auction Galleries, New Orleans, Louisiana.
  Note: For further listings on auctioneers, appraisers, dealers and experts on all types of jewelry refer to Maloney's Antiques & Collectibles Resource Directory by David J. Maloney (Krause Publications).

Auction Houses with Special Jewelry Sales:

Antiquorum USA, Inc.
609 Fifth Avenue, Suite 503
New York, New York 10017

Bonham & Butterfield
220 San Bruno Avenue
San Francisco, CA 94103

William Doyle Galleries
175 East 87th Street
New York, New York 10128

DuMouchelles
409 East Jefferson
Detroit, MI 48226

Jackson's International Auctioneers
& Appraisers
2229 Lincoln St.
Cedar Falls, IA 50613

Sloan Auctioneers & Appraisers
886 NW 18th Terrace, Suite 100
Miami, FL 33172

Skinner Inc.,
357 Main St.
Bolton, MA 01740

Weschler's Auctioneers &
Appraisers
909 "E" Street NW
Washington, DC 20004

On The Cover:

Top left: Victorian coiled snake bracelet in gold and platinum with diamond accents - $7,050. Courtesy of Skinner, Inc., Bolton, Massachusettes.
Top Right: A costume jewelry butterfly pin in mother-of-pearl in a goldplate mount - $55-75. Courtesy of Marion Cohen, Albertson, New York.
Bottom Left: A Victorian enamel & diamond portrait pin - $2,200. Courtesy of Alderfers, Hatfield, Pennsylvania.
Bottom Right: A costume jewelry dress clip decorated with deep blue marquise-cut rhinestones, ca. 1930s. Courtesy of Marion Cohen, Albertson, New York.

CHAPTER 1
Antique Jewelry (1800-1920)

General

Antique French Diamond Bar Pin

Bar pin, diamond, a very slender bar bead-set w/a line of tiny rose-cut diamonds, platinum-topped 18k gold mount, partial French guarantee stamp (ILLUS.)............. **$441**

Edwardian Pearl & Diamond Bar Pin

Bar pin, diamond & pearl, designed as six tapering diamond-set loops each surround a pearl, all centered by a circle of diamonds around a larger pearl, old European- and mine-cut diamonds, platinum-topped 14k gold mount, Edwardian era, early 20th c. (ILLUS.)...................... **$1,116**

Ornate Edwardian Bar Pin

Bar pin, diamond, seed pearl & platinum, composed of openwork arched & oblong side panels centered by a narrow bar all centered by a wheel-like ring, mounted overall w/bead- and bezel-set old European-cut diamond mélée & seed pearls, platinum-topped 14k gold mount, Edwardian, England, early 20th c. (ILLUS.) **$1,528**

Arts & Crafts Garnet & Amethyst Pin

Bar pin, garnet, amethyst & 14k gold, Arts & Crafts style, long oblong form centered by a cabochon amethyst flanked by rose-cut garnets bezel-set among leaves & berries, signed, early 20th c. (ILLUS.) **$646**

French Antique Garnet Bar Pin

Bar pin, garnet, diamond & 14k gold, centering a sugarloaf garnet surrounded by rose-cut diamonds, three large garnets at each end & set throughout w/faceted garnets, French hallmarks, missing one stone (ILLUS.)... **$1,058**

Bar Pin with Large Center Garnet

Bar pin, garnet, diamond & 15k gold, the center set w/a large garnet surrounded by 18 round diamonds flanked by gold bar ends, one diamond replaced, Victorian (ILLUS.)... **$413**

Fine Moonstone & Gem-set Bar Pin

Bar pin, moonstone, diamond & seed pearl, the thin 14k gold bar w/seed pearl tips centered by a large sugarloaf-shaped moonstone framed by a band of old European-cut diamonds & seed pearls, 19th c. (ILLUS.)... **$1,645**

Antique Peridot & Seed Pearl Bar Pin

Bar pin, peridot, seed pearl & 14k gold, the thin gold bar bezel-set w/a row of three peridot accented w/seed pearl-set leaf designs, 2 1/8" l. (ILLUS.) **$300-500**
Bar pin, ruby & diamond, long narrow form centered by a line of bezel-set oval rubies surrounded by forty-two old European- and full-cut diamonds weighing 2.28 cts., platinum-topped 14k gold mount, letter mark & Austrian guarantee mark, ca. 1910 .... **$3,525**

Fine Amethyst, Seed Pearl & Gold Victorian Bracelet

Gold & Enamel Art Nouveau Barrette

Barrette, plique-a-jour enamel & 14k yellow gold, Art Nouveau style, long oval shape enclosing undulating gold leaves & an iris blossoms highlighted by a small diamond & framed by lavender enamel, hallmark of Riker Bros., early 20th c., 5/8 x 1 7/8" (ILLUS.).. **$1,528**

Jadeite Archaic-style Belt Ornament

Ornate Gem-set Gold Belt Buckle

Belt buckle, gem-set 14k yellow gold, Art Nouveau style, the two lobed & rounded sections stamped w/scrolling designs of stylized fish & cattails, accented w/old mine-cut diamonds & small circular-cut red spinels, hallmark of Sloan & Co., late 19th - early 20th c. (ILLUS.) **$1,293**

Belt ornament-pendant, jadeite, carved Archaic-style, a flattened rectangular milky white plaque w/a curved bottom end, carved in low-relief on the front & back w/a dragon & geometric design, China, antique, 1 1/8 x 2 1/4" (ILLUS., top next column)....................................... **$441**

Victorian Amethyst & Gold Bracelet

Bracelet, amethyst & 14k gold, bangle-type, the hinged flat band widely swelled at the top & set w/a stylized blossoms composed of pear-shaped facet-cut amethyst petals around a large central oval-cut amethyst, a cluster of smaller circular-cut amethysts at each side, interior circumference 6 1/4" (ILLUS.) **$1,175**

Bracelet, amethyst, seed pearl & 15k gold, centered by a large prong-set oval amethyst framed by a band of seed pearls & looping scrolls set w/seed pearls, completed by a wide tightly arranged fancy link gold bracelet, 19th c., 7" l. (ILLUS., top of page) **$3,290**

Antique 18k Gold and Aquamarine Bracelet

Bracelet, aquamarine & 18k gold, composed of three heavy link chains finished w/a square cannetille work clasp bezel-set w/circular & pear-shape foil-backed aquamarines, minor evidence of solder, 7 1/4" l. (ILLUS., top of page)................. **$1,116**

Sloan & Co. Art Nouveau Opal Bracelet

Bracelet, black opal & gold, bangle-type, Art Nouveau style, the narrow band flaring to forked leaves flanking an engraved gold frame enclosing a bezel-set black opal, mark of Sloan & Co., New York, New York, repair to hinge, lower half bent (ILLUS.).. **$764**

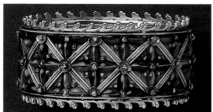

Rare Renaissance-style French Bracelet

Bracelet, chrysoberyl, enamel, diamond & gold, cuff-style, Renaissance Revival style, the wide band set w/cat's-eye quatrefoil designs punctuated by rose-cut diamond florettes joined by applied wire-work on a pale blue enameled ground, white & black enamel accents, gadrooned edge, hallmark of Falize Freres, France & French guarantee stamps, enamel loss, one diamond & cat's-eye missing, 19th c., inside circumference 6 1/2" (ILLUS.) **$56,400**

Early 20th Century Bangle Bracelet

Bracelet, diamond & 14k gold, bangle-type, a simple engine-turned hinged gold band bezel-set w/five old European-cut diamonds, marked by Riker Bros., early 20th c., interior circumference 7 1/4" (ILLUS.).............................. **$1,880**

Delicate Antique Diamond Bracelet

Bracelet, diamond & 14k gold, bangle-type, the back half a solid band & the front half a delicate flaring openwork design of leaves centered by a flower bead- and bezel-set overall w/old European- and mine-cut diamonds, diamonds weighing about 1.99 cts., platinum-topped 14k gold mount, interior circumference 6 1/2" (ILLUS.).. **$2,585**

Entwined Band French Antique Diamond Bracelet

Flower-mounted Victorian Gold Bracelet

Bracelet, diamond, enamel & yellow gold, bangle-type, the wide tapering foliate-engraved bangle mounted w/a large engraved oval plaque fitted w/a large stylized daisy-like flower & leaves trimmed w/opalescent pink & green enamel & rose-cut diamond accents, Tiffany & Co., New York, in original box w/an inscription dated 1866, interior diameter 5 3/8" (ILLUS.) **$2,468**

Bracelet, diamond & gold, the central arched section composed of a seven-section entwined band design w/each loop centered by a bezel-set old European-cut diamond, the borders set w/rose-cut diamonds, silver-topped 18k gold mount, completed by a gold curb link chain, in a fitted box from a French jeweler, 6 7/8" l. (ILLUS., top of page) **$2,115**

Antique Pearl & Diamond Bangle Bracelet

Bracelet, diamond, pearl & gold, bangle-type, the thin band centered by a large pearl flanked by graduated bands of alternating pearls & bezel-set old mine-cut diamonds, diamonds weighing about 1.04 cts., silver-topped 14k gold mount, interior circumference 6 1/4" (ILLUS.)........ **$999**

Bracelet, emerald, diamond & 14k gold, the wide snake chain centered by a crossed wide ribbon design set w/emerald-cut emeralds & 12 small old mine-cut diamonds, inscribed 1863, later safety, minor solder, 7 1/2" l. (ILLUS., bottom of page).. **$2,938**

Bracelet, enamel & 14k gold, bangle-type, the hinged ring engraved w/floral, foliate & bow designs, black tracery enamel highlights, interior w/minor dents, 19th c., interior circumference 5 7/8" d. **$235**

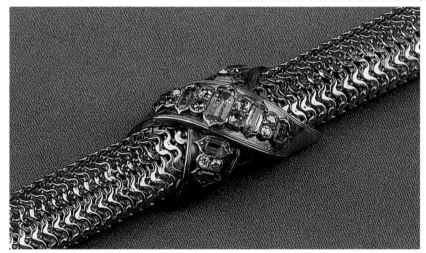

Snake Chain Bracelet with Emerald- and Diamond-set Ribbon Cross

Early Enamel, Pearl & Gem-set European Bracelet

Bracelet, enamel, pearl, diamond, emerald & 14k yellow gold, the central plaque framed by pointed & scrolled blue enamel panels accented w/freshwater pearls & enclosing a squared openwork panel set asymmetrically w/a large emerald bead & old European-cut diamonds, fitted on an arched 14k gold link bracklet, Austro-Hungarian assay mark & initials of the maker, 19th c., 6 1/2" l. (ILLUS. of part, top of page) **$1,528**

Russian Topaz & Enamel Bangle Bracelet

Bracelet, enameled 14k gold & pink topaz, bangle-type, the narrow band centered by a bezel-set oval pink topaz flanked by a repeated design of diamonds enameled in red, white & blue, Russian assay mark, late 19th - early 20th c., interior diameter 6 1/4" (ILLUS.) **$2,350**
Bracelet, enameled 18k gold, composed of round dished plaques each centered by a

gold knot surrounded by royal blue guilloché enamel & joined by trace links w/floral enameled spacers, French guarantee stamps & a hallmark (ILLUS., bottom of page).. **$940**

Rare French Enameled 18k Gold Bracelet

Bracelet, enameled 18k yellow gold, composed of four hinged panels each decorated w/polychrome enameled classical motifs centering a different ancient Greek figure, signed by Delarue, Paris, France & w/French guarantee stamps, 19th c., 6 7/8" l. (ILLUS.) **$8,225**

Enameled Gold Round Plaque Bracelet

Art Nouveau Fancy Link & Pearl Bracelet

Bracelet, freshwater pearl & 14k gold, Art Nouveau style, composed of scrolled & looping links centered by pearls, marked by Bippart, Griscom & Osborn, Newark, New Jersey, 7 1/2" l. (ILLUS., top of page) **$705**

w/small garnets, silver gilt mount, interior circumference 6 1/4" (ILLUS.)................... **$588**

Nice Late Victorian Garnet Bracelet

Fine Antique Garnet Bracelet

Bracelet, garnet, bangle-type, a narrrow band swelling at the top & centered by a round floret bead-set w/large rose-cut garnets w/bands of garnets down the sides against a ground set overall

Bracelet, garnet, narrow gold-filled band widening at the top w/arched pointed notch sides centering a florette of large garnets surrounded by tiny garnets & trimmed w/bands of large garnets along the sides, late 19th c., top 2 x 2 1/4" (ILLUS.).............. **$403**

Art Nouveau Gold Link Bracelet with Moth

Bracelet, gem-set 14k gold, Art Nouveau style, each squared openwork link decorated w/swirling vines, the center mounted w/a spread-winged gold mouth w/a bezel-set oval sapphire set on its shoulder & the wings set w/scattered diamonds, 6 1/2" l. (ILLUS., above) **$3,500-4,500**

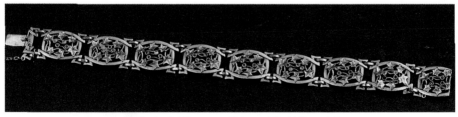

Delicate Art Nouveau Gem-set Gold Bracelet

Bracelet, gem-set 18k gold, Art Nouveau style, composed of oblong openwork links enclosing stylized vines & ivy w/tiny rose-cut diamond & emerald berries, French import stamp, late 19th - early 20th c., 7 1/8" l. (ILLUS., above) **$2,350**

Elaborate Openwork Enameled & Gem-set Swiss Bracelet

Bracelet, gem-set enamel, composed of large figure-8 open likes each enameled in various colored & centering a small blossom w/seed pearls surrounding a turquoise center, the large squared central openwork plaque composed of very ornate leafy scrolls enameled in various colors & centered by a large oval-cut aquamarine framed by a band of alternating seed pearls & turquoise beads, 18k gold & silver mount, made in Switzerland w/European & French import stamps, 6 3/8"l. (ILLUS., top of page) **$3,055**

Unusual Egyptian Revival Gem-set Scarab Link Bracelet

Bracelet, gem-set gold, Egyptian Revival style, composed of stylized scarab links set w/bands of sapphires, rubies & rose-cut diamonds, alternating w/squared links each set w/a cushion-cut light blue sapphire, silver-topped 18k gold mount, mark of French maker & guarantee stamps, dent on underside, 7 1/4" l. (ILLUS., above) **$1,175**

Victorian Braided Gold Bracelet

Bracelet, gold, 14k, bangle-type, hinged bangle w/four-leaf clover mount & seed pearl stem over an interlocking loop design, three green stone accents, Edwardian **$264**

Bracelet, gold (14k) & diamond, the flat braided gold strap completed by an oval clasp bead-set w/three full-cut diamonds, applied wirework accents, Victorian, later clasp, 7" l. (ILLUS., above) **$470**

Gold & Enamel Link Bracelet

Bracelet, gold (14k), enamel & seed pearl, composed of circular engraved gold links surmounted by blue enamel circles each set w/a seed pearl, one link is a drop, 7 1/2" l. (ILLUS.)... **$940**

Fine Victorian Gold Mesh Bracelet

Bracelet, gold (14k) & enamel, slide-type, wide flat adjustable mesh band w/the flat slide enameled w/blue palmettes centered by a pearl on a black-enameled ground, foxtail fringe (ILLUS.)................ **$1,998**

Bracelet, gold (14k) & sapphire, bangle-type, a narrow band w/delicate openwork scrolls set around the sides w/five bezel-set round sapphires, Edwardian era, England, interior circumference 7" d. **$382**

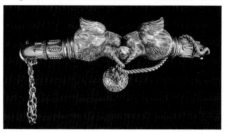

Hinged Victorian Gargoyle Bracelet

Bracelet, gold (14k yellow), circular tubular form w/a section of two facing gargoyle heads w/a small diamond six-prong setting above a ball drop, hinged to open, small safety chain, unmarked, Victorian, 2 1/4 x 2 1/2" (ILLUS.) **$2,300**

Bracelet, gold (18k), bangle-type, Art Nouveau style, a narrow solid band engraved overall w/leafy scrolls & accented by bezel-set circular-cut blue stones, interior circumference 7 1/4" **$558**

Bracelet, gold (18k), slide-type, a wide mesh strap completed by a buckle w/ropetwist highlights, foliate-engraved accents & fringe, evidence of solder on the back of the buckle, 19th c., 8 1/2" l. (ILLUS., bottom of page)....................... **$1,175**

Bracelet, gold (18k yellow), Arts & Crafts style, each open link w/three lily pad designs, Continental assay & hallmarks, early 20th c., 7" l. **$705**

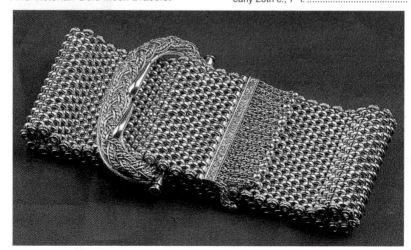

Fine Antique Gold Slide Mesh Bracelet

Very Rare Hardstone Intaglio & Gold Bracelet

Bracelet, hardstone intaglios & 18k yellow gold, composed of nine oval segments set w/a carnelian, banded agate, sard or jasper intaglios within a gold wire & bead-work frame joined by knot links & completed by a cylindrical clasp, by Ernesto Pierret, w/an additional intaglio link, 19th c., 6 1/2" l. (ILLUS., top of page)........... **$22,325**

Victorian Etruscan Revival Bracelet

Bracelet, lapis lazuli & 18k gold, Etruscan Revival, bangle-type, the wide band decorated on one half w/a curved lapis tablet & on the other w/delicate bead & wire-work designs (ILLUS. of half)................. **$3,408**

Early American Memorial Bracelet

Bracelet, memorial-type, an oval 10k bright-cut mount enclosing a pen & ink & hair-work scene of a lady standing by a memorial monument under a willow tree, the reverse w/an inscription noting the name of someone from Philadelphia & dated 1793, completed by a wide silk velvet ribbon, 5 3/4" l. (ILLUS.)................................. **$823**

Peridot & Gold Art Nouveau Bangle

Bracelet, peridot & 14k gold, bangle-type, Art Nouveau style, the very narrow band w/engraved & pierced latticework sections set w/three square step-cut peridot (ILLUS.)... **$470**

Bracelet, peridot & 14k yellow gold, bangle-type, Art Nouveau style, the openwork gold frame decorated w/stylized looping leaves alternating w/six bezel-set step-cut peridot, Whiteside & Blank hallmark, early 20th, interior circumference 7 5/8" d. (ILLUS. top with other Art Nouveau bangle bracelet, page 20) **$1,293**

Fine Platinum, Gold Snake Bracelet

Bracelet, platinum, 14k gold & diamond, designed as a coiled snake w/a platinum & yellow gold mesh body, the head set w/an old European-cut diamond weighing approx. 1.01 cts., rose-cut eyes offset by dark patination, stamped "PD," 11 1/2" l. (ILLUS.) **$7,050**

English Bracelet Composed of Reverse-painted Crystal Plaques

Bangle-style Spinel & Diamond Bracelet

Bracelet, red spinel, diamond & gold, bangle-type, a narrow hinged mount prong-set on the top w/a band of graduating oval-cut spinels alternating w/pairs of small old mine-cut diamond mélée, silver-topped 14k gold mount, 19th c. (ILLUS.) **$1,763**

Bracelet, reverse-painted crystal & 9k gold, composed of five circular reverse-painted crystal plaques depicting ducks, a pheasant, quail & partridge, joined by scrolling links, English hallmarks & maker's mark, boxed, 7 1/2" l. (ILLUS., top of page) **$2,350**

Edwardian Sapphire & Pearl Bracelet

Bracelet, sapphire, cultured pearl & 14k gold, bangle-type, hinged, the top band decorated w/entwined gold bands w/each loop enclosing a circular-cut sapphire alternating w/a pearl, Edwardian era, early 20th c., evidence of solder, interior circumference 6" (ILLUS.) **$470**

Gold, Diamond & Sapphire Bangle

Bracelet, sapphire, diamond & 14k gold, bangle-type, simple hinged gold band bezel-set w/three old European-cut diamonds alternating w/two circular-cut sapphires, Edwardian (ILLUS.) **$3,525**

Bracelet, sapphire & diamond, centering a sapphire cabochon framed by rose-cut diamonds, flanked by hinged plaques w/single-cut diamonds & channel-set sapphires, platinum-topped 18k gold mount, Edwardian era, early 20th c., 7 1/4" l. **$1,410**

Bracelet, sapphire & diamond, narrow oval links alternating w/five bezel-set cushion-cut sapphires or five old European-cut diamonds, millegrain accents, ca. 1915, 7 3/4" l. **$3,643**

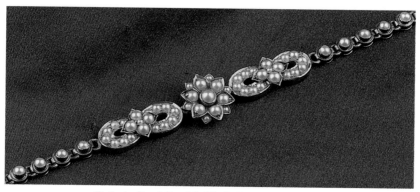

Delicate Seed Pearl & 18k Gold Antique Bracelet

Blue "Vauxhall Glass," Pearl & Gold Bracelet

Bracelet, seed pearl & 18k gold, composed of a slender link chain set w/seed pearls centered by two double-loop & floret mounts set w/seed pearls flanking the central floret further set w/seed pearls, 7" l. (ILLUS., bottom previous page) **$646**

Bracelet, seed pearl, sapphire & 18k yellow gold, composed of rectangular foliate links w/lines of seed pearls spaced by bezel-set French-cut sapphires, ca. 1900, 7 3/8" l. **$1,998**

Bracelet, silver, bangle-type, the hinged ring w/applied bead & ropetwist accents, minor break at edge, interior circumference 7 1/8" **$264**

Bracelet, silver & Scottish agate, composed of carnelian, banded agate, milky chalcedony & jasper plaques joined by shaped links w/scroll- and rocaille designs, suspending an engraved heart-form charm, Scotland, mid-19th c., 7 1/4" l. **$353**

& a bracelet composed of small square hinged gold plaques each w/flower & leaf engraving, w/later safety chain, England, mid-19th c., 7 1/4" l. (ILLUS., top of page)... **$353**

Russian Enamel & Gold Locket-Bracelet

Bracelet with locket, enamel, diamond & gold, bangle-style, the top w/a large round hinged locket decorated in the center w/a round blue enamel boss w/a leaf sprig design highlighted w/small rose-cut diamonds enclosed by a scalloped flora-form frame, the tapering sides engraved w/delicate florals, Russian assay marks, 19th c., interior circumference 5 3/4" (ILLUS.) **$1,410**

Two Art Nouveau Bangle Bracelets

Bracelet, turquoise & gold, bangle-type, Art Nouveau style, a large central oval bezel-set turquoise cabochon flanked by stylized lotus blossoms, Sloan & Co. hallmark & dated 1887 (ILLUS. bottom with other Art Nouveau bangle bracelet) **$1,058**

Bracelet, "Vauxhall Glass," pearl & 15k gold, centered by a large dark blue glass oval plaque centered by a small sprig w/a baroque pearl & an old single-cut diamond mélée flower, a simple gold frame

Antique Carved Black Onyx Bracelets

Bracelets, carved black onyx, bangle-type, each carved w/a repeating design of pyramidal squares, unsigned, in signed Tiffany & Co. fitted box, interior circumference 5 1/2", pr. (ILLUS., previous page) **$823**

Bracelets, enamel & 14k gold, buckle-form hinged bangle-type, wide w/overall black enamel, the gold clasp section w/engraved edges, second half 19th c., interior diameter 6", pr. (loss to enamel) **$1,175**

One of Two Early Enameled Bracelets

Bracelets, enamel & gold, bangle-style, engraved floral & foliate devices on a black enameled background, 18k yellow gold mount, 5 7/8" interior diameter, Victorian, pr. (ILLUS. of one) **$1,645**

Bracelets, gem-set 14k gold, bangle-type, each hinged ring set w/cabochon coral & seed pearl accents, elephant designed terminals, India, interior circumference 6 3/4", pr. **$529**

Fine Etruscan Revival Gold Bracelets

Bracelets, gold (14k), bangle-type, Etruscan Revival style, wide hinged band w/border bands of ropetwist accents, oxidation, tarnish, 19th c., interior circumference 5 3/4", pr. (ILLUS.) **$1,058**

Bracelets, gold (14k), turquoise & enamel, bangle-type, the hinged ring decorated w/black enamel tracery & engraved accents, the top w/an engraved gold ring surrounding a cluster of turquoise cabochons, second half 19th c., interior diameter 6", pr. **$1,175**

Brooch, amethyst & 14k gold, Arts & Crafts style, a large oval bezel-set amethyst set in a rectangular gold frame decorated w/pierced heart-shaped leaves & berry clusters, designed & signed by Josephine Hartwell Shaw, early 20th c. **$3,408**

Fine Edwardian Amethyst & Diamond Brooch

Brooch, amethyst & diamond, oblong quatrefoil design centered by a clipped-corner amethyst within a pierced frame bead- and bezel-set overall w/old mine-, single- and European-cut diamonds, platinum & 18k gold mount, in a fitted box marked "Jays of London," Edwardian, missing brooch attachment (ILLUS.) **$5,405**

Victorian Amethyst & Seed Pearl Brooch

Brooch, amethyst, ruby, seed pearl & 18k yellow gold, centered by a large oval-cut amethyst framed by split seed pearls & circular-cut rubies, gold mount, in original fitted box, Victorian (ILLUS.) **$823**

Krementz & Co. Amethyst & Pearl Brooch

Brooch, amethyst, seed pearl & 14k yellow gold, a large oval facet-cut amethyst enclosed in an openwork looped gold mount accented by seed pearls, hallmark of Krementz & Co., late 19th - early 20th c. (ILLUS.) **$705**

Brooch, aquamarine & 14k gold, a large cartouche form composed of gold openwork engraved scrolls, four aquamarines set around the sides w/a scrolling wirework drop pendant mounted w/another aquamarine, second half 19th c. **$1,528**

Victorian Banded Agate Brooch

Brooch, banded agate, diamond & 14k gold, the horseshoe-shaped mount set w/round banded agate cabochons & accented w/tiny rose-cut diamonds, 1 3/8" l. (ILLUS.).. **$1,528**

Arts & Crafts Black Opal & Gold Brooch

Brooch, black opal & 14k gold, Arts & Crafts style, a long oval bezel-set black opal enclosed by a wide pierced frame w/a scrolling leaf & blossoms design (ILLUS.) **$1,528**

Brooch, cat's-eye chrysoberyl, memorial-type, bezel-set w/oval cabochon w/14k gold ropetwist frame, verso w/locket containing hair... **$382**

Fine Antique French Horse Head Brooch

Brooch, chalcedony, diamond & 18k gold, brown translucent chalcedony carved as a horse head w/gold reins & bridle ac-

cented w/rose-cut diamonds, French guarantee stamp (ILLUS.)...................... **$3,408**

Flower-shaped Gem-set Antique Brooch

Brooch, citrine & diamond, designed as a five-petaled flower w/incised citrine petals, old European- and rose-cut diamonds in & around the center & around the outer border of the petals & down the stem, silver-topped 18k gold mount, French guarantee stamp, 1 3/4" l. (ILLUS.).......................... **$3,643**

Antique Citrine & Seed Pearl Brooch

Brooch, citrine & seed pearl, centered by a large round facet-cut citrine framed by a band of seed pearls, silver-gilt mount, 1 1/8" d. (ILLUS.) **$382**

Group of Antique Coral Jewelry Pieces

Brooch, coral & 18k yellow gold, Hellenistic-inspired design, a round gold frame enclosing a ring of small coral beads round an engraved gold band centered by a larger coral bead, ca. 1860 (ILLUS. bottom center with other antique coral jewelry pieces, previous page) **$1,093**

Ornate Art Nouveau Gem-set Brooch

Brooch, demantoid garnet, ruby, pearl & gold, Art Nouveau style, an ornate S-scroll mount w/scrolling detail & bezel-set w/scattered green garnets, rubies & pearls, three teardrop pearl pendants along the bottom, unsigned, from Marcus & Co., boxed, 1 3/8 x 1 1/2" (ILLUS.) **$7,050**

Nearly Round Diamond Crescent Brooch

Brooch, diamond & 14k gold, crescent-type, a rounded & nearly closed tapering crescent bead- and prong-set w/a graduated band of old mine- and European-cut diamonds weighing about 1.13 cts., 1" l. (ILLUS.) **$588**

Circle & Bow Diamond Brooch

Brooch, diamond & 14k white gold, circle & bow design, bead-set overall w/full- and old mine-cut diamonds, millegrain accents, diamonds weighing about 1.28 cts., 1" d. (ILLUS.) **$646**

Brooch, diamond, conch pearl & gold, designed as a detailed flower spray, the numerous leaves & petals of the flower set overall w/old mine-, European- and single-cut diamonds, the center of the flower set w/a pink conch pearl & a pink conch pearl flower bud, silver-topped gold mount **$2,233**

Fancy Diamond & Pearl Openwork Brooch

Brooch, diamond & cultured pearl, a ribbon bow & leaf mount w/an openwork arched bottom band set overall w/full- and single-cut diamonds & centering a prong-set old European-cut diamond drop weighing 1.25 cts., the upper half accented w/ten cultured pearls, 14k white gold mount, 1 5/8" l. (ILLUS.) **$2,468**

Rare Early Diamond-set Frog Brooch

Brooch, diamond & demantoid garnet, modeled as a small frog, the body set overall w/old European-cut diamonds weighing about 1.65 cts., bezel-set green garnet eyes, platinum-topped 18k gold mount, signed by Tiffany & Co., early 20th c. (ILLUS.) **$16,450**

Diamond & Gem-set Butterfly Brooch

Brooch, diamond, gem-set & gold, model of a butterfly, the wings & body bead-set w/opals, rose-cut diamonds & circular-cut sapphires, emerald & ruby mélée, silver-topped 14k yellow gold mount, one mélée w/chip, ca. 1910 (ILLUS.) **$1,763**

Rare Edwardian Starburst Brooch

Brooch, diamond & gold, a large starburst design pavé-set w/81 old European-cut diamonds weighing about .926 cts., platinum-topped 14k gold mount w/remov-

able pin stem, Edwardian, England, early 20th c. (ILLUS.) **$22,325**

Early Diamond Bow Brooch with Drops

Brooch, diamond & gold, bow-form, the top four-loop fancy openwork gold bow collet-set w/table- and rose-cut diamonds, suspending a small bow pendant topped w/scrolls also set w/diamonds & suspending another cross-form pendant w/scrolling details further set w/diamonds, gold mount, diamonds possibly foiled, later pin stem, evidence of solder, 1 3/4 x 3 7/8" (ILLUS.) **$3,819**

Dramatic Floral Spray Diamond Brooch

Brooch, diamond & gold, designed as a large floral spray w/a multi-petaled flower above a pair of multi-lobed leaves, prong- and bead-set w/old mine-, European-, single- and rose-cut diamonds, French import stamps, silver-topped 18k gold mount, 3" l. (ILLUS.) **$3,055**

Long-armed Diamond Starburst Brooch

Brooch, diamond & gold, starburst-style, the long pointed arms each bead-set w/old European-, mine- and rose-cut diamonds weighing about 1.11 cts., silver-topped gold mount, 1 3/8" d. (ILLUS.)........ **$588**

Small Diamond Starburst Brooch

Brooch, diamond & gold, starburst-style, the multiple short pointed arms each bead-set w/old mine- and rose-cut diamonds, silver-topped 14k gold mount, diamonds weighing about 1.10 cts., 3/4" l. (ILLUS.)... **$823**

Rare Diamond, Gold & Pearl Bow Brooch

Brooch, diamond, pearl & 18k gold, model of a large looping bow, bead-set w/90 old mine-cut diamonds weighing about 10.75 cts., five of the diamonds enclosing a large central white pearl, 19th c., w/detachable pin stem, 2 x 2 1/2" (ILLUS.)
.... **$14,100**

Fine Delicate Edwardian Gem Brooch

Brooch, diamond, pink topaz & gold, the delicate design w/a large undulating ribbon bow framing an oval wreath suspending single diamond drop, set overall w/rose-, single- and old European-cut diamonds, the wreath framing a bezel-set oval-cut pink topaz drop, millegrain accents, platinum & 18k gold mount, missing one diamond, evidence of solder, Edwardian, early 20th c. (ILLUS.) **$7,050**

Brooch, diamond, sapphire & 14k gold, gem-set model of insect, wings & body collet & bead-set w/twenty-nine rose-, old mine- and old European-cut diamonds & twenty oval & circular-cut sapphires, ruby eye, rose gold legs & antennae, detachable silver-topped rose, gold mount........ **$3,525**

Antique Caldwell Gem-set Crescent Brooch

Brooch, diamond, sapphire & gold, crescent-shaped, the long gently curved mount set w/a graduated band of alternating cushion-cut blue sapphires & old European-cut diamonds, platinum-topped gold mount, No. D8401, signed by J. E. Caldwell, Philadelphia, 2 7/8" l. (ILLUS.).. **$1,528**

Fine Georgian Diamond Lyre Brooch

Brooch, diamond & silver, lyre-form, the frame & top collet-set w/graduating old mine-cut diamonds, twisted gold wire strings, silver mount, diamonds weighing about 3.23 cts., Georgian, England, late 18th - early 19th c., later center element & pin stem, 1 1/4" l. (ILLUS.)................... **$3,525**

Art Nouveau Calla Lily Blossom Brooch

Brooch, enamel & 18k yellow gold, Art Nouveau style model of a calla lily, the pale shaded blue to white enameled petal centered by a stamen & base bead-set w/yellow full-cut diamond mélée, early 20th c. (ILLUS.)....................................... **$1,116**

Brooch, enamel, diamond & 18k gold, the purple enameled flowerhead centered by a prong-set old European-cut diamond, signed by Tiffany & Co., approximate weight .75 cts., second half 19th c. (enamel loss).. **$2,115**

Enamel & Diamond Butterfly Brooch

Brooch, enamel & diamond, model of butterfly, red, yellow, blue & black basse taille enamel wings & old mine-cut diamond body, ruby eyes, rose-cut diamond accents, silver-topped 14k gold mount, Austro-Hungarian hallmarks (ILLUS.)..... **$6,463**

French Art Nouveau Enameled Brooch

Brooch, enamel & moonstone, Art Nouveau style, the round center plaque enameled w/lavender & pink lilies & green leaves on a deep brown ground, a narrow gold frame w/a small bezel-set moonstone at each side, signed "G. Candelier - Limoges," France, late 19th - early 20th c. (ILLUS.).......................... **$1,058**

Art Nouveau Dogwood Blossom Brooch

Brooch, enameled 14k gold & diamond, Art Nouveau style, designed as a five-petal dogwood blossom enameled in white & centered by a small diamond, on a short gold stem, 1 1/4" w. (ILLUS.).................... **$529**

Signed Yellow Enameled Pansy Brooch

Brooch, enameled 14k gold & diamond, Art Nouveau style, designed as a pansy blossom enameled in dark yellow, light yellow, white & dark purple, centered by a full-cut diamond, marked Dees, 1 1/4" w. (ILLUS., previous page) **$1,998**

Delicate Enameled Gold Brooch

Brooch, enameled 14k gold & diamond, delicate gold oval frame decorated w/ribbon & garland designs set w/pear- and circular-cut diamonds on a bluish green guilloché enamel ground (ILLUS.).............. **$441**

Brooch, enameled 14k gold & diamond, designed as a pansy blossom enameled in lavender & off-white & centered by a small diamond, mark of maker, possibly Carrington & Co., Newark, New Jersey, 1" w. **$1,116**

Enameled Gold & Pearl Mermaid Brooch

Brooch, enameled 14k gold & freshwater pearl, Art Nouveau style, an openwork design of a swimming mermaid w/swirling hair & red basse taille enameled tail, a freshwater pearl mounted below her extended arm, diamond accents (ILLUS.) **$411**

Art Nouveau Brooch with Maiden Head

Brooch, enameled 14k gold & seed pearl, Art Nouveau style, designed w/the profile bust of an Art Nouveau maiden w/a butterfly wing-like headdress enameled in shad-

ed green to yellow w/red dots, against an openwork vining good mount set w/seed pearls, unsigned, 1 1/4" l. (ILLUS.) **$2,820**

Marked Pansy Basket Brooch

Brooch, enameled 14k gold & seed pearl, designed as a low wide basket w/a high arched handle & filled w/gold leaves & three small enameled pansy blossoms, one in maroon, one in yellow & the third in dark purple, all centered by a seed pearl w/two other seed pearl accents, mark of A. J. Hedges, Newark, New Jersey, 1 3/4 x 2" (ILLUS.) **$1,528**

Brooch, enameled 18k gold & diamond, Art Nouveau style, designed as a pansy blossom w/the top two petals enameled in very dark purple & the lower three enameled in lavender shaded to white & accented w/tiny dots & dark purple accents around the center old European-cut diamond, marked by Tiffany & Co., 1 1/4" w. **$3,408**

Lovely Enameled Portrait & Diamond Brooch

Brooch, enameled gold & diamond, a round plaque enameled in color w/a bust portrait of a lovely red-haired lady wearing a diamond-set diadem in her hair, framed across the upper half w/two arches set w/rose- and old single-cut diamonds ending in diamond-set balls, platinum & 18k gold mount, early 20th c., 1 1/2" w. (ILLUS.) **$2,820**

Portrait Brooch of Emperor Franz Josef

Brooch, enameled, rectangular w/rounded corners, featuring a color half-length portrait of Austrian Emperor Franz Josef as a young man wearing a cavalry uniform featuring the medal of the Order of the Golden Fleece, scrolling openwork 10k gold frame, reinforced pin stem, mid-19th c., 1 1/2 x 1 3/4" (ILLUS.)........................... **$323**

Art Nouveau Enameled Butterfly Brooch

Brooch, enameled silver, Art Nouveau style, in the form of a butterfly w/the gilt filigree wings highlighted by enamel in gold, blues & lavender, silver filigree body & head, marked "800 - 79SE," early 20th c. (ILLUS.) **$316**

Unusual Antique Gold Filigree Brooch

Brooch, filigree 18k gold, a rounded stylized flower design composed of tight swirls of gold wire filigree accented around the edge w/six tiny flat blossoms, suspending two filigree bellflower drops on fine link chains, compartment in the back, 19th c., 1 3/8" d. (ILLUS.)................. **$323**

Unusual Pearl & Diamond Flower Brooch

Brooch, freshwater pearl, diamond & 14k gold, Art Nouveau style, designed as a very stylized four-petal flower, each petal a baroque freshwater pearl in white or pink, centered by an old mine-cut diamond & w/a gold stem, evidence of solder at pin stem, 1 1/4" l. (ILLUS.).............. **$470**

Early Target-form Garnet & Gold Brooch

Brooch, garnet & 18k gold, target-form, the center w/a large cabochon pyrope garnet framed by a wide decorative gold band w/applied bead & wirework designs, locket compartment in the back, locket glass cracked, 19th c., 1 3/8" d. (ILLUS.)............ **$294**

Antique Garnet & Diamond Bow Brooch

Brooch, garnet, diamond & 18k yellow gold, designed as a bow centered by a faceted rectangular garnet w/the ribbon set w/old European-, single- and mine-cut diamonds, two cultured pearl accents, gold mount, late 19th - early 20th c. (ILLUS., previous page) **$823**

Large Garnet & Pearl Spider Brooch

Brooch, garnet, pearl & diamond, model of a large spider, a large cabochon almandite garnet forming the body, a pearl head & rose-cut diamond eyes & gold legs, 14k yellow gold mount, ca. 1920 (ILLUS.).. **$588**

Gem-set Gold Salamander Brooch

Brooch, gem-set 14k gold, in the shape of a gold salamander pavé-set down the body w/opal cabochons, step-cut peridot accent on the head, ca. 1920, 2" l. (ILLUS.).... **$529**

Fancy Gem-set Arts & Crafts Brooch

Brooch, gem-set 18k gold, Arts & Crafts style, the delicate openwork lacy gold mount in a winged design, set in the center top w/a ring of circular-cut amethysts enclosing a large oval-cut amethyst, surrounded by various bands of gems including blue, purple & yellow sapphires, peridots, amethysts, rubies, green tourmalines, aquamarines & seed pearls, three gem-set pendant drops at the bottom, designed & signed by Frank Gardiner Hale, early 20th c., 2 x 2 1/2" (ILLUS.) **$10,575**

Brooch, gold (10k), designed as a hand w/a red stone ring holding a card reading "Souvenir," replaced clasp, pin stem original, 19th c., 1 3/4" l. **$441**

Antique Gold Ram's Head Brooch

Brooch, gold (14k), a curved bar terminating in a realistic ram's head w/curling horns, 19th c. (ILLUS.)............................... **$588**

Antique Feathery Pinwheel Gold Brooch

Brooch, gold (14k) & diamond, designed as an ornate feathery scroll pinwheel centered by an old European-cut diamond, 19th c., 1 1/4" d. (ILLUS.) **$382**

Brooch, gold (14k) & diamond, stickpin-type bar w/ribbon swags suspended by five antique & Art Nouveau full-cut diamond-set stickpin heads, diamond flowerhead surmount, stickpins w/hallmarks for "Carter, Howe & Co." and "Dieges & Clust."... **$646**

Brooch, gold (14k) & diamond, two rounded intertwined engraved gold bands suspending a pair of long tassels, at the center a large round boss w/a textured surface centered by a star enclosing a small rose-cut diamond, second half 19th c. **$294**

Art Nouveau Gold Medallion Brooch

Brooch, gold (14k yellow), Art Nouveau style, a round medallion depicting a profile bust of Hermes framed by openwork loop frame, the reverse depicting an oval on a fruiting branch, European hallmark, late 19th - early 20th c. (ILLUS.) **$588**

Art Nouveau Gold Figural Brooch

Brooch, gold (18k) & diamond, Art Nouveau style, a large square gold plaque chased w/a design of three angels w/a censer & casket amid swirling incense, edged w/a narrow border of rose-cut diamonds, French guarantee stamp, late 19th - early 20th c., pin stem closure replaced (ILLUS.)........................... **$940**

Brooch, gold (18k), enamel & pearl, Renaissance Revival style, oval form composed of small openwork scrolls decorated w/black & white enamel & set in the center & around the sides w/seven pearls, a hair compartment on the back, marked by T.B. Starr, second half 19th c. **$1,645**

Plique-à-Jour & Gold Dragonfly Brooch

Brooch, gold (18k) & plique-à-jour, Art Nouveau-style model of a dragonfly w/a yellow gold body set w/one oval blue sapphire, the shoulder of the wings, mouth, eyes & body set w/small round diamonds, early 20th c. (ILLUS.) **$1,725**

Antique Round 18k Gold Brooch

Brooch, gold (18k), round design centered by a bombé form w/millefiori gold work centering a reclining amorino within a ropetwist & wirework frame, designed by Michelangelo Caetani, hallmark for Castellani, minor losses to petals, slight damage to back of frame at pin stem (ILLUS.) **$1,763**

Fine Georgian Painted Mourning Brooch

Brooch, gold & hand-painted, mourning-type, a thin gold mount & frame enclosing a long oval h.p. scene of a memorial obelisk centered by a covered urn above initials against a landscape of hairwork poplar trees & inkwork details, the back inscribed & dated 1782, Georgian era, England, 1 1/4" l. (ILLUS.) **$2,468**

Carved Jadeite & Gold Butterfly Brooch

Brooch, green jadeite & 14k gold, in the shape of a butterfly w/a gold body & flexible antennae, carved & pierced jadeite wings, 2" w. (ILLUS., previous page) **$383**

Rare Arts & Crafts Designer Brooch

Brooch, green tourmaline, seed pearl & 14k gold, Arts & Crafts style, centered by a long rectangular fancy-cut green tourmaline flanked by scroll & floret gold ends accented w/seed pearls, unsigned piece by Edward Oakes, early 20th c., 5/8 x 1 1/2" l. (ILLUS.) **$5,581**

Antique Agate & Diamond Oval Brooch

Brooch, landscape agate & diamond, a long oval agate mounted in a thin gold frame enclosed by an openwork gold frame set w/tiny rose-cut diamonds, partial European assay marks, 18k gold mount, evidence of minor solder, 3/4 x 1 1/2" (ILLUS.) **$558**

Antique French Lapis & Gold Brooch

Brooch, lapis lazuli & 18k gold, centered by a large cabochon lapis framed by a ring of small gold beads & a heavy smooth gold ring, long rounded side bars each enclosing three gold beads, unsigned but w/French import stamps & in a fitted & signed Mellerio box, 2 1/4" l. (ILLUS.) **$705**

Limoges Enamel Cherub & Gold Brooch

Brooch, Limoges enamel & 15k gold, the round enameled center decorated w/a white cherub w/palette & canvas against a black ground, the scalloped gold frame applied w/bead & wirework designs, first half 19th c., 1" d. (ILLUS.) **$676**

Brooch with Fly on Malachite Sphere

Brooch, malachite, enamel & 14k gold, designed as a gold fly w/black enamel trim perched atop a large malachite sphere supported in a U-shaped gold mount w/ball terminals & a bead drop, 19th c. (ILLUS.) **$470**

Micromosaic Agnus Dei Brooch

Brooch, micromosaic & 14k gold, the round center in polychrome tesserae depicting a recumbent lamb w/banner on a red platform representing the Agnus Dei, within a wide gold frame ornately decorated w/ropetwist & grape leaves, 19th c., 1 1/4" d. (ILLUS., previous page) **$411**

Micromosaic Butterfly Brooch

Brooch, micromosaic, a round wide gilt-metal frame w/wirework & bead accents centering a round color design of a butterfly on a white ground (ILLUS.) **$1,293**

Fine Arts & Crafts Gold & Moonstone Brooch

Brooch, moonstone & 14k gold, Arts & Crafts style, the oblong gold mount decorated w/leaves & delicate scrolls, centered by an oval moonstone flanked by round cabochon moonstones, unsigned work of Edward Oakes, 1 1/2" l. (ILLUS.) **$5,875**

Fine Intaglio Moonstone & Pearl Brooch

Brooch, moonstone intaglio, seed pearl & 14k gold, centered by an oval moonstone carved w/a scene of warriors making offerings to the gods, within a delicate openwork gold frame w/scroll accents & set w/seed pearls, 1 3/4" l. (ILLUS.)........ **$2,350**

Edwardian Opal & Diamond Brooch

Brooch, opal & diamond, oval opal framed by seed pearls & old European-cut diamonds, 14k gold mount, early 20th c., hallmark for Krementz & Co., w/original Tiffany & Co. box (ILLUS.) **$1,293**

Fine Victorian Diamond Flower Brooch

Brooch, opal, diamond, ruby & 14k yellow gold, modeled as a long-stemmed flower, the carved six-petal opal flower centered by an old European-cut diamond surrounded by a small ring of ruby mélées, a second stem topped by a teardrop-shaped opal, a pair of large serrated leaves set w/old mine-cut diamonds, the double stems & ribbon wrap band also set w/diamonds, backing w/silver-topped 14k yellow gold, late 19th c. (ILLUS.) **$3,163**

Antique Gem-set Ribbon Bow Brooch

Brooch, opal, emerald, diamond & 14k gold, designed as a large openwork ribbon bow set w/opals, emeralds & circular-cut diamonds, suspending two cross-form drops w/matching decoration, replaced pin stem, later diamonds, 19th c. (ILLUS.).............. **$1,058**

Art Nouveau Gold Iris Brooch

Brooch, pearl, diamond & 14k yellow gold, Art Nouveau style, the openwork fanned frame enclosing an iris blossom flanked by scrolling leaves, accented w/old European-cut diamond mélée & pearls, late 19th - early 20th c. (ILLUS.) **$500**

Rare Early Peridot & Diamond Brooch

Brooch, peridot & diamond, the center bezel-set w/a large oval-cut peridot framed by 12 old mine-cut diamonds weighing about 2.40 cts., silver-topped 18k gold mount, 19th c., 1 1/4" l. (ILLUS.) **$5,288**

Victorian Pietra Dura Floral Brooch

Brooch, pietra dura & 14k yellow gold, flat oval black plaque inlaid w/a sprig of lily-of-the-valley in white & green, narrow gold mount w/tiny acorn & ropetwist accents, replaced pin stem, 19th c. (ILLUS.)
.... **$294**

Victorian Pietra Dura Floral Brooch

Brooch, pietra dura, a large oval plaque depicting a large floral bouquet w/a rose, lily-of-the-valley and forget-me-nots on a black ground, mounted in a ribbon & floret gilt wirework frame, mid-19th c., 2 x 2 1/2" (ILLUS.) **$646**
Brooch, pink topaz & 14k gold, a squared rounded scrolling mount w/wirework details & projecting scroll shells at two sides, the center set w/a large facet-cut topaz surrounded in the mount by four smaller oval topazes alternating w/small round topaz, second half 19th c............. **$1,116**

Early Miniature Portrait Brooch

Brooch, platinum, 18k gold & diamond, miniature portrait-type, the oval plaque h.p. w/a half-length portrait of a lady in 18th c. costume & an elaborate hairdo, rose-cut diamond frame, Edwardian era, early 20th c. (ILLUS.) **$588**
Brooch, platinum & diamond, bead & prong-set throughout w/seventy-six rose, single- and full-cut diamonds, approx. total wt. 1.70 cts., French hallmark, Edwardian **$2,000**

Extremely Fine Cartier Diamond Brooch

Brooch, platinum & diamond, the garland form bezel- and bead-set w/51 old European-cut & mine-cut diamonds, approx. 10.44 cts., produced by Cartier, signed & w/original standing triptych (ILLUS.) **$27,025**

Brooch, plique-à-jour enamel, diamond & gems, Art Nouveau model of a dragonfly, the green & blue enamel wings set en tremblent, rose-cut diamond, cabochon ruby & faceted emerald accents, in a platinum-topped 14k yellow gold mount, early 20th c. **$4,994**

Victorian Gem-set Gold Brooch

Four-petal Sapphire & Diamond Flower Brooch

Brooch, sapphire & diamond, designed as a stylized flower w/four petals formed by large pear-shaped faceted sapphires & centered by a old European-cut diamond, the curved stem further set w/old European-cut diamond mélée, in a silver-topped 14k gold mount, 19th c., 1 1/2" l. (ILLUS.) **$1,293**

Early Antique Miniature Portrait Brooch

Brooch, portrait miniature & 14k gold, the oval silhouette profile portrait of a gentleman w/gilt accents mounted in an openwork scrolling gold frame, hair compartment in the back, first half 19th c., 1 3/8 x 1 5/8" (ILLUS.) **$588**

Brooch, ruby, pearl & 14k rose gold, the gold shield-shaped mount set w/a band of round-cut rubies flanked by rows of seed pearls, the scrolled top & lower section further set w/seed pearls, late 19th c. (ILLUS., top next column) **$460**

Ring-shaped Scottish Agate Brooch

Brooch, Scottish agate & 15k yellow gold, a flattened ring set w/alternating jasper & carnelian tablets & pointed scroll panels, the center w/a large openwork gold X mounted w/a gold scrolling crown, Scotland, 19th c., 1 1/2" d. (ILLUS.) **$529**

Bicolor Gold & Seed Pearl Grape Brooch

Brooch, seed pearl & 18k bicolor gold, designed as a long cluster of seed pearl grapes suspended from textured gold leaves & vine, 1 1/2" l. (ILLUS.) **$705**

Unusual Seed Pearl-Set Jaguar Brooch

Brooch, seed pearl & gold, designed as the head of a jaguar w/an open mouth, pavé-set overall w/tiny seed pearls, ruby eye, silver-topped 14k gold mount, 1 3/4" l. (ILLUS.) **$1,880**

Early Shakudo, Gold & Enamel Brooch

Brooch, Shakudo, enamel & 18k gold, the large round central disk depicting a raised design of a Japanese Samurai w/sword & fan, within a polychrome blue & white enamel frame w/red stone accents, the reverse w/a locket compartment, minor enamel loss, 19th c., 1 1/2" d. (ILLUS.) **$1,175**

Carence Crafters Arts & Crafts Brooch

Brooch, sterling silver & agate, Arts & Crafts style, a rectangular openwork band centered by a cabochon agate & decorated w/repoussé Celtic designs, mark of Carence Crafters, early 20th c., 1 1/2" l. (ILLUS.) **$705**

Scottish Agate & Silver Brooch

Brooch, sterling silver & agate, in the shape of a Saint Andrews cross w/the center silver cross highly engraved & framed by two cut stones & two square, Scotland, ca. 1870 (ILLUS.)...................... **$144**

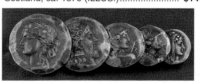

Art Nouveau Silver Medallions Brooch

Brooch, sterling silver, Art Nouveau style, designed as a bar of overlapping graduated medallions each molded in relief w/a bust portrait of an Art Nouveau maiden or a man, No. 598, mark of Geo. W. Shiebler & Co., early 20th c., 2 5/8" l. (ILLUS.) **$235**

Artist-signed Arts & Crafts Brooch

Brooch, sterling silver & lapis lazuli, Arts & Crafts style, the narrow oblong openwork bar decorated w/looping scrolls centered by a large oval lapis cabochon, designed by James Winn & signed, 2 1/4" l. (ILLUS.) **$940**

Fine Early Topaz & Gold Bow Brooch

Brooch, topaz & 14k gold, oblong bow shape, each side set w/a large pear-shaped topaz framed w/engraved gold floral designs, an engraved gold button in the center, back w/evidence of solder, 19th c., 1 3/4" l. (ILLUS.) **$940**

French Antique Double Circle Brooch

Brooch, turquoise, seed pearl & 18k gold, designed as two graduated interlocking circles w/the smaller top one decorated w/a band of split seed pearls & the larger lower one decorated w/a band of cabochon turquoise, suspending a flexible ropetwist fringe w/pearl drops, applied gold bead & ropetwist accents, French guarantee stamps & hallmarks, in a fitted inscribed box (ILLUS.) **$2,233**

Brooch, turquoise, seed pearl & 18k yellow gold, set overall w/turquoise cabochons within a scrolling gold frame w/seed pearl accents, three flexibly-set drops, French guarantee stamp, 19th c. **$940**

Fancy Amethyst & Gold Brooch-Pendant

Brooch-pendant, amethyst & 18k gold, the arched fancy openwork gold frame w/ornate scrolling leaves accented by three large cabochon amethysts, suspending a detachable matching teardrop pendant connected w/four swags of snake chain & centering a large teardrop cabochon amethyst, 2 x 2 3/4" (ILLUS.) **$999**

Art Nouveau Amethyst & Gold Brooch

Brooch-pendant, amethyst, seed pearl & 14k gold, Art Nouveau style, centered by a large oval amethyst within a scrolling gold frame w/wiretwist & seed pearl accents, late 19th - early 20th c. (ILLUS.) **$529**

Edwardian Citrine & Seed Pearl Brooch

Brooch-pendant, citrine, seed pearl & 14k gold, a large bezel-set rectangular step-cut citrine framed by two rows of seed pearls, Edwardian era, early 20th c., 1 1/4" l. (ILLUS.)..$881

Victoran Flower-form Brooch-Pendant

Brooch-pendant, diamond & 18k gold, an openwork stylized seven-point flower form bezel-set overall w/rose-cut diamonds, 19th c. (ILLUS.) $881

Wheat-shaped Diamond Brooch

Brooch-pendant, diamond & gold, designed as a sheaf of wheat on a long leafy stem set overall w/72 old mine-cut & 57 rose-cut diamonds, silver-topped 14k gold mount, evidence of solder at pin stem, 19th c., 2 3/4" l. (ILLUS.) $1,763

Rare Early Diamond & Pearl Brooch

Brooch-pendant, diamond, pearl & gold, designed w/an openwork bow atop a pair of overlapped hearts suspending a leaf cluster & a white pearl drop, set overall w/old mine- and rose-cut diamonds w/each heart centered by a white pearl, diamonds weighing about 3.28 cts., platinum-topped 14k gold mount, signed by Howard & Co., early 20th c., bow & pin stem detachable, 1 1/4 x 1 3/8" (ILLUS.) $14,100

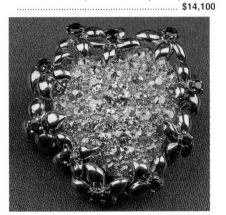

Early Starr Diamond & Sapphire Brooch

Brooch-pendant, diamond, sapphire & gold, the heart-shaped center pavé-set w/old European- and mine-cut diamonds weighing about 2.49 cts., the uneven border composed of four-petal gold blossoms each centered by a small blue sapphire, platinum & 14k gold mount, from T.B. Starr, 1 1/4" w. (ILLUS.) $5,288

Victorian Brooch with Dog Portrait

Brooch-pendant, enamel & 14k gold, a domed round crystal covering a painted enamel head portrait of a brown & white St. Bernard, signed & dated 1862, within a narrow gold ropetwist frame, 1 1/4" d. (ILLUS.)... **$1,528**

Pretty Art Nouveau Orchid Brooch

Brooch-pendant, enameled 14k gold & diamond, Art Nouveau style, designed as a realistic orchid blossom enameled in deep rose & pink & centered by an old European-cut diamond framed by gold stamens, 1 1/2" w. (ILLUS.) **$2,585**

Delicate Enameled Portrait Brooch

Brooch-pendant, enameled 18k gold & diamond, a flat round disk centering a small h.p. image of a maiden w/a flower garland framed by light green guilloché enamel overlaid w/a delicate platinum overlay bead-set w/rose-cut diamonds, a seed pearl border frame, Edwardian era, early 20th c., No. 3443 (ILLUS.) **$940**

Purple Pansy Brooch-pendant with Pearls

Brooch-pendant, enameled gold & seed pearl, Art Nouveau style, designed as a pansy blossom w/the petals enameled in dark purple shaded white & yellow, centered by a seed pearl & each petal bordered by seed pearls, w/pendant hook, 1 1/8" w. (ILLUS.).................................... **$1,175**

Brooch-pendant, gold (14k) & enamel, Art Nouveau style, round, decorated w/a profile of a classical woman accented by chased gold hair w/enameling on her face & earring, ca. 1900............................ **$999**

Brooch-pendant, gold (14k), seed pearl & enamel, the large top section in an inverted horseshoe form banded w/black enamel & enclosing a large florette w/black enamel centered by inset gold leaves & seed pearl blossoms, a ring drop at the bottom enclosing another smaller enameled rosette centered by a seed pearl & suspending a smaller round enamel drop centered by an inlaid star, in a fitted box from Savage & Lyman Jewellers, Montreal, Canada, second half 19th c. **$588**

Outstanding Opal & Diamond Brooch

Brooch-pendant, opal, diamond & demantoid garnet, centered by a large oval Australian peacock opal framed by two narrow rows of bead-set single- and old European-cut diamonds, w/calibre-cut demantoid garnets in four crossed bands, platinum-topped 14k gold mount, removable brooch fittings, ca. 1910 (ILLUS.)........... **$18,800**

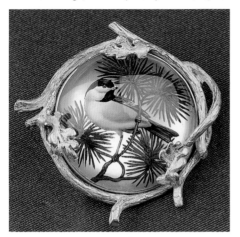

Fine Reverse-painted Crystal Brooch

Brooch-pendant, reverse-painted crystal & 18k gold, the large round domed crystal reverse-painted w/a scene of chickadee on a pine bough, mounted in a gold twig & leaf frame, American-made & signed, 1 1/4" d. (ILLUS.) **$2,703**

Antique Gem-set Delicate Gold Brooch

Brooch-pendant, tourmaline, diamond & 14k gold, a lacy scrolling openwork flora-form gold mount centered by a prong-set cushion-cut green tourmaline flanked at the sides by faux pearls & above & below w/old European-cut diamonds weighing about 1.24 cts., 1 3/4" d. (ILLUS.) **$2,703**

Buckle pin, gold (14k), Art Nouveau style, flattened & slightly curved wide oval form w/low-relief sinuous vine motifs, a pair of narrow bars extending across the top from one end, a hinged pin closure at the back, inscribed w/owner's name, also signed by maker Drosten, ca. 1900 .... **$558**

Buttons, sterling silver gilt, Art Nouveau style, each depicting a fairy w/strawberry blossom, signed "RF", 1" d., set of six **$353**

Lava Cameo of Garibaldi

Cameo, carved lava & gold, oval grey lava carved in relief w/the profile bust of Giuseppe Garibaldi, 19th c. Italian patriot, together w/a silk banner dated 1847 celebrating the reforms of King Carlo Alberto of Sardinia & Piedmont, Italy, mid-19th c. (ILLUS. of cameo) **$705**

Unusual Double Cameo Bracelet

Cameo bracelet, carved hardstone & 14k gold, the narrow open two-band bracelet topped by two oval cameos, each carved in white to black w/different scenes of sea cherubs, each in an oval frame w/delicate beading & separated by a lacy wirework panel, 19th c., interior circumference 6 3/8" (ILLUS.) **$1,528**

Lovely Victorian Agate Cameo Brooch

Cameo brooch, agate & 18k gold, a large oval cameo carved w/the profile bust of a classical woman w/diamond & pearls in her upswept hair, French maker mark, evidence of minor solder on the back, nicks, 19th c., 2" l. (ILLUS., previous page) **$823**

Cameo brooch, carved coral & 14k gold, a delicate openwork scroll-trimmed gold frame enclosing a coral cameo carved w/a detailed bust portrait of a woman, Italy, ca. 1880 (ILLUS. top center with other antique coral jewelry pieces, page 22) **$316**

Victorian Shell Cameo with Landscape

Fancy Gold & Coral Cameo Zeus Brooch

Cameo brooch, carved coral & 18k gold, the ornate mount cast w/leafy scrolls & a scrolling ground centered by a long full-leaf carved coral portrait of the god Zeus, in the box of a Geneva, Switzerland, jewelry, 1 1/4 x 1 3/4" (ILLUS.) **$1,768**

Lovely Hardstone Portrait Cameo

Cameo brooch, hardstone, a large deeply carved profile bust of a classical lady w/a floral garland in her hair against the dark brown background, in a delicate scrolling 14k gold frame accented w/seed pearls, French guarantee stamp, 19th c. (ILLUS.) **$2,703**

Antique Medusa Head Cameo Brooch

Cameo brooch, carved shell & 14k gold, the oval cameo carved in bold relief w/the head of the Gorgon Medusa, mounted in an ornate oval gold frame w/pointed arches & florets alternating w/wirework beads, 1 1/2" l. (ILLUS.) **$750-850**

Cameo brooch, carved shell, oval, cameo-carved w/a landscape showing a medieval man leading a rearing stallion, a stone castle in the background, in a gold-plated mount, late 19th - early 20th c. (ILLUS., top next column) **$316**

Fine Onyx Cameo Brooch

Cameo brooch, onyx & 18k gold, the oval onyx cameo carved w/the profile bust of an elegant lady w/fancy curly hair in the 18th c. style, mounted in a delicate wire-work gold frame, 14k gold pin stem, 19th c. (ILLUS.) **$588**

Fine Edwardian Coral Cameo Brooch

Cameo brooch-pendant, coral, diamond & 14k gold, a large oval coral cameo carved in bold-relief w/the head of a classical maiden, framed by a narrow band of 36 old European-cut diamonds, platinum-topped 14k gold mount, Edwardian era, England, early 20th c., 1 3/4" l. (ILLUS.) **$1,116**

Agate Cameo & Gold Earrings

Cameo earrings, agate cameo & 14k gold, pendant-type, each oval agate cameo-cut from deep orange to milky white w/the head of Janus, later mounted as earrings, pr. (ILLUS.) **$881**

Fine Antique French Cameo Earrings

Cameo earrings, carved hardstone & 18k gold, pendant-type, each w/a round cameo carved w/the profile bust of a classical woman in white on black w/a brown leaf wreath in her hair, framed by a narrow etched gold band & a overlapping gold loop border, French guarantee stamps, 1" d., pr. (ILLUS.) **$764**

Antique Coral Cameo Earrings

Cameo earrings, coral & gold, pendant-type, the round carved coral cameo depicting a classical lady mounted in an engraved gold band w/an applied ropetwist border, 19th c., pr. (ILLUS.) **$940**

Cameo locket, tortoiseshell & 14k gold, centered by a cameo carved w/a cherub, suspended on a 14k gold fancy trace link chain, Victorian, locket 2" l., ... **$558**

Fine Victorian Fringe-style Pendant Cameo Necklace

Cameo necklace, shell cameos, freshwater pearl, rock crystal & gilt metal, festoon-style, composed of a gilt metal paper clip-style link chain alternating w/small gilt ribbon bow links or round rosette links each suspending pairs of delicate trace link chains that suspend a repeating series of pendants consisting of two oval shell cameos carved w/the head of a classical woman & a larger central round cameo w/a similar carved portrait, the cameos alternating w/pendant purple foil-backed rock crystal cabochons, each pendant suspending a small freshwater pearl drop, in a period case, missing one pearl, 19th c., 15 1/4" l. (ILLUS., bottom previous page)............... **$1,410**

Early Hardstone Cameo in Fancy Mount

Cameo pendant, carved hardstone, enamel & 18k yellow gold, the oval cameo boldly carved w/the bust portrait of a classical lady, the gold frame trimmed w/polychrome champlevé enamel on the front & back, nick on the cameo face, 19th c. (ILLUS.) **$1,116**

Cameo pendant, hardstone & 14k gold, a carnelian agate cameo within an oval frame w/applied foliate designs & a flexible fringe, suspended on a gold chain, Victorian, 18" l. (pendant bail missing suspended element)................................... **$441**

Lovely Victorian Hardstone Cameo

Cameo pendant, hardstone & 14k yellow gold, the oval cameo w/a black ground boldly carved w/a large profile bust of a classical lady w/fabric headwrap trimmed w/a dark brown floral sprig, in a wide oval mount w/a twisted wire band, boxed, 19th c. (ILLUS.)... **$1,880**

Rare Cameo in Gem-set Enameled Frame

Cameo pendant, the oval shell cameo carved w/a scene of a classical woman driving a chariot, mounted in a flaring oval frame decorated w/polychrome champleve enamel & suspending a pearl, hung on two thin gold chains from a top segment centered by a cabochon ruby & suspending a smaller pearl, further enameling on the back, 20k yellow gold mount, 19th c. (ILLUS.).................. **$2,820**

Fine Hardstone Cameo Pendant & Gold Chain

Cameo pendant & chain, carved hardstone, the pendent centered by an oval cameo w/a profile bust portrait of a lady in Renaissance dress, the wide 14k gold frame highlighted by seed pearls, rose-cut diamonds & bead & wiretwist accents, suspended from an 18k gold heavy ribbed trace link chain, completed by an integral bead clasp possibly added later, 19th c. (ILLUS.) **$2,938**

Fine Victorian Shell Cameo Pendant-Brooch

Cameo pendant-brooch, shell cameo & 14k bicolor gold, the large oval cameo carved w/a finely detail bust of a Grecian lady, wide yellow & rose gold frame w/scroll & bead accents, 19th c. (ILLUS.) **$470**

Fine Victorian Agate Cameo Pendant

Cameo pendant-locket, carved agate & 18k gold, Etruscan Revival style, the oval carved carnelian agate cameo depicting a dancing classical lady, within a wide gold frame decorated w/applied beads & ropetwist accents, the wide top loop also trimmed w/beading, locket compartment in the back contains blonde hair, mid-19th c. (ILLUS.) **$1,116**

Fine Pair of Victorian Shell Cameos

Cameo pins, carved shell, large oval pair w/facing portraits of a Victorian couple, one showing a profile bust portrait of a gentleman facing right & wearing a fancy coat & cravat, the other w/a bust portrait of a lady facing left w/a cap on her pulled-back hair & wearing a high-collared dress, each housed in a simple gold frame w/small hallmarks that may be French, the man w/invisible cracks, the lady w/two visible cracks, 2nd half 19th c., in original presentation boxes, each 2 x 2 1/2", the pair (ILLUS.) **$920**

Rare Christ Cameo & Diamond Ring

Cameo ring, carved agate, 18k gold & diamond, centered by an oval agate cameo depicting the head of Christ, framed by sixteen old mine-cut diamonds weighing about 4.00 cts., the shoulder w/diamond & ruby bishop's & archbishop's symbols, w/ring guard, 19th c., size 10 (ILLUS.)..... **$5,758**

Cameo ring, carved shell & 14k. gold, the cameo carved w/the doves of Pliny, small edge loss, size 4 1/2" **$411**

Chain, bone & 14k gold, composed of alternating engraved baton & cylindrical bone links, completed by a ropetwist chain, 29" l. **$705**

Elaborate Enameled & Gem-set Renaissance Revival Chain

Chain, gem-set & enamel, Renaissance Revival style, composed of groups of three enameled links w/a long oblong enameled link decorated w/a white panel framed by black & deep red leaves flanked by smaller oval enameled links w/deep red, white & black bands, the groups alternating w/small rectangular plaques w/enamel trim around a collet-set gem on the front & back including a foil-back sapphire, ruby, emerald, pearl, turquoise, diamond, amethyst, coral, moonstones, opal & pink topaz, minor enamel loss, later hook closure, 26 3/4" l. (ILLUS. of part, top of page)................. **$18,800**

Chain, gold (18k), Art Nouveau style, composed of navette-shaped links w/scrolling wirework joined by trace link chain, 62" l. **$2,585**

Chain, gold (18k), composed of trace links textured w/dots completed by a tubular clasp, 19th c., 16 1/4" l. **$294**

Chain, turquoise & 14k gold, Art Nouveau style, the delicate trace link gold chain punctuated by scrolled leaf links & small bezel-set cabochon turquoise links, 54" l. (ILLUS., bottom of page)........................ **$2,820**

Charm bracelet, gold, gem & hardstone, a wide bracelet of oblong yellow gold links suspending 17 charms including a small book-shaped locket dated 1888, an inta-

Unusual Victorian Charm Bracelet

glio-cut stone w/bust, small square charm w/diamond & blue stone, large oval cut amethyst-style stone, gold horse-shaped fob w/green jade inset (damaged head), gold heart w/diamond chip, revolving yellow stone w/intaglio-cut bust, drilled 1849 gold one dollar coin, oval pietra dura flower, green stone slide chain clasp, small round cameo of woman, intaglio-cut jasper stone, engraved gold disk, small locket, oval pendant w/red (possibly ruby) & diamond teardrops, small basket w/a turquoise & gold globe w/a seed pearl holder, late 19th c., 7" l. (ILLUS.) **$2,530**

Art Nouveau Turquoise & Gold Chain

Rare Gem-set Gold Art Nouveau Choker

Early Turquoise & Gold Choker

Lovely Enameled Gold Chatelaine

Chatelaine, enameled 14k gold, a leafy-scroll openwork waist clasp suspending three trace link chains each trimmed w/small blue enameled blossom, the chains suspending a cylindrical gold needlecase, a cylindrical adjustable mechanical pencil case enameled w/the figure of a classical woman on a blue ground & a folding button hook, hallmark of the maker Carter, Howe & Co., retailed by Black, Starr & Frost, early 20th c. (ILLUS.).. **$1,880**

Choker, gem-set 14k yellow gold, Art Nouveau style, composed of openwork looped & serpentine links highlighted w/seed pearls, diamonds, rubies, sapphires or turquoise, joined by trace link chains, American hallmark, late 19th - early 20th c., 13" l. (ILLUS. of part, bottom previous page) **$3,819**

Choker, turquoise & 14k yellow gold, composed of six large oval turquoise cabo-

chons joined by triple delicate trace link chains, ca. 1900, 13" l. (ILLUS. of part, top of page)... **$764**

Antique Clasp with Later Pearl Bracelet

Clasp, painted porcelain & 14k gold, an oval porcelain plaque painted w/a scene of a young girl seated in a landscape, mounted in an oval gold frame decorated w/gold beads, joined to a later multi-strand cultured pearl bracelet, overall 6 1/8" l. (ILLUS.) **$353**

Rare Pair of 18k Gold Coach Covers

Coach covers, gold (18k), Etruscan Revival style, each hinged sphere applied overall w/fine wirework decoration, 19th c., pr. (ILLUS.).. **$1,645**

Rare Antique Emerald & Gold Cross

Cross, gold (18k) & emerald, the large cross decorated at the end of each arm w/a round medallion depicting Luke, John, Mark & Paul, open scrolls set at the corners, the inner arms prong-set w/bands of graduated step-cut emeralds w/the largest one at the very center, suspended from an antique 14k gold double strand smooth link chain, 19th c., overall 31 1/2" l. (ILLUS.).................................... **$6,463**

Early Victorian Maltese Cross Pendant

Cross pendant, chalcedony & gold, in the shape of a Maltese cross, the wide flaring & scalloped arms formed of thin pieces of milky chalcedony centered by a delicate gold flower & stem cluster surrounding an oval mixed-cut pale green chalcedony cabochon, a scroll-decorated pendant loop, ca. 1840, 2" w. (ILLUS.) **$558**

Cross pendant, diamond, ruby & gold, the wide cross set in the arms w/six large European-cut diamonds outlined in calibré-cut rubies, millegrain accents, platinum-topped 14k gold mount, suspended from a later 14k white gold chain, Edwardian era, early 20th c., cross 3/4" l. (ILLUS., top next column)..................................... **$1,880**

Diamond & Ruby Early Cross Pendant

Cross pendant, gem-set 18k gold, the top center & end of each arm bezel-set w/a large circular-cut amethyst or emerald, four pearls near the center, applied bead & wirework accents, 19th c. **$2,938**

Cross pendant, sapphires & 14k gold, gem-set cross w/circular-cut sapphires, cross suspended on gold chain w/five square step-cut sapphires, bloomed gold mount, signed "Tiffany & Co.," 32" l. **$3,819**

Fine Antique Diamond Cross Pendant

Cross pendant-brooch, diamond & 18k gold, the gold mount set w/ten old European- and mine-cut diamonds weighing about 3.75 cts., each arm w/a pointed & forked tip accented w/black enamel, 2 1/8" l. (ILLUS.) **$3,525**

Cuff buttons, diamond & gem-set 18k gold, each bead-set w/a sapphire, diamond & split pearl leaf, rose-cut diamond accents, Dutch hallmarks, pr. **$1,175**

Cuff buttons, labradorite & 18k gold, each set w/a round labadorite cabochon framed by ropework, unsigned, in original fitted box for Pierret, Rome, Italy, antique, 1" d., pr.. **$235**

Art Nouveau Lion Head Cuff Links

Cuff links, diamond & 14k gold, Art Nouveau style, each designed as a winged lion head w/old European-cut diamond eyes & another diamond in its open mouth, signed by Schwartz Bros., pr. (ILLUS.) **$529**

Cuff links, enameled 14k gold, each end in the shape of a card suite, a spade, heart, diamond or club & enameled on a white ground, signed w/initials of maker & English karat stamp, Edwardian era, early 20th c., enamel loss, one link w/ivory tone, pr. **$470**

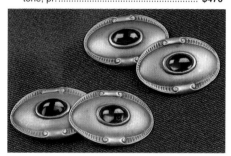

American Garnet & Gold Cuff Links

Cuff links, garnet & 14k gold, Arts & Crafts style, each double link bezel-set w/a cabochon garnet within an oval gold frame w/tiny scroll designs, inscribed "Tommie '22," American-made, pr. (ILLUS.) **$323**

Art Nouveau 14k Gold Cuff Links

Cuff links, gold (14k), Art Nouveau style, each double link w/an oval top decorated w/a geometric & garland design, marked by The Brassler Company, Newark, New Jersey, late 19th - early 20th c., pr. (ILLUS.) **$235**

Gold Art Nouveau Cuff Links

Cuff links, gold (14k yellow), Art Nouveau style, a double-link design w/the oval segments stamped w/the head of a roaring lion, partial American hallmark, possibly Krementz & Co., pr. (ILLUS.) **$470**

Gold & Ancient Coin Cuff Link

Cuff links, gold (18k) & ancient coin, each set w/a silver denarius depicting a helmeted Roma, signed by Wiese, partially worn French guarantee stamps, pr. (ILLUS. of one) **$1,998**

Unusual Carved Labradorite Cuff Links

Cuff links, labradorite & 14k gold, the large oval slightly iridescent black stone carved w/the face of a monkey w/red stone eyes, simple gold frame, 1 1/4" l., pr. (ILLUS.) **$2,468**

Platinum-topped Gold Cuff Links

Cuff links, platinum-topped 14k gold, the double links designed as engine-turned disks, American-made, signed, ca. 1915, the set (ILLUS.) **$558**

Early Quartz-set Gold Cuff Links

Cuff links, quartz & 14k yellow gold, the oval top set w/gold quartz tablets, signed "H & Co.," one link w/a dent in terminal, 19th c., pr. (ILLUS.) **$323**

Ear pendants, gold (14k) & turquoise cabochon, hemisphere & sphere design, bow & hanging tassel suspended, bezel & gypsy-set throughout w/turquoise cabochons, applied wirework accents, 10.5 dwt., Victorian (evidence of solder, small dents, missing elements) **$104**

Ornate Gold & Amethyst Victorian Earrings

Earrings, amethyst & 14k gold, ornate oblong gold leaf & coiled wirework frame

enclosing a large collet-set pear-shaped amethyst w/a smaller amethyst above & below, Victorian, missing tops, pr. (ILLUS.) **$1,645**

Early Diamond-shaped Amethyst Earrings

Earrings, amethyst & diamond, pendant-style, the fancy-cut diamond-shaped amethyst top suspending a long tapering diamond-shaped amethyst drop, rose-cut diamond highlights, silver-topped 14k gold mount, 19th c., chip, later screwback findings, pr. (ILLUS.) **$1,116**

Antique Carnelian & Gold Earrings

Earrings, carnelian & 18k gold, day/night pendant-style, the top set w/a round cabochon carnelian framed by gold leafy scrolls above a central drop composed of gold leaves & fruit above the bottom drop w/a pair of gold leaves above a long teardrop carnelian, 19th c., 2" l., pr. (ILLUS.) **$1,293**

Antique Carved Coral Pendant Earrings

Earrings, carved coral, pendant-type, carved w/a ram's head top suspending a long drop carved w/a grotesque mask & grapes & scrolling vines, later 14k gold findings, 19th c., pr. (ILLUS.) **$1,998**

Earrings, coral, pearl & 14k yellow gold, pendant-type, composed of a top coral bead suspending a cluster of three small coral beads & four natural pearls around a large round coral bead, all above three long tear-form coral drops, ca. 1890, pr. (ILLUS. left & right with other pieces of antique coral jewelry, page 22) **$920**

Earrings, coral, seed pearl & gilt-metal, pendant-style, of abstract design mounted w/seed pearls & suspending a coral bead, 19th c., 3" l., pr. **$206**

Diamond & Gold Pendant Earrings

Earrings, diamond & 18k gold, pendant-type, the top composed of ornate flaring scrolls bead-set w/full-cut diamonds, suspending a long tear-shaped gold drop, patinated silver & gold mounts, diamonds weighing about 1.88 cts., 1 3/4" l., pr. (ILLUS.) **$1,116**

Pair of Gold, Pearl & Diamond Earrings

Earrings, diamond, freshwater pearl & 14k gold, pendant-type, the top w/a pair of scrolls topped by a small rose-cut diamond & suspending three freshwater pearls, suspending an openwork scrolling drop set w/rose-cut diamonds & three freshwater pearl drops, Victorian, 1 3/4" l., pr. (ILLUS.) **$411**

Extraordinary Antique Diamond Earrings

Earrings, diamond & gold, pendant-type, the floret-form top suspending a long independent frame designed as a garland surrounding a central cascade, set overall w/112 old mine-cut, 12 rose-cut and two pear-cut diamonds, silver-topped 14k gold mounts, later findings, pr. (ILLUS.) **$31,725**

Early Diamond & Platinum Earrings

Earrings, diamond, platinum & 18k yellow gold, pendant-style, composed of two graduated circles bezel-set w/old European-cut diamonds w/single-cut diamond highlights, total weight about 3.50 cts., pr. (ILLUS., previous page) **$8,813**

Early Diamond & Tahitian Pearl Earrings

Earrings, diamond & Tahitian pearl, the oblong openwork top set w/large & small old mine- and rose-cut diamonds, suspending a large Tahitian pearl measuring about 14.00 x 1.55 mm, silver-topped 18k gold mount, 19th c., pr. (ILLUS.) **$2,468**

Earrings, enameled 18k gold, Poissarde-type, each centering a plaque depicting a polychrome champleve enamel pansy & words "A Moi," w/star & lyre designs, French guarantee stamps **$940**

One of Two Gold & Garnet Earrings

Earrings, garnet & 14k gold, pendant-type, the openwork scrolling top suspending a delicate openwork branch suspending three openwork drops, set overall w/bezel-set table-cut garnets, illegible hallmarks, chips, pr. (ILLUS. of one) **$999**

Arts & Crafts Jadeite & Gem Earrings

Earrings, gem-set jadeite & 18k gold, Arts & Crafts style, pendant-type, flat pierce-carved green jadeite plaque w/floral designs attached to a gold four-petal cap & suspended from a round flower-form top each highlighted by small demantoid garnets, citrine & sapphire mélée, 1 3/4" l., pr. (ILLUS.) **$1,058**

Earrings, gold (18k), Etruscan Revival style, pendant-type, each w/ornate ropetwist accents, minor dents, 1" l., pr. **$323**

Earrings, gold (18k), pendant-type, the floret tops suspending conical forms w/applied wirework & foliate fringe, 3" l., pr. **$529**

Victorian Gold Leaf-form Earrings

Earrings, gold (18k) & seed pearl, pendant-type, the small round top suspending a large stylized leaf-shaped plaque w/engraved border accents & centering a raised design of a ring & three-lobe leaf design accented by a seed pearl & gold bead, partial mark of the maker, 19th c., 1 3/4" l., pr. (ILLUS.) **$1,116**

Rare Grisaille Enamel & Gold Earrings

Earrings, grisaille enamel & 18k gold, pendant-type, the wide gold oval mount centered by a grisaille enameled scene of a dancing cherub, the border & upper loop finely detailed w/C-scrolls & applied bead & wirework, in a fitted box, 1 3/4" l., pr. (ILLUS.)... **$5,581**

Earrings, paste & 15k gold, each collet-set w/a cushion-cut paste, suspending a later seed pearl drop, one w/dent on back, minor solder to findings, 19th c., 7/8" l., pr. **$264**

Fine Art Nouveau Pearl & Gold Earrings

Earrings, pearl & 18k gold, Art Nouveau style, pendant-type, the top designed as an open flower & leaves centered by a small European-cut diamond & suspending a foliate designed gold framework enclosing a rounded blister pearl, European hallmarks, late 19th - early 20th c., 2 5/8" l., pr. (ILLUS.) **$4,994**

Fine Pearl & Diamond Pendant Earrings

Earrings, pearl, diamond & gold, pendant-type, a pearl- and diamond-set link suspending a round drop centered by a large button pearl framed by a ring of old European- and mine-cut diamonds, diamonds weighing about 1.70 cts., silver-topped 14k gold mount, 1 1/8" l., pr. (ILLUS.)..... **$2,350**

Victorian Pink Coral Carved Earrings

Earrings, pink coral, the top carved as a small fly above a suspended carved flower over three teardrops, gilt-metal mounts, 19th c., pr. (ILLUS.)...................... **$294**

Ruby, Diamond & Gold Earrings

Earrings, ruby, diamond & gold, a round openwork gold frame bezel-set w/rubies surrounded by rose-cut diamonds, one small ruby missing, ca. 1890, pr. (ILLUS.) **$633**

Lapis & Gold Castellini Fibula

Fibula, lapis lazuli & 18k gold, a thin ringed bold bar centered by a long oval lapis cabochon within a gold frame, hallmark of Castellini, 2" l. (ILLUS.).......................... **$353**

Antique French Fob Chain with Bloodstone Accents

Fob chain, bloodstone & 18k gold, the double foxtail chain mounted w/two oval slides set w/bloodstone & suspending a watch key & oval swivel fob also set w/bloodstone, engraved foliate & trefoil designs, French guarantee stamps & maker's mark, 13" l. (ILLUS., top of page) **$940**

Fine Art Nouveau Gold Hair Comb

Hair comb, tortoiseshell, 14k yellow gold & seed pearl, Art Nouveau style, the top w/a curved rectangular gold frame enclosing a blossom & leaf vine accented w/seed pearls, the long-toothed comb of tortoiseshell, hallmark of Sloan & Co., ca. 1900 (ILLUS.) **$1,645**
Jabot pin, diamond, pearl & 18k gold, each fan-shaped end w/pavé-set diamond

mélée framing a golden & ivory-toned cultured pearl, pearl possibly natural, Edwardian, England, early 20th c **$3,878**

Aquamarine, Pearl & Diamond Lavaliere

Lavaliere, aquamarine, pearl & diamond, designed w/two white pearl drops suspending small leaves set w/old mine-cut diamonds all above the large cushion-cut aquamarine drop, millegrain accents, platinum-topped 14k gold mount, completed w/a delicate platinum trace link chain, Edwardian, England, early 20th c., 16" l. (ILLUS.) **$1,645**

Lovely Edwardian Diamond Lavaliere

Lavaliere, diamond & platinum, an openwork heart-shaped top bead- and bezel-set w/old European- and mine-cut diamonds suspending an openwork teardrop further set w/diamonds & suspending a large diamond solitaire, on a delicate trace link chain, Edwardian, England, early 20th c., 15 1/2" l. (ILLUS.)............................... **$3,290**

Fine Edwardian Opal Lavaliere

Lavaliere, opal & diamond, the teardrop-shaped long opal suspended from an old European- and rose-cut diamond bow, completed by a delicate fancy link chain, platinum-topped 18k gold mount, Edwardian era, early 20th c., overall 15" l. (ILLUS.) **$3,500-4,500**

Turquoise, Enamel & Pearl Lavaliere

Lavaliere, turquoise, enamel & pearl, Art Nouveau style, the looping openwork pendant enameled in pale blue & centered by a heart-shaped turquoise & w/two freshwater pearl drops w/diamond mélée accent, suspending a turquoise teardrop, on a delicate trace link gold chain, hallmark of Krementz & Co., early 20th c., 15" l. (ILLUS.)........................... **$1,763**

Engraved & Gem-set Gold Locket

Locket, gem-set 14k gold, the round flat gold disk finely engraved w/leafy scrolls & blossoms, highlighted by a circle of tiny circular-cut peridot & scattered old mine-cut diamonds, opens to a compartment, 1 1/4" d. (ILLUS.) **$1,645**

Art Nouveau Gold Locket

Locket, gold (14k yellow), Art Nouveau style, rounded scroll-bordered design centered by a bold-relief helmeted head of a Roman soldier, old European-cut diamond highlight, late 19th - early 20th c. (ILLUS.).. **$353**

Gold Locket with Lady & Cherub Scene

Locket, gold (18k), Art Nouveau style, a flat disk embossed w/a scene of a lady & cherub framed by C-scrolls & swags, rose-cut diamond accents, signed "Holyss," late 19th - early 20th c. (ILLUS.) **$999**

French Gold, Pearl & Diamond Locket

Locket, gold, pearl & diamond, oval set w/an outer band of pearls around a large stylized flower set w/24 partial-cut diamonds & a central pearl, scrolled top for hanging ring, French hallmarks, 19th c. (ILLUS.).. **$403**

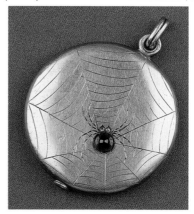

Antique Locket with Spider Design

Locket, sapphire, diamond & 14k gold, the large round gold disk etched w/a design of a spider web w/a large spider to one side, the body formed by a sapphire cabochon & the eyes by small rose-cut diamonds, 1 3/4" d. (ILLUS.) **$1,116**

Victorian Gold Locket & Book Chain

Locket on book chain, gold (14k), the chain composed of alternating applied wirework & polished round links suspending a cartouche-shaped locket w/wirework trim & centering an oval panel enclosing two rounded wirework panels flanking a band of seed pearls, late 19th c., 18 1/4" l. (ILLUS. of part) **$940**

Art Nouveau Gold Lorgnette

Lorgnette, 14k gold, Art Nouveau style, the oval top w/a top screw-knob bordered & centered by bands of fine floral scrolls continuing down the undulating handle & grip, w/an 18k gold bloom, early 20th c., 4 1/4" l. (ILLUS., top of page).................... **$441**

Gold & Diamond Art Nouveau Lorgnette

Lorgnette, gold (14k) & diamond, the oval gold case & long handle ornately embossed as iris blossoms & vining leaves accented w/old mine-cut diamond mélée around the blossom, late 19th - early 20th c. (ILLUS.)... **$1,116**

Muff chain, pinchbeck, composed of textured round trace links completed by a barrel clasp, first half 19th c., 42" l. (ILLUS., bottom of page)... **$1,293**

Necklace, agate & 15k yellow gold, composed of hinged narrow rectangular engraved gold plaques each set w/two agate, jasper or bloodstone panels flanking a foil-backed cabochon, Scotland, 19th c., 16" l. (ILLUS. of part, top next page)
.... **$8,519**

Early Pinchbeck Muff Chain

Rare Scottish Stone & Gold Necklace

Antique Amethyst & Fancy Gold Necklace

Necklace, amethyst & 14k gold, composed of 12 oblong links w/ornate openwork scrolling gold mounts enclosing large oval fancy-cut amethysts, the central link suspending a matching detachable link enclosing a teardrop-cut amethyst, 15 1/2" l. (ILLUS.) **$3,408**

Fine Amethyst & Gold Antique Fringe-style Necklace

Necklace, amethyst & 14k gold, fringe-type, a fine trace link chain suspecting a repeating design of amethysts w/a small gold bellflower link suspending a marquise-cut amethyst alternating w/gold S-scrolls flanking a large facet-cut oval amethyst suspending a marquise-cut amethyst, the front center w/the largest oval & marquise-cut drops, engraved accents, 16 3/4" l. (ILLUS.) **$3,819**

Krementz Art Nouveau Necklace

Rare Castellani Gold & Amethyst Necklace

Necklace, amethyst & 18k gold, archeolog-
ical-style fringe-type, a design of multiple
small round cabochon amethyst drops interspersed w/beads & rondels strung on
a foxtrail chain, S-form closure, mark of
Castellani, small dents, losses to several
beads, 15 1/2" l. (ILLUS.)..................... **$30,550**

Necklace, amethyst, seed pearl & 14k gold,
Art Nouveau style, a long delicately
scroll-pierced band tapering to a point at
each end & centered by a faceted oval
amethyst & accented w/seed pearls, suspending a pierced scrolling drop mounted w/a pear-shaped amethyst, completed by a trace link chain, mark of
Krementz & Company, Newark, New Jer-
sey, dated 1909, 15" l. (ILLUS.)................ **$764**

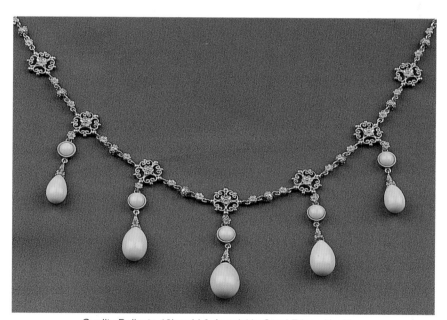

Quality Delicate 18k gold & Angelskin Coral Fringe Necklace

Necklace, angelskin coral & 18k gold, fringe-style, composed of a fine gold chain accented w/tiny florets &
beaded balls accented by seven scrolling floret links w/the center five each suspending a round coral cabochon above a large coral tear-shaped drop, the end completed by a foxtail chain, 19th c., 15 3/4" l.
(ILLUS.) **$2,350**

Very Fine Aquamarine & Gold Antique Fringe Necklace

Necklace, aquamarine & 15k gold, fringe-type, designed as a graduating fringe of prong-set round, rectangular & cushion-cut aquamarines joined at the front by six lacy loop links, signed w/initials of the maker, 19th c., 15 1/4" l. (ILLUS.) **$4,348**

Green Carved Nephrite Dragon Necklace

Necklace, carved nephrite, the long green serpentine sides each carved as a dragon joined at the front w/small links & a carved fruit-form cabachon, in a silver mount (ILLUS.) **$2,115**

Extraordinary Carved Ruby & Diamond Necklace

Necklace, carved ruby, diamond & platinum, composed of ornate openwork platinum links w/geometric, feath-
er-style & ribbon designs set overall w/old European-, mine- and single-cut diamond mélée, the openwork
links joining 12 graduating oval carved rubies w/stylized floral & geometric designs all centered by a large
oval cameo-carved ruby featuring the bust profile of a lady, seed pearl accents, gemstones weighing about
9.27 cts., ca. 1920, 15 1/2" l. (ILLUS.) **$22,325**

Fine East Indian Citrine & Seed Pearl Necklace

Necklace, citrine, seed pearl & 18k gold,
composed of three swags of faceted oval
citrine beads interspersed w/strands of
seed pearls, gathered at the ends by bars
highlighted w/red enamel cabochons, In-
dia, 13 3/4" l. (ILLUS., above) **$2,585**
Necklace, cultured pearl, composed of 47
pearls w/ivory overtones ranging in size
from 7.60 to 7.80 mm, completed by a
14k gold clasp w/old European- and
rose-cut diamonds, 17 1/2" l. (ILLUS.,
next column) **$470**

Early Cultured Pearl Necklace

Necklace, diamond, citrine & 14k gold, Art Nouveau style, a large oblong facet-cut citrine flanked by large leafy scrolls continuing into the leafy scroll chain accented by collet-set small diamonds, European hallmark, ca. 1900, 16" l..................... **$5,288**

Necklace, diamond, graduating geometric scroll design links bead-set w/rose-cut diamonds, silver-topped 18k gold mount, 15 1/4" l. **$7,050**

Edwardian Diamond & Ruby Necklace

Necklace, diamond & ruby, negligee-style, two rose-cut diamond flower terminals framed by calibré-cut rubies suspended from knife-edge bar links highlighted by bezel-set full- and rose-cut diamonds, millegrain accents, completed by a fancy link chain, platinum & 18k gold mount, Edwardian, w/original fitted Parisian jeweler's box, 20" l. (ILLUS. of part)............ **$4,935**

Ornate Gold & Emerald Necklace

Necklace, emerald, seed pearl & 18k yellow gold, a central scrolled filigree plaque centered by a bezel-set cabochon emerald & accented for three seed pearls, suspending three drops, two w/a small gold oval suspending an emerald cabochon & the long central one w/an emerald cabochon above a gold scroll mount set w/two cabochon emeralds, suspended on a delicate trace link gold chain further set w/two cabochon emeralds, T-form closure, 19th c., 16 1/2" l. (ILLUS.) **$2,468**

Art Nouveau Freshwater Pearl & Gold Necklace

Necklace, freshwater pearl & 14k gold, Art Nouveau style, fringe-style w/the delicate looped & scrolling gold chain set w/white pearls w/rose overtones, centered by a large baroque pearl drop flanked by two delicate trace link chains suspending further pearls, late 19th - early 20th c., 16 1/2" l. (ILLUS.) **$1,293**

Art Nouveau Freshwater Pearl & Diamond Necklace

Necklace, freshwater pearl & diamond, Art Nouveau style, fringe-type design w/a delicate trace link chain suspending a band of alternating large oblong pearls & smaller rounded pearls, the large pearls on links topped by a small old mine-cut diamond, ribbed barrel clasp, early 20th c., 14 1/4" l. (ILLUS., top of page) **$2,763**

Necklace, garnet, a central long scrolled mount w/a six-petal blossom at the center set overall w/round & pear-shaped rose-cut garnets, suspending three drops, each w/a cluster of three garnets above a single round garnet suspending a teardrop garnet, the links in the chain each set w/a round garnet, gilt-metal mount, second half 19th c., 16 1/2" l. **$1,116**

Fine Fancy Link Antique Garnet Necklace

Necklace, garnet, fringe-type, the side links composed of small florets set w/garnets, the central group of seven large links each set in an openwork design of a crescent enclosing a star & each suspending a floral-shaped garnet drop, gilt mount, 15 1/2" l. (ILLUS.) **$764**

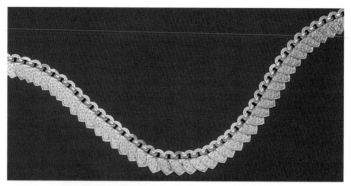

Necklace of Etched Padlock-shaped Gold Links

Fine Victorian Garnet Necklace

Necklace, garnet, graduated wide form set overall w/faceted garnets in a graduating florette design, gilt-metal mount, Victorian, one stone missing, 14 1/2" l. (ILLUS. of part).. **$1,763**

Necklace, gold (14k), composed of oval wirework links w/floret & flattened bead accents, 18 1/4" l. **$705**

Necklace, gold (14k yellow), composed of a graduating fringe of gold teardrops suspended from a trace link chain, 19th c., 15" l. **$2,468**

Necklace, gold (15k), composed of overlapping flat gold padlock-shaped links engraved w/foliate designs, 16 1/4" l. (ILLUS., top of page)............................. **$2,468**

Necklace, gold (18k), composed of large graduating quatrefoil links each w/a domed center w/a sunburst design of alternating solid & filigree panels, the same sunburst design continues on the flat sides of each link with bead highlights, late 19th c., 16" l. (ILLUS., bottom of page) **$2,233**

Fancy Filigree Quatrefoil Link Victorian Necklace

Necklace, gold (18k), diamond & enamel, Art Nouveau-style, delicate trace link chain w/figure of woman in blue enamel dress suspended, framed by curving branches w/pink & blue plique-a-jour enamel leaves, bezel-set w/seven old European-cut diamonds & bead-set w/rose-cut diamond highlights, freshwater pearl terminal, 18" l. **$4,935**

Necklace, gold (18k), slide-type, the fancy link rope chain mounted w/an engraved slide w/foliate terminals, second half 19th c., 36" l. **$999**

Art Nouveau Gold, Diamond & Enamel Necklace

Necklace, gold, diamond & enamel, Art Nouveau style, delicate trace link chain, suspended figure of woman in blue enamel dress, framed by curving branches w/pink & blue plique-a-jour enamel leaves, bezel-set w/seven old European-cut diamonds & bead-set w/rose-cut diamond highlights, freshwater pearl terminal, 18" l. (ILLUS.) **$4,935**

Arts & Crafts Gem-set Gold Necklace

Necklace, moonstone, aquamarine & 14k gold, Arts & Crafts style, the front centered by a large oblong moonstone cabochon flanked by cushion-cut aquamarines, joined by bar spacers & completed by a long tapering fancy link chain, double trefoil clasp inscribed w/a

phrase from the Song of Solomon, nick to reverse of moonstone, early 20th c., 15 1/2" l. (ILLUS.) **$3,231**

Extraordinary Antique Pearl & Diamond Necklace

Necklace, natural pearl, diamond & gold, composed of 18 graduated flower-form links each centered by white pearls ranging in size from 8.50 to 9.90 mm, the flower petals set w/old European-cut diamonds weighing about 34.06 cts., silver-topped 15k gold mount, unsigned work of Carrington & Co., England, original fitted box, second half 19th c., 15 1/2" l. (ILLUS.) **$143,500**

Necklace, onyx & enameled gold, composed of graduating open carved onyx rings each suspending a bulbous onyx drop & joined by small diamond-shaped floral-engraved & black-enameled links, the three central links enclosing a second smaller link, 19th c., 14" l. (ILLUS., top next page) **$2,350**

Necklace, pearl, cultured, 101 white pearls graduated in size from 3.75-7.01 mm, completed by openwork 18k white gold barrel clasp w/diamond accents, Continental hallmark, 22" l. **$382**

Necklace, pearl, cultured, composed of 46 white pearls w/rose overtones measuring approx. 8.05-8.20 mm, completed by 18k gold X-form clasp, signed "T & Co." for Tiffany & Co., w/original suede pouch, 16 1/4" l. **$2,233**

Necklace, platinum, aquamarine, diamond & seed pearl, fringe-style, an upper band composed of circular-cut aquarmarines alternating w/seed pearl links, the lower band composed of a seed pearl chain connected to the upper band w/two-leaf diamond-set links or larger seed pearls, suspending several larger pear-shaped faceted aquamarine drops, platinum-topped 14k gold mount, completed by a later 14k white gold curb chain, Edwardian era, overall 18 3/8" l. (ILLUS., second next page) **$2,468**

Necklace, platinum, diamond & seed pearl, negligee-style, the chain suspending a long drop composed of delicate leaves, scrolls & a blossom, all set w/old European- or mine-cut diamonds, this suspending a short diamond-set drop flanked by two long matching drops of slightly varying lengths also set w/diamonds & seed pearls, 14k white gold fancy link chain, Edwardian era, England, 19 1/2" l. (one mélée missing) **$3,055**

Onyx Ring & Enameled Gold Victorian Necklace

Aquamarine, Seed Pearl, Diamond & Platinum Edwardian Fringe Necklace

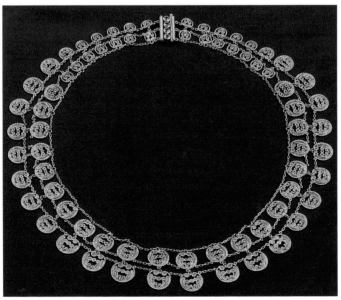

Extraordinary Plique-a-Jour Enamel & Gold Filigree Necklace

Delicate Edwardian Seed Pearl & Gold Fringe Necklace

Necklace, plique-a-jour enamel & 18k gold, composed of a double row of delicate filigree circles enclosing openwork green enameled leaf & dot designs, joined by trace links & completed by a later circular-cut ruby clasp, ca. 1910, 18 3/4" l. (ILLUS., bottom previous page) **$24,675**

Necklace, seed pearl & 14k gold, fringe-style, the delicate link chain set w/seed pearls & suspending in the front alternating seed pearl-set beads & small leaves, a round pearl-set flowerhead at the center front, Edwardian era, early 20th c., 14 3/4" l. (ILLUS., top of page) **$1,058**

Necklace, seed pearl, enamel & 14k gold, festoon-style decorated w/floral, foliate & bow designs, applied bead & ropetwist accents, black tracery enamel & seed pearl accents, suspended from a double box-link chain, evidence of solder, 19th c., 14 3/4" l. **$1,410**

Fancy Antique Silver & Turquoise Choker-type Necklace

Necklace, silver & turquoise, choker-type, the choker band composed of ornate openwork scroll & lattice sections joined by light blue turquoise cabochons & centered by a scroll-framed larger turquoise cabochon, suspending two silver links spaced w/oval turquoise cabochons each suspending two teardrop-shaped turquoise cabochons, ca. 1900, 13" l. (ILLUS.) **$1,175**

Tiffany Turquoise & Gold Bead Necklace

Necklace, turquoise & 18k gold, Arts & Crafts style, composed of groups of bluish-green tumbled turquoise w/matrix egg-shaped beads alternating w/oval scrolling openwork gold beads, signed by Tiffany & Co., one small turquoise bead possibly replaced, ca. 1915, 33" l. (ILLUS., top of page)............................ **$17,625**

Necklace, turquoise & 18k gold, snake-form, composed of flexible links, bezel-set w/turquoise cabochons, circular-cut ruby eyes, very minor solder evidence at pin near head, Victorian, 15 3/4" l. (ILLUS. of part, next column) **$3,055**

Gold & Turquoise Snake Bracelet

Rare Bow-shaped Diamond Necklet

Necklet, platinum & diamond, designed as a long hinged bow w/upward curling ends & a circular center w/swirled leaves, bead- and bezel-set overall w/old European- and single-cut diamonds, diamonds weighing about 6.65 cts., millegrain accents, suspended from a 10k white gold chain, 17" l. (ILLUS.) **$5,875**

Arts & Crafts Amazonite-set Pendant

Pendant, amazonite & 14k gold, Arts & Crafts style, the delicate oblong gold mount w/slender leafy vines & tiny beads enclosing four bezel-set long oval amazonite cabochons framing a large rectangular cabochon, suspended on a gold foliate frame enclosing a teardrop amazonite cabochon, early 20th c. (ILLUS.) **$1,410**

Amethyst, Seed Pearl & Gold Pendant

Pendant, amethyst, seed pearl & 15k gold, designed as a gold ribbon bow set w/seed pearls suspending an amethyst briolette drop, suspended from a delicate 14k gold trace link chain, Edwardian era, early 20th c., overall 16 3/4" l. (ILLUS. of pendant) **$999**

Pendant, black onyx & rose gold, mourning-type, inscribed "Charles Lord Southampton, obt 22 March 1797" & "George Lord Southampton, obt 24 June 1810," centering a glass compartment containing locks of hair, enameled crown design bail, early 19th c. **$259**

Carved Jadeite Gold-framed Pendant

Pendant, carved jadeite, emerald, diamond & 14k gold, a long rectangular orange jadeite plaque carved w/exotic foliage, mounted in a serpentine gold frame decorated w/leaf-like designs accented w/single-cut diamonds & four small emeralds, 3 1/2" l. (ILLUS.) **$881**

Early Bird & Heart Diamond Pendant

Pendant, diamond & 9k gold, designed as a small bird suspending a large heart, both set overall w/rose-cut diamonds, engraved back, w/a later 14k gold chain, ca. 1900 (ILLUS.) **$1,645**

Elegant Diamond & Pearl Pendant

Pendant, diamond, pearl & gold, an open-work looping design decorated w/four larger old European-cut diamonds & 70 old single- and rose-cut diamond mélée, the top loop centered by a pearl measuring 7.20 mm, also w/an oblong pearl drop, in a platinum-topped 18k gold mount, suspended from a delicate platinum trace link chain, Edwardian era, early 20th c., pearls not tested for origin, pendant 1 3/4" l. (ILLUS.)........................ **$2,350**

Rare Art Nouveau Emerald Pendant

Pendant, emerald, diamond & enamel, Art Nouveau style, a large central cabochon

emerald & a teardrop emerald drop, the cabochon within a gold scroll mount framed by 47 old European-cut diamonds, platinum-topped 18k gold mount, chased & engraved on the reverse, by Marcus & Co., later pin stem, some enamel loss (ILLUS.) **$17,625**

Pearl-edged Enameled Pansy Pendant

Pendant, enameled gold, diamond & seed pearl, Art Nouveau style, designed as a pansy blossom enameled in dark purple shading to white & centered by an old mine-cut diamond, the petals edged by tiny seed pearls, suspended from a flattened curb link chain, mark of Crane & Theurer, chain unsigned, overall 18" l. (ILLUS.).. **$940**

Carbuncle-set Enameled Gold Pendant

Pendant, gem-set & enameled 18k gold, the oblong cartouche-form gold frame centered by a large bezel-set carbuncle & accented w/dotted bands of white enamel & wire & beadwork accents, a pointed drop at the bottom also trimmed w/enamel, suspended from a bar & loop link further trimmed w/white enamel, mark of Edwin Streeter, successors to Hancock & Co., original fitted box, 19th c. (ILLUS.)... **$2,233**
Pendant, gold (14k), opal & enamel, Art Nouveau-style, oval opal framed by a pink guilloché enamel lotus design, two diamond accents, suspended by a 14k

gold trace link chain, hallmark for Krementz & Co. (crack to opal)........................ **$705**

Gold Art Nouveau Maiden Head Pendant

Pendant, gold (18k), Art Nouveau style, round disk stamped in relief w/the head of an Art Nouveau maiden w/flower-filled flowing hair, early 20th c., 1 1/8" d. (ILLUS.) **$264**

Pendant, gold (18k), guilloché enamel & diamond, the 18k gold locket w/pale blue guilloché enamel in a radiating design set in the center w/an old European-cut diamond surrounded by an open ring w/leaf sprigs further set w/diamonds, a narrow outer rim band further set w/small rose- and old European-cut diamonds, suspended from a platinum chain w/blue enamel baton links trimmed w/seed pearls, Edwardian era, locket w/French guarantee stamp, chain 20" l. **$2,705**

Gem-set Large Lapis Lazuli Pendant

Pendant, lapis lazuli & gem-set 18k gold, bulla-style, centered by a very large lapis cabochon framed by projecting button pearls & rose-cut diamonds, blue enamel accents, a locket in the back, 1 3/4" d. (ILLUS.).. **$1,058**

Gorham Art Nouveau Moonstone Pendant

Pendant, moonstone & 14k gold, Art Nouveau style, a long oval openwork gold mount w/scrolling cattails suspending a long narrow oval cabochon moonstone, mark of Gorham Mfg. Co., Providence, Rhode Island, late 19th - early 20th c. (ILLUS.) **$588**

Fine Ivory, Diamond & Emerald Pendant

Pendant, painted ivory, emerald, diamond & gold, a large central oval ivory plaque h.p. in color w/a scene of the circumcision of Christ, enclosed in an openwork scrolling gold frame & bail set w/old mine-cut diamonds & bezel-set step-cut emeralds, silver-topped 14k gold mount, 19th c., 1 3/4 x 2 1/2" (ILLUS.).................. **$823**

Early French Paste & Enamel Pendant

Pendant, paste, enamel & silver, the large oval central mother-of-pearl plaque painted en grisaille w/a scene of two Cupids, the frame composed of a ring of cut paste stones, a locket compartment on the back, French assay mark, 19th c. (ILLUS.) **$881**

Edwardian Pendant with Large Amethyst

Pendant, platinum, diamond & amethyst, the flexibly set oval-cut large amethyst framed by a double ring of old European, rose- and single-cut diamonds, suspended from a diamond-set looped circle & fancy link chain, millegrain accents, Edwardian, England, early 20th c., 28 1/4" l. (ILLUS.).. **$4,348**

Art Nouveau Plique-a-Jour Pendant

Pendant, plique-a-jour enamel & 14k gold, the wide stylized spade-form gold pendant centered by the molded face of an Art Nouveau maiden framed by blossoms & serpentine vines enameled in white opalescence & accented w/small full-cut

diamonds, suspending cultured pearl drop, minor solder near pendant bail, 1 3/4" l. (ILLUS.) **$11,175**

Rock Crystal & Seed Pearl Heart Pendant

Pendant, rock crystal, seed pearl & 15k gold, rounded almost heart-shaped crystal cabochon framed around the edge of the mount w/seed pearls, 19th c., 1 1/4" l. (ILLUS.)... **$823**

Pendant, ruby, freshwater pearl & 14k gold, bezel-set w/faceted rubies, engraved on the back, suspending a later fringe of freshwater pearls, 2 1/4" l. **$353**

Pendant, sapphire, pearl & diamond, bezel-set w/an oval-cut sapphire, five white pearls & 27 rose- and old mine-cut diamond accents, silver-topped 18k gold mount, suspended from later antique seed pearl & silver chain w/tarnish **$441**

Pendant, seed pearl, onyx & 14k gold, designed as a starburst set w/seed pearls, a compartment in the back, on a later grosgrain cord w/black tracery enamel & seed pearl slide, pendant 1 5/8" w., overall 29" l. **$529**

Pendant, silver, ivory & coral, designed as cluster of silver leaves & scrolling tendrils w/two fluted ivory bellflowers suspended, accented by three coral beads, probably designed by Dagobert Peche, Wiener Werkstatte, Austria, early 20th c. **$3,525**

Rare, Unique Alexandrite Pendant

Pendant-brooch, alexandrite & diamond, rectangular form prong-set in the center w/a very large cushion-shaped alexandrite weighing 11.18 cts., framed by old European-cut diamond mélée, diamonds weighing about 1.44 cts., brooch fitting detachable, evidence of minor solder at closure of pendant hook, natural color stone, 19th c. (ILLUS.) **$110,500**

Pendant-brooch, bloodstone, rose-cut diamond, ruby & 18k gold, the oval bloodstone surmounted by a rose-cut diamond & cabochon ruby floral design within an 18k gold pierced, chased & engraved floral & foliate frame set w/rose-cut diamonds & rubies, French import stamp, Victorian **$489**

Pendant-brooch, chalcedony, ruby & enamel, oval chalcedony carved w/four intaglio classical figures within a Holbeinesque polychrome floral enamel frame set w/three circular cut rubies, 18k gold mount **$1,840**

Star-shaped Diamond & Gold Pendant

Pendant-brooch, diamond & 14k gold, designed as a five-point star prong-set overall w/old European- and mine-cut diamonds, diamonds weighing about 2.20 cts. (ILLUS.) **$2,703**

Pendant-brooch, diamond & 14k gold, starburst pendant/brooch set w/fifty old mine-cut diamonds, 14k gold mount, hallmark for Krementz & Co., ca. 1900 .... **$2,990**

Tiffany Starburst Pendant/Brooch

Pendant-brooch, diamond & 18k gold, starburst design, set w/fifty-five old European-cut diamonds, 18k gold mount, signed "Tiffany & Co." (ILLUS.) **$7,168**

Antique Cross-form Diamond Pendant

Pendant-brooch, diamond & 18k yellow gold, in the shape of a Latin cross set throughout w/old European- and old mine-cut diamonds in the gold mount, 19th c., total weight 3.00 cts. (ILLUS.) **$2,233**

Pendant-brooch, diamond, bow design w/five loops, each set w/nine old mine-cut diamonds & centered by an old European-cut diamond, 18k gold mount, ca. 1895 .... **$1,955**

Pendant-brooch, diamond & demantoid garnet, model of a leaf bead-set w/circular-cut demantoid garnets within a gold ring decorated w/nine bezel-set old mine-cut diamonds, platinum-topped 18k gold mount **$3,055**

Rare Antique Diamond & Emerald Brooch

Pendant-brooch, diamond, emerald & gold, the lacy openwork four-lobe mount accented w/tiny scrolls & set w/three large old European-cut diamonds & accented w/smaller European- and mine-cut diamonds, the center bezel-set w/a large rectangular step-cut emerald, diamonds weighing about 4.62 cts., silver-topped 18k gold mount, removable brooch fitting (ILLUS.) **$19,975**

Antique Diamond Swallow Pendant

Pendant-brooch, diamond & gold, designed as a flying swallow, bead-set w/rose-cut diamond mélée, cabochon pink stone eye, engraved feathers, silver-topped 14k gold mount, missing one diamond, 2" l. (ILLUS.)...................................... **$353**

Pendant-brooch, diamond & gold, oval frame containing portraits of young girls painted front & back, silver-topped 18k gold mount designed as a bow set w/old mine-cut diamonds, Edwardian, England **$1,410**

Lovely Edwardian Diamond Pendant

Pendant-brooch, diamond & platinum, designed as a large round leafy wreath suspending an open ring surrounding a round drop centered by a large diamond, bezel-set w/four large old mine-cut diamonds weighing about 1.90 cts. the flexible frames set overall w/small rose-cut diamonds, millegrain accents, Edwardian, early 20th c. (ILLUS.) **$6,756**

Diamond and Sapphire Pendant-Brooch

Pendant-brooch, diamond & sapphire, centered by oval sapphire measuring approximately 10.10 x 7.85 x 5.05 mm, surrounded by fifty-eight old mine-, old European- and single-cut diamonds, approx. total wt. 5.56 cts., silver-topped 14k gold mount (ILLUS.)....................................... **$8,225**

Pendant-brooch, diamond & seed pearl, the round openwork design centered by a large old European-cut diamond surround by old mine- and rose-diamonds, all framed by a ring of seed pearls, diamonds weighing 1.50 cts., suspended from a later 14k white gold chain, Edwardian era, early 20th c., pendant 1 1/4" d. **$3,173**

Antique Enamel & Seed Pearl Pendant

Pendant-brooch, enamel, seed pearl & gold, an oval narrow frame set w/tiny seed pearls enclosing an openwork leaf & blossom wreath surround a rectangular plaque painted en grisaille w/a scene of two cherubs, suspended from three flattened open-link chains attached to the upper pin mount bordered by seed pearls & decorated w/a flower, 18k gold & silver-gilt mount, 19th c. (ILLUS.) **$1,528**

Pretty Art Nouveau Pansy Pendant

Pendant-brooch, enameled 14k gold, diamond & seed pearl, Art Nouveau style, designed as an enameled dark purple & white pansy blossom centered by a diamond & edged w/a thin band of seed pearls (ILLUS.)....................................... **$1,528**

Pendant-brooch, enameled 14k gold & seed pearl, designed as a green-enameled four-leaf clover centered by an old mine-cut diamond, the stem & borders trimmed w/seed pearls, mark of Krementz & Co., Newark, New Jersey, 1 1/4" l. **$646**

Art Nouveau French Pendant-Brooch

Pendant-brooch, enameled 18k gold, diamond & pearl, Art Nouveau style, designed as an openwork rounded cluster of swirling gold leaves framing a pale purple-enameled iris blossom centered by the gold head of an Art Nouveau maiden w/flowing hair, a drop at the bottom w/a small rose-cut diamond suspending a baroque pearl, engraved mount, No. 5041, French guarantee stamp (ILLUS.)........... **$2,820**

Pendant-brooch, ivory & gem-set 14k gold, a figure of Buddha w/circular-cut sapphire, ruby, emerald & single-cut diamond highlights & a cabochon green stone accent, engraved foliate designs, 3 1/2" h. **$646**

Intaglio Moonstone & Diamond Pendant

Pendant-brooch, moonstone, diamond & gold, the central oval flat-topped moonstone intaglio-carved w/a bust figure of Diana, flanked by four old mine-cut diamonds, 14k gold mount, 3/4 x 7/8" (ILLUS.).. **$1,410**

Pearl & Diamond Heart-shaped Pendant

Pendant-brooch, seed pearl, diamond & 14k gold, heart-shaped, pavé-set w/seed pearls centering seven old European-cut diamond mélée, early 20th c., mark of Krementz & Co., Newark, New Jersey, 7/8" l. (ILLUS.).............................. **$823**

Pendant-frame, gold (14k), designed w/oak leaf & acorn designs, the back engraved "To our dear daughter Katharine Sayre Van Duzer Burton...A souvenir of our golden wedding," 1900, 3" l. **$705**

"Lover's Eye" Maltese Cross Pendant

Pendant-locket, chalcedony & 14k gold, "Lover's Eye" type, designed as a Maltese cross of carved chalcedony tablets centered by a gold square enclosing a portrait of a blue eye, framed by ornate gold cannetille work, ca. 1830, small chips (ILLUS.) **$2,350**

Enameled Gold & Ctirine Pendant

Pendant-locket, citrine & enameled gold, the oval piece centered by a large oval-cut citrine framed by two narrow white-enameled bands & a black enameled band highlighted w/tiny gold beads, an outer ropetwist gold border, a cylindrical link enameled w/black & white triangles below the top bail further enameled w/white & black bands, 2 3/4" l. (ILLUS., previous page) **$1,058**

Antique Enamel & Seed Pearl Locket

Pendant-locket, enamel, seed pearl & silver-gilt, the oval center panel enameled w/a scene of Eros w/his quiver & a basket of flowers framed by bands of small seed pearls within a thin black & white-dotted enamel border band, a seed pearl-set bow pin at the top, French assay stamp & partial hallmark, 19th c. (ILLUS.)............. **$1,175**

Etruscan Revival Gold Pendant-Locket

Pendant-locket, gold (18k), Etruscan Revival style, flattened oval form decorated w/a central diamond & a border of diamond devices against a background finely decorated w/bead & wirework, 19th c., 2 1/2" l. (ILLUS.) **$1,528**

Antique Micromosaic Pendant-Locket

Pendant-locket, micromosaic & 14k gold, a scroll-engraved rectangular plaque w/gold scroll & bead trim, centered by an oval panel w/polychrome tesserae depicting a pair of white doves among leafy branches on a deep red ground, 19th c. (ILLUS.).. **$764**

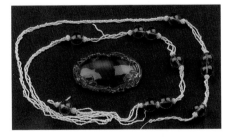

Early Chinese Amber & Pearl Pendant

Pendant-necklace, amber & seed pearl, a large oval Chinese Tao Kuang period amber pendant carved around the edges w/archaic dragons, suspended from a multi-strand seed pearl necklace highlighted by amber beads, antique Chinese, seed pearl chain broken, w/fitted paisley velvet-covered box (ILLUS.) **$1,116**
Pendant-necklace, antique glass intaglio & 18k gold, the oval glass intaglio depicting a classical scene, suspending a freshwater pearl, pendant 1 1/2" l., completed by a 14k gold curb-link chain **$470**

Very Rare Arts & Crafts Opal Pendant

Pendant-necklace, black opal, diamond & 14k gold, Arts & Crafts style, the delicate fancy link gold chain fitted w/an oblong gold slide decorated w/tiny pine cones & leaves & enclosing an oblong black opal, suspending an ornate long gold-frame pendant w/open leafy scrolls w/tiny pine cones flanking a large almond-shaped black opal above an openwork spear-point frame set w/five old European-cut diamonds suspending a black opal teardrop, mark of William Bramley, Montreal & "14B," 15" l. (ILLUS.) **$17,625**

Black Opal and Diamond Necklace

Pendant-necklace, black opal & diamond, delicate trace link chain suspending a pendant w/two bezel-set harlequin black opals & thirty-one bead & bezel-set single-cut diamonds, millegrain accents and pierced gallery, platinum-topped 18k gold mount, platinum chain, 16 1/2" l. (ILLUS.) **$3,525**

Coral & Gold Antique Pendant Necklace

Pendant-necklace, coral & 18k yellow gold, a large angelskin coral teardrop suspended from an oval gold frame trimmed w/applied bead- and wirework designs enclosing an angelskin coral cabochon, suspended from a trace link gold chain, minor wirework loss, 19th c., 17" l. (ILLUS.) **$1,293**

Rare Edwardian Diamond & Pearl Pendant

Pendant-necklace, diamond, pearl & platinum, the filigree pendant designed as a ribbon bow atop a long triangular banded drop, set overall w/bands of old European- and mine-cut diamonds accented by pearls, suspended from a baton link chain punctuated by bezel-set diamonds alternating w/pearls, millegrain accents, Edwardian era, early 20th c., missing pin, necklace extended by later 14k white gold trace link chain, 17 1/4" l. (ILLUS.).......... **$6,756**

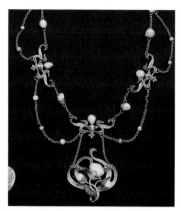

Pretty Art Nouveau Fairy Pendant

Pendant-necklace, gold (14k bicolor) & enamel, reeded trace link chain suspended by three foxtail tassel pendants & medallion w/enamel cherubs, all joined by swags, black tracery enamel accents, Victorian, 16 1/2" l. **$764**

Outstanding Enamel & Pearl Necklace

Pendant-necklace, enamel, pearl & 14k yellow gold, Art Nouveau style, the bottom pendant in the form of stylized freshwater pearl blossoms on scrolling leafy stems enameled in shaded orange & pale green & trimmed w/tiny seed pearls, suspended on delicate trace link chains below a necklace composed of three leafy scroll enamel & pearl blossoms along double delicate trace link chains accented w/seed pearls, Bippart Griscom & Osborn, late 19th - early 20th c., 15 1/2" l. (ILLUS.) **$4,406**

Victorian Gold & Seed Pearl Pendant-Necklace

Pendant-necklace, gold (14k yellow) & seed pearl, the shield-shaped pendant w/fine applied bead & wirework scroll designs & seed pearl accents w/a locket compartment in the back, the fancy link chain engraved w/scroll & floral designs, Victorian (ILLUS. of part) **$764**

Victorian Gold Necklace with Fancy Mount

Pendant-necklace, enameled 15k gold, composed of a long fancy oblong link chain fitted w/a large geometric mount centering an oval plaque set w/a stylized leafy flower w/a beaded frame, the sides w/engraved designs & black tracery enamel highlights, each end of the chain completed by a foxtail drop, barrel closure, Victorian, 17 1/4" l. (ILLUS. of part) **$764**

Pendant-necklace, gem-set 18k gold, Art Nouveau style, the pendant in the form of an Art Nouveau fairy in gold w/carved pink tourmaline wings & full-cut accents, suspended from a thin ball chain necklace w/bright-cut stars, pendant 1 5/8" l., overall 18" l. (ILLUS., top next column)... **$1,645**

Early Lalique Glass Pendant-Necklace

Pendant-necklace, molded glass, Art Nouveau style, the arrowhead-shaped foil-backed plaque designed as a nude maiden reclining among flowers, suspended from a light blue enamel baton link chain, small losses to enamel, signed, pendant 2 x 2", overall 20" l. (ILLUS., previous page) **$3,819**

Unique Enameled Art Nouveau Pendant

Pendant-necklace, plique-a-jour enamel, 18k gold & diamond, Art Nouveau style, designed as the gold dancing figure of an Art Nouveau maiden wearing a swirled long gowl enameled in turquoise & gold, the figure flanked by heavy gold vines curling up to suspend a pair of three-petaled blossoms w/blue & lavender plique-a-jour enamel & accented w/old-European- and rose-cut diamonds, the base suspending a long freshwater pearl drop, the whole suspended by a pair of trace links joined to another three-petal blossom suspending a diamond drop, later trace link chain, overall 18" l. (ILLUS.).................... **$7,931**

Fine Kalo Arts & Crafts Silver Pendant

Pendant-necklace, sterling silver & amethyst, Arts & Crafts style, the ornate openwork silver pendant decorated w/scrolling leafy vines & Glasgow roses, centering a large oval mixed-cut amethyst, suspended on a paper clip-style silver chain, mark of the Kalo Studios, overall 18" l. (ILLUS. of pendant) **$2,703**

Pendant-necklace, sterling silver & enamel, Art Nouveau style, tripartite abstract-form pendant decorated en plein w/blue & green enamel, suspended from a baton-link chain, hallmarks for Chester, date letter for 1911, maker "C.H.," England **$323**

Pendant-necklace, sterling silver & green agate, shaped pendant centered by an oval green agate, suspended from a silver paper clip chain, pendant stamped on reverse "TF (for Theodor Fahrner) - 935 - Déposé," 21" l. **$1,528**

American Art Nouveau Turquoise Pendant

Pendant-pin, turquoise & 14k gold, Art Nouveau style, a bezel-set oval cabochon turquoise within a frame of scrolled stylized leaves & vines, worn mark of A.J. Hedges & Co., Newark, New Jersey (ILLUS.) **$235**

Edwardian Amethyst, Pearl & Diamond Pin

Pin, amethyst, seed pearl & diamond, the center prong-set w/a cushion-cut amethyst framed w/an openwork arched loop frame set w/tiny single- and old European-cut diamonds & enclosing eight seed pearls, Edwardian era, early 20th c., 1" l. (ILLUS.).. **$940**

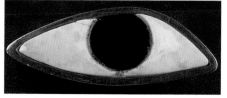

Ancient Egyptian Eye Set as a Pin

Pin, an ancient Egyptian alabaster & obsidian eye from an ancient Egyptian anthropoid coffin, mounted in a modern 18k gold mount w/a 14k gold pin stem, ca. 700 B.C., 2 5/8" l. (ILLUS., previous page) **$3,173**

Carved Carnelian Horse Head Pin

Pin, carved carnelian & 14k gold, carved as the head of a racing horse, gold mount, mark of Enos Richardson & Co., 1 1/4" l. (ILLUS.) **$470**

Art Nouveau Citrine, Pearl & Gold Pin

Pin, citrine, seed pearl & 14k gold, Art Nouveau style, an openwork scrolled wing-form gold mount resembling stylized lotus leaves centered by a large bezel-set oval fancy-cut orange citrine, seed pearl highlights around the edges, late 19th - early 20th c. (ILLUS.) **$499**

Art Nouveau Stylized Floral Garnet Pin

Pin, demantoid garnet & 14k gold, Art Nouveau style, designed as a stylized openwork scrolling floral spray w/three garnet-set blossoms & small garnets down the stem, European assay & maker's marks (ILLUS.) **$470**

Antique Diamond & Gold Starburst Pin

Pin, diamond & 14k gold, a starburst design centered by a large old mine-cut diamond surrounded by six smaller diamonds & w/each ray set w/graduated diamonds, diamonds weighing about 1.60 cts., 1 3/4" w. (ILLUS.) **$1,763**

Figural Swallow Pin with Diamonds

Pin, diamond, colored diamond & gold, in the shaped of a flying swallow w/long pointed wings & tail feathers, set w/colorless old European-, rose-, single- and full-cut diamonds & yellow diamonds, silver-topped gold mount, 2 1/2" w. (ILLUS.) **$940**

Pin, diamond, demantoid garnet & 18k gold, model of a flying goose, the large wings pavé-set w/circular-cut round garnets & the body pavé-set w/old European- and mine-cut diamonds, a ruby eye, platinum-topped gold mount, Edwardian, England, early 20th c. **$12,925**

Lovely Art Nouveau Enameled Pin

Pin, diamond, enamel & 18k gold, Art Nouveau style, designed as a pair of large scrolled leaves enameled in bluish green & framed by looping leaves & arching blossoms & buds bead-set w/single-cut diamond, suspending a freshwater pearl drop, early 20th c. (ILLUS., previous page) **$2,233**

Fine American Diamond Crown Pin

Pin, diamond & gold, designed as a crown w/five points each topped by a single diamond, the openwork mount set overall w/bead-set old European-cut diamonds, diamonds weighing about 1.33 cts., platinum-topped gold mount, signed by J.E. Caldwell & Co., Philadelphia, 1 1/2" w. (ILLUS.) **$1,880**

Antique Diamond & Ruby Snake Pin

Pin, diamond & ruby, designed as a delicate looped snake, the body set w/rose-cut diamonds, the head gypsy-set w/a circular-cut ruby, green stone eyes, platinum-topped 14k gold mount (ILLUS.) **$558**

Rose-cut Diamond Serpent Pin

Pin, diamond & ruby, designed as coiled rose-cut diamond serpent w/ruby eyes, silver-topped, 14k gold mount, Austro-Hungarian hallmarks (ILLUS.) **$1,058**

Diamond & Seed Pearl Pin

Pin, diamond & seed pearl, designed as a diamond baton tied w/ribbon, bead-set w/fifty-nine old mine-cut diamonds, seed pearl & millegrain accents, silver-topped 18k gold mount, (ILLUS.) **$646**

Fine Edwardian Diamond Pendant

Pin, diamond, the openwork form of foliate designs bead- and bezel-set overall w/old European- and single-cut diamonds, millegrain accents, platinum-topped 18k gold mount, Edwardian, England, early 20th c. (ILLUS.) **$4,230**

Hedges & Co. Enameled Pansy Pin

Pin, enamel & 14k gold, Art Nouveau style, model of a pansy flower enameled in dark purple & white, centered by a seed pearl, mark of A. J. Hedges & Co., Newark, New Jersey, early 20th c., 1 1/8" w. (ILLUS.)... **$705**

Enamel & Diamond Portrait Pin

Pin, enamel & diamond, a large central round enamel plaque h.p. w/a bust portrait of a costumed lady w/diamonds inset

into her headdress & shoulder, within an outer band of 40 rose-cut diamonds, set in 18k yellow gold (ILLUS.) **$2,200**
Pin, enamel & diamond, flying mallard w/basse taille enamel head, body & wings bead-set w/old mine-, rose- and single-cut diamonds, silver-topped 18k gold mount, w/fitted Asprey box.............. **$1,880**

Rare Hedges Wasp-shaped Pin

Pin, enamel & gem-set 14k yellow gold, in the shape of a flying wasp, the long wings w/polychrome basse taille enamel studded w/old European-cut diamond mélée, long gold body & legs, small demantoid garnet eyes, hallmark of A. J. Hedges, Newark, New Jersey, late 19th - early 20th c., 2 1/8" w. (ILLUS.)...................... **$3,290**

Art Nouveau Enameled Dragonfly Pin

Pin, enamel & gem-set gold, Art Nouveau style, designed as a flying dragonfly, the wings & long body decorated in brown basse taille enamel, demantoid garnet eyes, hallmark of Riker Bros., late 19th - early 20th c., 1 3/8 x 1 3/4" (ILLUS.)....... **$1,763**

Art Nouveau Enameled Pansy Pin

Pin, enamel & gold, Art Nouveau style, designed as a single pansy blossom enameled in purple, yellow & white & centered by a small seed pearl, 14k gold mount, hallmark of A. J. Hedges, chip to enamel, late 19th - early 20th c. (ILLUS.) **$1,058**

Art Nouveau Lotus & Leaves Pin

Pin, enamel, pearl & 14k yellow gold, Art Nouveau style, designed as a white lotus blossom centered by a seed pearl on long stems issuing pale green basse taille enamel leaves, hallmark of Krementz & Co., late 19th - early 20th c., 1 3/8 x 2" (ILLUS.).................................. **$1,763**

Pretty Art Nouveau Enameled Flower Pin

Pin, enameled 14k gold, Art Nouveau style, designed as a three-petaled blossom enameled in peach & yellow & attached to a green-enameled bud stem & a gold curled stem w/two green-enameled leaves, small freshwater pearl accents, small enamel chip, late 19th - early 20th c. (ILLUS.) **$764**

Delicate French Enameled Gold Pin

Pin, enameled 18k gold, an openwork design w/a long oval frame w/a narrow band enameled in white w/tiny gold dots, the center filled w/a gold ribbon-tied flower & leaf bouquet, signed by L. Gautrait w/mark of maker & French guarantee stamps, 1 3/8" l. (ILLUS.).......................... **$646**

Art Nouveau Enameled Beetle Pin

Pin, enameled 18k gold & diamond, Art Nouveau style, modeled as a beetle w/red & green enameled wings, the center of the body, shoulders & eyes set w/old European-cut diamonds & seed pearls, some enamel loss, missing one seed pearl, late 19th - early 20th c. (ILLUS.)..................... **$1,116**

Unusual Enameled Cherub Pin

Pin, enameled & gem-set 14k gold, the top enameled in color w/a two cherubs w/a torch & letter above a wide fan-shaped lower panel w/two gold spearpoint drops, accented w/seed pearls & red & green stone accents, enamel losses (ILLUS.) **$1,058**

Rare Edwardian Mallard Duck Pin

Pin, freshwater pearl, enamel & 18k gold, modeled as a Mallard duck drake, the front body & neck decorated w/enamel, the rear body formed by a large freshwater pearl, rose-cut diamond eye, the back w/engraved feathers, Edwardian era, England, early 20th c., 1" l. (ILLUS.) **$1,528**

Victorian "Regard" Heart-shaped Pin

Pin, gem-set 14k gold, "Regard" type, a heart shape set w/gems & simulated stones forming the acronym, applied wirework floral & foliate designs, the reverse w/a locket compartment, replaced pin stem, 19th c. (ILLUS.) **$1,410**

Pin, gold (10k yellow) & black enamel, oval cartouche-shaped floral & scroll-etched gold frame w/black enamel border band, frames a half-length Daguerreotype portrait of a young female child, ca. 1850s, 1 5/8 x 2" **$132**

Pin, gold (14k) & coral, a wide gold ring decorated w/applied beads & wirework, centered by a large angelskin coral cabochon, second half 19th c. **$176**

Pin, gold (14k), diamond & seed pearl, designed as a sword & scabbard connected by a trace link chain, the handle set w/seed pearls & four prong-set old European-cut diamonds, further seed pearls at the top, Edwardian, ca. 1905 .... **$235**

Pin, gold (14k), enamel & diamond, Art Nouveau style, in the shape of a dogwood blossom w/the petals decorated w/black enamel, the center w/an old European-cut diamond weighing .50 cts., American mark, ca. 1900 .... **$764**

Fine Castellani Gold Circle Pin

Pin, gold (15k), circle-type, designed as a beast w/a bead & wirework collar devour-

ing its tail, flexible pendant bead in the center, hallmark of Castellani, Italy, 19th c. (ILLUS.)... **$2,988**

Pin, gold (18k) & diamond, a tapering silver-topped baton set w/graduated bead-set rose-cut diamonds, entwined w/an engraved yellow gold slender rope tipped by a pearl, French guarantee mark, late 19th c. **$323**

Art Nouveau Griffin Pin

Pin, gold (18k) & diamond, Art Nouveau-style, designed as griffin clutching an old European-cut diamond, rose-cut diamond accents, marker's mark "GC" (ILLUS.)..... **$2,350**

Fancy French Gold & Diamond Pin

Pin, gold (18k yellow) & diamond, a long crescent-shaped openwork scrolling gold frame w/figural ram head terminals flanking an openwork flower & ribbon trophy topped by a bezel-set old European-cut diamond, French guarantee stamp, 19th c. (!ILLUS.)... **$1,175**

Early Gold & Pearl Lover's Eye Pin

Pin, gold & seed pearl, "Lover's Eye" design, a double oval row of seed pearls set in gold enclosing a small oval picture of a painted blue eye, late 18th - early 19th c., 1" l. (ILLUS.) **$3,819**

Crescent-shaped Opal & Diamond Pin

Pin, opal, diamond & gold, crescent-shaped, set w/graduated cabochon opals & rose-cut diamonds, Edwardian, England, early 20th c., evidence of solder (ILLUS.).. **$1,116**

Edwardian Circle Pearl Pin with Swan

Pin, pearl & enamel, circular ring composed of freshwater pearls enclosing the model of a swan composed of a large freshwater pearl & the neck & head in blue & white basse taille enamel, 14k gold mount, Edwardian, England, early 20th c. (ILLUS.)... **$646**

Pin, pietra dura & 14k gold, the oval plaque depicting a dove carrying a ribbon, the gold frame applied w/grape leaf designs, evidence of solder at pin stem **$764**

Antique Ruby & Diamond Wide Crescent Pin

Pin, ruby, diamond & 14k gold, crescent-shaped, a wide crescent bead-set along the outside edge w/a line of circular-cut rubies & set along the inner edge w/a line of rose-cut diamonds (ILLUS.) **$999**

Fine Gorham Art Nouveau Gold Pin

Pin, sapphire, diamond & 18k gold, Art Nouveau style, designed as a stylized gold heart w/ruffled edges around a design of embossed undulating leafy vines & two blossoms each centered by an old European-cut diamond, the center of the pin set w/a cushion-cut blue sapphire, Gorham Mfg. Co. mark (ILLUS.) **$9,694**

Antique American Crescent Pin

Pin, sapphire, seed pearl & 14k gold, crescent-shaped, prong-set w/circular-cut sapphires alternating w/seed pearls, hallmark of Bippart, Bennett & Co., Newark, New Jersey, early 20th c. (ILLUS.) **$235**

Rare Early Tiffany Oval Pin

Pin, sapphire, seed pearl & platinum, oval openwork filigree platinum mount centered by a cluster of cushion- and circular-cut blue sapphires, radiating bands of seed pearls, signed by Tiffany & Co., New York, ca. 1915 (ILLUS.) **$14,100**

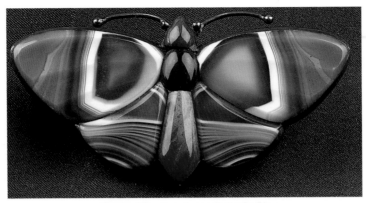

Unusual Scottish Agate Butterfly Pin

Pin, Scottish agate, in the form of a butterfly w/the body & wings composed of various pieces of patterned agate, silver mount, Scotland, mid-19th c., 2 3/8" w. (ILLUS., top of page) **$1,998**

American Seed Pearl Starburst Pin

Pin, seed pearl, diamond & gold, a starburst design centered by an old European-cut diamond mélée, the arms pavé-set w/seed pearls, American hallmark, 19th c. (ILLUS.) **$382**

Pin, turquoise, diamond & 14k gold, a round narrow mount set w/small old mine-cut diamonds & centered by a large turquoise cabochon, open gallery, second half 19th c. **$646**

Art Nouveau Pinwheel Pin

Pin-pendant, enameled 14k gold & seed pearl, Art Nouveau style, designed as a rounded paneled openwork ring enclosing a five-petal pinwheel, decorated overall w/polychrome enamel highlighed by seed pearls & tiny old mine-cut diamonds, suspended from a delicate 14k gold fancy link chain, late 19th - early 20th c., 16" l. (ILLUS.) **$206**

Pins, enamel & 14k gold, Art Nouveau style, each designed w/the enameled face of an Art Nouveau maiden w/flowing hair, mark of Krementz & Co., Newark, New Jersey, early 20th c. boxed, set of 3 .... **$529**

Early French Enamel & Pearl Pomander

Pomander, enameled 18k gold & seed pearl, small rectangular box w/the front decorated w/a polychrome enameled scene of a seated cherub leaning on a closed book atop a monument inscribed "Gare-a-vous," framed by a band of split seed pearls, the sides & back w/geometric, scroll & foliate engraving w/black & white enamel accents, opening to a pierced grille designed as a lute among roses & leafy vines, French guarantee stamps & partial mark of the maker, later pendant bail, small loss to grille, France (ILLUS.)... **$5,288**

Man's Antique Amethyst & Gold Ring

Ring, amethyst & 14k gold, man's, the top bezel-set w/a large step-cut amethyst within a foliate mount w/lion's paw shoulders, later shank, size 11 1/2 (ILLUS.)....... **$764**

Antique Amethyst Gold-inlaid Ring

Ring, amethyst & 14k gold, the top w/a large oval amethyst w/an inlaid gold flower on a leafy stem, the blossom centered by a small old European-cut diamond, size 7 1/2 (ILLUS.)... **$499**

Antique Amethyst, Gold & Pearl Ring

Ring, amethyst, seed pearl & 14k gold, the top set w/a faceted oval amethyst decorated w/a gold & diamond floral design, the wide rectangular gold mount accented w/seed pearls & decorated w/flower & leaf engraving, 19th c., size 7 1/2 (ILLUS.) **$411**

Ring, black enamel & 18k gold, memorial-type, the top w/an enameled urn design, the shank inscribed & dated 1760, the back w/a hair compartment, size 5 1/2, some repair to reverse & enamel loss, to-

gether w/an early silver wedding band w/engraved accents, size 5 3/4, England, 18th c., the two... **$881**

Ring, carnelian agate & 18k gold, locket-type, designed as an oval agate tablet opening to a locket compartment, foliate shoulders, size 7 1/4 .... **$294**

Rare Cat's-eye Chrysoberyl Ring

Ring, cat's-eye chrysoberyl & diamond, centered by a large prong-set cabochon chrysoberyl framed by 11 old mine-cut diamonds weighing about 2.20 cts., 18k gold mount, Edwardian era, early 20th c., size 5 (ILLUS.) **$6,169**

Very Rare Early Two-stone Diamond Ring

Ring, colored & colorless diamond two-stone design, prong-set w/a large orangey-brown old European-cut diamond weighing about 2.56 cts. beside a colorless old European-cut diamond weighing about 2.70 cts., open gallery & shoulders set w/diamond mélée, millegrain accents, girdle nicks on colored diamond, signed by Tiffany & Co., early 20th c., size 6 1/4 (ILLUS.) **$41,125**

Ring, demantoid garnet & 18k gold, the gold band bezel set w/circular-cut green garnets, 19th c., size 7 1/2 .... **$499**

Delicate Diamond & Gold Diamond Ring

Ring, diamond & 14k gold, a delicate leafy scroll openwork top set w/old European-, full- and single-cut diamonds, size 8 1/2 (ILLUS., previous page) **$382**

Victorian Navette-form Diamond Ring

Ring, diamond & 14k gold, the long navette-shaped top prong-set w/23 old mine-cut diamonds weighing about 2.16 cts., Victorian, size 7 (ILLUS.) **$1,058**

Fine Rounded Diamond-set Ring

Ring, diamond & 14k gold, the round flora-form top centered by a large old European-cut diamond weighing about 3.49 cts. & surrounded by petals prong-set w/12 full-cut diamonds weighing about 5.29 cts., size 7 3/4 (ILLUS.)........................... **$7,638**

Fine Antique Diamond Solitaire Ring

Ring, diamond & 18k gold, solitaire old mine-cut diamond weighing about 1.50 cts., size 5 1/4 (ILLUS.)......................... **$2,820**

Old Diamond-set Gold Ring

Ring, diamond & 18k yellow gold, the top composed of thin bands mounted w/twenty-seven old European-, old mine- and single-cut diamonds, total weight 1.60 cts. (ILLUS.)..................................... **$646**

Antique Diamond & Amethyst Ring

Ring, diamond & amethyst, the top set w/a ring of eight pear- and cushion-shaped rose-cut diamonds surrounding a later amethyst cabochon, silver-topped 14k gold mount, size 6 (ILLUS.) **$1,528**
Ring, diamond, an oblong silver-topped 18k gold mount composed of pairs of open-work scrolls collet-set w/rose-cut diamonds, 19th c., size 3 3/4 .... **$499**

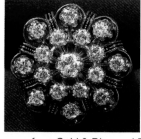

Blossom-form Gold & Diamond Ring

Ring, diamond & enameled 14k gold, designed as a rounded stylized openwork blossom head set w/rows of 17 full-cut diamonds, black enamel accents, size 7 1/2 (ILLUS.)... **$470**

English Diamond Ring

Ring, diamond, floret composed of nine old mine-cut diamonds weighing approx. 0.89 cts., scrolling openwork white metal & 18k yellow gold mount, English karat stamp, size 2, shank indistinctly inscribed (ILLUS.)... **$764**

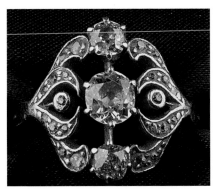

Antique Openwork Diamond Ring

Ring, diamond & gold, the openwork top decorated w/scrolls flanking a row of three large old mine-cut diamonds, the sides bead-set overall w/small diamonds, silver-topped gold mount, diamonds weighing about 1.20 cts., size 8 3/4 (ILLUS.) **$1,058**

Antique Diamond & Pearl Ring

Ring, diamond & pearl, prong-set w/a white pearl surrounded by seven old European-cut diamonds, platinum-topped 18k gold mount, in a J. E. Caldwell & Co. box, size 7 (ILLUS.) **$1,293**

Long Antique Diamond & Ruby Ring

Ring, diamond, ruby & gold, the long top centered by a round cluster of old European-cut diamonds flanked w/double curves further set w/diamonds w/a teardrop cabochon ruby accent, foliate shoulder & pierced scrolling gallery, silver-topped 18k gold mount, size 7 1/2 (ILLUS.).................... **$705**

Ring, diamond & ruby, the narrow navette-shaped top centered by a marquise-cut diamond surrounded by bands of channel-set rubies & bead-set single-cut diamonds, platinum-topped 18k gold mount, size 8 1/2 (ILLUS. below with other Edwardian diamond ring) **$999**

Navette-shaped Sapphire & Diamond Ring

Ring, diamond, sapphire & 14k gold, the long navette-shaped top centered by a prong-set oval-cut blue sapphire surrounded by old mine-cut diamond mélée, 19th c., one diamond replaced w/single-cut, bend to band, size 8 1/4 (ILLUS.) **$705**

Ring, diamond, the elongated openwork top bead- and bezel-set w/old European- and single-cut diamonds weighing about 1.15 cts., silver-topped 18k gold mount, Edwardian era, early 20th c., size 4 1/4 .... **$1,175**

Two Fine Edwardian Rings

Ring, diamond, the long navette-form head bead and bezel-set w/old European- and single-cut diamonds, millegrain accents, platinum-topped 14k gold mount, size 6 1/2 (ILLUS. top with Edwardian diamond & ruby ring)...................................... **$705**

Rare Antique Emerald & Diamond Ring

Ring, emerald, diamond & 18k gold, a three-stone top w/a central old mine-cut diamond weighing about 1.11 cts. flanked by pear-cut emeralds, in an open scrolling mount, emeralds w/minor nicks, size 6 1/4" (ILLUS.) **$7,050**

Fine Antique Emerald & Diamond Ring

Ring, emerald & diamond, the top centered by a bezel-set foil-backed oval-cut emerald flanked by small old mine-cut diamonds, the shoulders decorated w/lion heads & leaves, reverse w/blue & green enamel accents, 15k gold mount, size 5 (ILLUS.)... **$9,400**

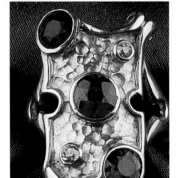

Unusual Antique Gem-set Gold Ring

Ring, garnet, diamond & 14k gold, the rectangular gold top w/serpentine ends & a textured ground accented by a row of three circular-cut garnets & two small old mine-cut diamonds, open shoulders, inscribed & dated 1871, size 6 (ILLUS.) **$499**

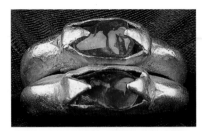

Ancient Vietnamese Gem & Gold Ring

Ring, gem-set high-carat gold, a double gold band w/each claw-set at the top w/two differently hued tumbled pink sapphire beads, together w/invoice from Spinks, London stating it dates from the Chaim period, Vietnam, 10th-11th centuries, size 4 1/4 (ILLUS.) **$2,938**

Ring, gold (18k), diamond & enamel, mourning-type, the round top centered by a small round compartment for a lock of hair surrounded by a circle w/four black enamel panels alternating w/four old mine-cut diamonds weighing .60 cts., the shank w/champlevé enameled rings, 19th c., size 5 1/4...................................... **$470**

Ancient Roman Gold & Carnelian Ring

Ring, gold & carnelian, Ancient Roman piece w/a plain hollow gold hoop flat on the interior & rounded on the exterior, expanding at the shoulders, set w/a convex oval carnelian engraved w/a standing draped figure of Fortuna, the goddess holding a cornucopia in one hand & sheaves of wheat & a ship's rudder in the other, ca. 1st century A.D. (ILLUS.)........ **$1,035**

Rare Early Tiffany Sapphire & Diamond Ring

Ring, Kashmir sapphire, diamond & gold, the oval top centered by a large cushion-cut blue sapphire weighing 1.17 cts., framed by a ring of old European- and mine-cut diamonds, platinum-topped 18k gold mount, signed by Tiffany & Co., early 20th c., size 2 1/2 (ILLUS.)................. **$9,400**

Early Limoges Enamel & Diamond Ring

Ring, Limoges enamel, 18k gold & diamond, the long narrow oval enameled plaque decorated w/the figure of an ancient Greek woman dancer w/a tambourine en grisaille w/rose tones, the narrow frame set w/rose-cut diamonds, shank w/scrolling shoulders, first half 19th c., size 6 1/4 (ILLUS.) **$1,116**

Rare Antique Diamond & Pearl Ring

Ring, natural pearl & diamond, bypass-style, the curled band set w/small old European-cut diamonds, one terminal prong-set w/a cushion-cut diamond weighing about 2.10 cts., the other terminal set w/a pearl meauring about 8.30 x 7.90 mm, size 5 1/2 (ILLUS.)........ **$7,638**

Edwardian Opal & Diamond Ring

Ring, opal, diamond & gold, the top centered by a prong-set large broadflash opal cabochon framed by 18 old mine-cut diamonds weighing about .72 cts., gold mount, slight crazing & tiny chip on opal, Edwardian era, early 20th c., size 4 1/4 (ILLUS.)...................................... **$881**

Antique Opal, Emerald & Gold Ring

Ring, opal, emerald & 14k gold, the oval top centered by an oval cabochon opal framed by cushion-cut emeralds, completed by a gold shank of multiple fused bands, size 6 1/4 (ILLUS.) **$1,058**
Ring, pearl, diamond & 18k gold, set w/five pearls interspersed w/rose-cut diamonds, the gallery w/engraved C-scrolls, 19th c., size 5 1/4...................................... **$999**

Edwardian Pearl & Diamond Ring

Ring, pearl, diamond & 18k yellow gold, a center white pearl framed by a ring of old European-cut diamond mélée, gold mount, pearl possibly natural, by Theodore B. Starr, Edwardian, England, early 20th c., size 6 1/4 (ILLUS.)................. **$1,293**

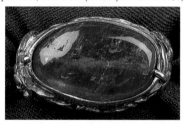

Arts & Crafts Pink Sapphire & Gold Ring

Ring, pink sapphire & 18k gold, Arts & Crafts style, bezel-set w/an oval tumbled pink sapphire bead, the gold shoulders, gallery & shank w/grape & leafy vine designs, early 20th c., size 3 1/4 (ILLUS.).............. **$2,115**

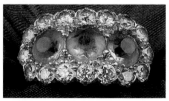

Pink Topaz & Diamond Antique Ring

Ring, pink topaz, diamond & gold, the oval top centered by a row of three circular-cut pink topaz framed by 16 full-cut diamonds weighing about 1.60 cts., platinum-topped 14k gold mount, topaz abraided, Edwardian era, early 20th c., size 6 1/4 (ILLUS.) **$1,116**

Extraordinary Diamond Solitaire Ring

Ring, platinum & diamond solitaire, prong-set w/a large old European-cut diamond weighing about 3.25 cts., flanked by diamond baguettes, size 5 (ILLUS.)........... **$25,850**

Fine Lavender Pearl & Diamond Ring

Ring, Quahog pearl, diamond & 18k gold, the top prong-set w/a lavender pearl framed by eight old European-cut diamonds weighing about 1.60 cts., Edwardian era, early 20th c., size 5 1/2 (ILLUS.) **$2,350**

Very Fine Ruby & Diamond Ring

Ring, ruby & diamond, a large central cushion-shaped ruby framed by ten old mine-cut diamonds, diamond-set shoulders, platinum-topped 18k gold mount, size 5 (ILLUS.)... **$10,575**

Ring, ruby & diamond, Art Nouveau style, bezel-set w/faceted cushion-shaped ruby measuring approx. 6.05 x 5.55 x 4.06 mm, flanked by old European-cut diamonds, approx. total wt. 1 ct., scrolling foliate 18k gold mount, size 7 1/4.............. **$4,406**

Antique Ruby & Diamond Ring

Ring, ruby & diamond, the round top centered by a cushion-cut ruby surrounded by a ring of rose-cut diamonds within a ring of circular-cut rubies, silver-topped 18k gold mount, size 3 3/4 (ILLUS.) **$1,200-1,800**

Gold & Sapphire Alligator Ring

Ring, sapphire & 14k gold, designed as a curled alligator w/engraved scales & the top of the head set w/a cabochon sapphire, size 7 1/4 (ILLUS.) **$470**

Ring, sapphire & 18k bicolor gold, an oval cut sapphire in an oval mount engraved w/delicate flowers & leaves, size 7 1/2 ...... **$999**

Ring, sapphire, diamond & 18k gold, bead-set w/four circular-cut sapphires alternating w/four old European-cut diamonds arranged in a checkerboard pattern, late 19th - early 20th c., size 6 1/2................ **$1,410**

Rare Early Tiffany Sapphire & Diamond Ring

Ring, sapphire, diamond & 18k gold, the three-stone top centered by a prong-set cushion-cut sapphire weighing 3.38 cts. flanked by old European-cut diamonds weighing about 1.40 cts., Tiffany & Co., ca. 1910, size 5 1/4 (ILLUS.)......... **$43,475**

Edwardian Sapphire & Diamond Ring

Ring, sapphire & diamond, the center w/a bezel-set cushion-cut blue sapphire framed by old single-cut diamonds, platinum-topped 18k gold mount, Edwardian era, early 20th c., size 5 1/2 (ILLUS.) **$2,585**

Ring, sapphire & diamond, the round top centered by a large round sapphire surrounded by a ring of ten old European-cut diamonds, 14k gold mount, w/a Bigelow, Kennard Co. box, early 20th c., size 8 1/2 .... **$1,058**

Kalo Amethyst & Silver Arts & Crafts Ring

Ring, sterling silver & amethyst, Arts & Crafts style, the top prong-set w/a large emerald-cut amethyst, the shoulders w/an arch & bead design, signed by Kalo Studios, early 20th c., size 6 3/4 (ILLUS.) **$705**

Fine Edwardian Turquoise & Diamond Ring

Ring, turquoise, diamond & 14k yellow gold, the oblong top centered by an oval turquoise cabochon surrounded by old European-cut diamonds, Edwardian, England, early 20th c., size 2 3/4 (ILLUS.) **$646**

Unusual Antique Ring with Locket

Ring with locket, gold (14k), fraternal order-type, the oval top cast in the shape of a Bacchus mask, opening to reveal a compartment, shoulders inscribed "sous le...la verité," 19th c., size 7 3/4 (ILLUS.)
.... **$1,058**

Art Nouveau Silver Slide Locket

Slide locket, silver, Art Nouveau style, a flattened waisted rectangular shape, the top embossed w/sinuous vine & abstract leaf designs highlighted by green cabochons, gilt interior, European assay marks, early 20th c., 1 3/8 x 2" (ILLUS.).... **$529**

Art Nouveau Black Opal Stickpin

Stickpin, black opal & 14k gold, Art Nouveau style, the oval opal top framed w/gold scrolled leaves, gold pin, marked by Walton & Co., early 20th c. (ILLUS.)
.... **$1,175**

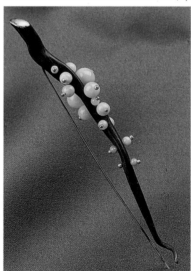

Early Coral Branch Stickpin

Stickpin, coral branch, designed as a long tapering dark coral branch decorated w/applied coral beads, 10k blackened mount, 3 1/2" l. (ILLUS.) **$1,058**

Art Nouveau Egyptian Head Stickpin

Stickpin, enameled 14k gold, the top designed as the head of an Egyptian woman wearing a diamond & blue stone headdress topped by a seed pearl, some enamel loss, late 19th - early 20th c. (ILLUS.) **$353**

Amethyst Dog Head Stickpin

Stickpin, gold (18k), amethyst, diamond & enamel, the top w/an amethyst carved as a spaniel head w/a rose-cut diamond collar & chain, hallmarks of Cabrelli, Paris, France (ILLUS.)...................................... **$2,350**

Jockey Head Moonstone & Gold Stickpin

Stickpin, moonstone & 18k gold, the top of moonstone carved in the shape of the head of a jockey wearing a gold cap & collar, later 14k gold pin stem, 19th c. (ILLUS.) **$1,528**

Horse Head & Crop Gold Stickpin

Stickpin, platinum, 14k gold & seed pearl, designed as a horse head atop a riding crop w/a seed pearl tip, Edwardian era, early 20th c. (ILLUS.)................................ **$264**

Rare Tiffany Sapphire & Diamond Stickpin

Stickpin, sapphire & diamond, the round top centered by a bezel-set cushion-cut sapphire framed by a ring of old European-cut diamonds, millegrain accents, platinum & 18k gold mount, signed by Tiffany & Co., early 20th c. (ILLUS.) **$4,348**

Set of Antique Gem-set Stickpins

Rare Edwardian Diamond Tiara

Stickpins, gem-set 14k gold, each bezel-set at the top w/a circular-cut hessonite garnet, amethyst, lavender spinel, pyrope garnet & lyacinth & jargoon zircons, 14k gold mounts, unsigned, fitted in a Tiffany & Co. signed cloth sleeve, the set (ILLUS., previous page) **$764**

Tiara, coral, composed of four tiers of faceted coral beads, gilt-metal mount, possibly French hallmarks, 19th c. **$3,525**

Tiara, diamond & platinum, designed as three intersecting floral garlands set throughout w/old European- and single-cut diamonds, w/a white metal tiara mount & later brooch attachment, evidence of solder, Edwardian, England, early 20th c., diamonds 7 1/4 cts. (ILLUS., top of page) **$15,275**

Vinaigrette-pendant, garnet & gilt-metal, oval w/the wide top frame composed of cast spiral rings centered by a large cabochon garnet, opens to a perforated compartment, late 19th c. (ILLUS., next column) **$382**

Watch chain, amethyst & 14k gold, the trace link chain w/bezel-set round amethysts, 51" l. **$1,293**

Victorian Garnet Vinaigrette-Pendant

Watch chain, gem-set 18k gold, composed of a foxtail chain mounted w/oval slides w/applied wirework accents, enamel & colored stone highlights, French guarantee stamps & partial mark of maker **$1,528**

Watch chain, gold (14k), composed of delicate circular links, 62" l. **$264**

Watch chain, gold (14k), composed of fancy narrow loop links, 38" l. (ILLUS., bottom of page)... **$646**

Watch chain, gold (14k), composed of round trace links highlighted by circular-cut cobalt blue glass, American maker's mark, late 19th c., 51" l. **$470**

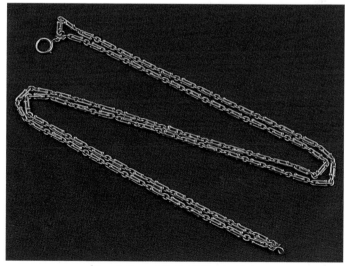

Fine Antique 14k Gold Watch Chain

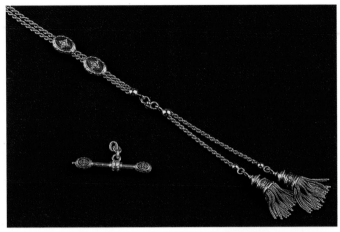

Fancy Antique Gold Watch Chain & Key

Watch chain & key, enamel & 18k gold, the fine ropetwist gold chain mounted w/two oval slides enameled w/a diamond design in white & light blue, suspending a pair of pendants w/foxtail fringe & trimmed w/blue enamel bands & fob concealing a retractable watch key, late 19th c., minor enamel loss, 24" l. (ILLUS., top of page) **$1,058**

Watch chain & pendant, gold (14k), the chain composed of rectangular trace links fitted w/an opal-set slide & suspending a pendant bezel-set w/three opal cabochons, overall 29" l. **$382**

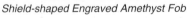

Shield-shaped Engraved Amethyst Fob

Watch fob, amethyst & 14k gold, the shield-shaped frame set w/an intaglio-carved amethyst w/an escutcheon & motto reading "En Dieu Est Tout," the mount w/C-scroll & rocaille designs, 19th c. (ILLUS.) **$470**

Watch fob, carnelian, silver & gold, the top carved as a seated carnelian puppy w/red stone eyes in a basket of silver & 18k gold decorated w/navette & fleur-de-lis designs, the bottom set w/a carnelian intaglio depicting a pair of hunting hounds in an English landscape, 19th c. (ILLUS., top next column) **$940**

Carnelian Puppy in Basket Watch Fob

Early 19th Century Citrine Watch Fob

Watch fob, citrine & gilt-metal, a large facet-cut oval citrine mounted in a heavy oval gilt-metal frame cast w/leaves & berries & swiveling within a matching U-form frame topped by a pointed link attached to a ball-form link suspended on a smaller ring connected to a wide top ring, ca. 1830, 3" l. (ILLUS.) **$823**

Figural Gold & Hardstone Watch Fob

Watch fob, hardstone & 18k yellow gold, the top designed as the figure of a gold prospector w/pick, shovel, pan & rifle, bottom w/a hardstone seal engraved w/a name, 19th c. (ILLUS.) **$411**

Very Ornate 18k Gold Watch Fob

Watch fob & chain, gold (18k), the long fob designed w/a base pendant in the shape of a seated squirrel grasping a nut, sus-

pended from three wide openwork chased & engraved links decorated w/ornate C-scrolls, ruffles & floral & leaf designs, the top w/a pair of short oval link chains joined at the hanging clip, signed by Tiffany & Co., original box, fob 6 1/2" l., the set (ILLUS. of fob) **$6,463**

Watch pin, gem-set 14k gold, Art Nouveau style, the scrolling foliate mount w/a cherub head, centering a cabochon turquoise framed by four seed pearls, engraved designs, 1 1/8" l. **$499**

Unique Hourglass Watch Pin

Watch pin, glass & 18k gold, designed as a tiny hourglass, the silvertone metal dial w/abstract numerals, hourglass w/running sands within a ropework frame, crystal w/slight bloom, pin stem detachable, Gubelin, 1 1/2" l. (ILLUS.) **$1,410**

Sets

Lapis & Gold Bracelet and Brooch Set

Bracelet & brooch, lapis lazuli & 18k yellow gold, the bracelet composed of lapis disks within scalloped frames joined by engraved arched & barbell links, matching brooch, brooch w/later pendant frame, small repair to the back, 19th c., brooch 1 1/8" d., bracelet 7 1/2" l., the set (ILLUS.) **$1,293**

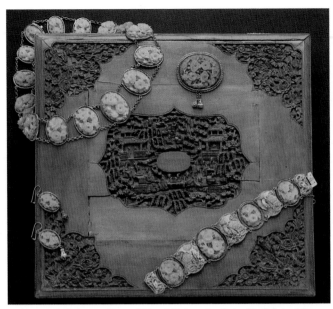

Unusual Chinese Carved Hornbill Jewelry Set with Original Box

Bracelet, choker, brooch & earrings, carved Hornbill, each piece composed of oval segments set w/floral-carved hornbill alternating w/gold bird-decorated plaques, China, ca. 1860, complete w/original fitted velvet-lined camphorwood box carved on the top w/a central landscape scene w/figures & temples, the corners w/delicate floral-carved panels, hallmarked, necklace, the set (ILLUS., top of page) **$5,288**

Brooch & earpendants, enamel, diamond, gem-set demi-parure, brooch w/flexible plaques decorated w/golden basse taille enamel & bezel-set w/five circular-cut citrines & ten old European-cut diamonds, pear-shape faceted citrine terminal, 18k gold mount, signed "Marcus & Co.," the set **$9,400**

Brooch & earrings, chalcedony, coral & 14k gold, the round brooch composed of an outer flat ring of milky chalcedony surrounding an ornately engraved gold disk centering a coral bead, the pendant earrings of similar design, the set (ILLUS.) **$999**

Brooch & earrings, chalcedony, coral & 14k gold, the round brooch w/an outer ring of milky chalcedony enclosing a ring of engraved gold centered by a coral bead, matching earrings, second half 19th c., the set **$646**

Fine Antique Garnet & Gold Suite

Brooch & earrings, garnet & 14k gold, the brooch centered by a large oval garnet cabochon framed w/an openwork rope-

Victorian Stone, Coral & Gold Set

work mount w/fancy link chain swags suspending three small gold teardrops, matching pendant-type earrings w/a single gold drop, the set (ILLUS.) **$1,175**

Fine Gold & Garnet Victorian Set

Brooch & earrings, gold (14k) & amethyst, the brooch designed as a ringed knot set w/a spray of amethyst berries, applied wire-twist decoration, a glass compartment on the back, the earrings of similar design, Victorian, the set (ILLUS.) **$1,410**

Brooch & earrings, gold (14k) & enamel, the brooch composed of an inverted U-form pin w/incurved sides & topped w/scrolls flanking a button, the sides w/a textured surface trimmed w/black enamel, suspending a long lyre-form drop w/a large central button drop flanked by tiny drop beads, also w/a textured surface & black enamel trim, the earrings matching the lyre-form drop, ca. 1872, the set
.... **$2,468**

Victorian Coral Shell-carved Set

Brooch & earrings, pink coral & 18k yellow gold, each piece carved as a scallop shell centering a coral bead, w/original fitted box from Howard & Co., Victorian, the set (ILLUS.)... **$2,115**

Fine Carved Coral Victorian Set

Brooch & earrings, pink coral, the brooch of squared shape boldly carved in the center w/the head of a classical lady framed by leafy roses & carved at each side w/another classical profile, suspending three carved coral teardrops, the longest central one carved w/a classical head, the matching earrings w/the small top carved as a classical head suspending a larger tapering carved plaque carved w/another classical head & suspending three carved coral teardrops, 14k yellow gold mounts, Victorian, the set (ILLUS.)... **$2,350**

Brooch & earrings, shell cameo & 14k gold, the brooch centered by an oval cameo carved w/a scene of lovers boating on a river, the pendant-type earrings carved w/a scene of a dog beneath a tree, ropework gold frames, some losses, original fitted box, 19th c., the set **$823**

Antique Cameo Brooch & Pendant

Cameo brooch & pendant, carved hardstone, seed pearl & 14k gold, the brooch centered by a large oval finely carved hardstone cameo depicting the bust of a lady in Renaissance dress, in a gold wiretwist frame accented w/delicate fanned gold rods & a pointed leaf finial all accented by seed pearls, the pendant of smaller matching design, pendant 1 1/2" l., brooch 2 1/4" l., the suite (ILLUS.) **$999**

Rare Complete Victorian Lava Cameo Jewelry Suite

Cameo necklace, bracelet, brooch & earrings; carved lava; the fringe-style necklace composed of numerous round & oval links each enclosing a carved lava cameo of a classical woman w/the largest oval cameo at the center front, also suspending three teardrop cameos; the bracelet also composed of lava cameo links; the brooch formed from a single cameo & the pendant earrings each suspending a small round cameo; gilt mounts, all in original fitted box, mid-19th c., earrings 1 1/8" l., brooch 1 1/2" d., bracelet 7 1/2" l., necklace 17 1/2" l., the suite (ILLUS., top of page) **$2,115**

Edwardian Opal Cuff Links & Shirt Studs

Moonstone & Gold Cuff Links & Studs

Cuff links & shirt studs, cat's-eye moonstone & 14k gold, the double-link cuff links bezel-set w/cabochon moonstones, the three bar-form shirt studs set w/matching moonstones, hallmark of Larter & Sons, the set (ILLUS.) **$881**

Cuff links & shirt studs, opal & 18k yellow gold; each stud w/a simple gold mount set w/a round opal, each cuff link w/a bar & two rounded mounts each set w/a dark bluish green opal, signed "M & Co.," Edwardian, England, early 20th c., the set (ILLUS., top next column) **$2,115**

Coral & Turquoise Earrings & Brooch Set

Unusual Complete Ornate Jeweled Suite of Victorian Jewelry

Earrings & brooch, white coral, turquoise & 14k gold, the pendant-type earrings designed as a cluster of engraved leaves suspending a carved coral flower bud, cabochon turquoise accents, the matching oblong & looping brooch w/a locket compartment, 19th c., the set (ILLUS., previous page) **$499**

Necklace, bracelet, brooch, ring & earrings, moonstone, sapphire & seed pearl, each piece composed of ornate leafy scroll silver-gilt oval & bar links, the oval links & large oval main panels centered by a cabochon moonstone framed by bands of tiny seed pearls & scattered circular-cut sapphires, Austro-Hungarian hallmarks, 19th c., ring size 6, necklace 17" l., the set (ILLUS., top of page) **$1,293**

Necklace, brooch, earrings & bangle, gold, turquoise & seed pearl; the necklace composed of ornate oblong scrolling gold links suspending a wide scrolled pendant decorated w/clusters of bead-set small cabochon turquoise & suspending a beaded chain & two scroll pendants; the loop earrings & other pieces of matching design all set w/small turquoise cabochons, from Bailey & Kitchen, Philadelphia, in original fitted box, second half 19th c., bangle & brooch w/losses, brooch 1 3/8" w., earrings 2 3/8" l., bracelet w/5 7/8" interior circumference, necklace 16 1/2" l., the suite (ILLUS., next column) **$2,585**

Fine Complete Suite of Turquoise-decorated Gold Jewelry

Coral & Gold Suite

Necklace & ring, coral & 14k gold, the necklace w/an arched & looping delicate gold frame w/tiny florette & shells designs & applied wirework & bead decoration all centered by a cabochon coral & suspending another cabochon coral, suspended on a delicate trace link chain, a matching coral cabochon ring w/a lacy gold mount, ring size 5 3/4, necklace 17 1/2" l., the set (ILLUS.) **$823**

Victorian Garnet Necklace & Pendant

Necklace & pendant, garnet, the necklace composed of clusters of rose-cut garnets, together w/a detachable oval pendant of rose-cut garnets, a glass compartment on the back, gilt-metal mounts, 19th c., 12" l. (ILLUS. of part) **$1,058**

Early Turquoise & Yellow Gold Set

Necklace, pendant & earrings, turquoise & 18k yellow gold, the cross-form pendant w/rounded arms set w/teardrop-shaped turquoise-set teardrops & a central ring, the necklace composed of graduated circular turquoise & wirework florette links, matching teardrop-shaped earrings, 19th c., boxed, small losses, 19th c. (ILLUS. of part) **$4,700**

18k Gold "Placque de Cou"

Necklace plaques, gold (18k), diamond & turquoise "Placque de Cou," Art Nouveau design, largest 2 x 7" rectangular curved openwork plaque centered w/carved turquoise woman's head w/chased flowing gold hair highlighted by old European-cut diamond blossoms, signed "Lalique," similar 2" square plaque also w/carved turquoise head & signed "Lalique," also a pair of smaller openwork plaques set w/diamond blossoms, accompanied by 18k gold flattened baton link chain, 20 1/2" l., two gold satin ribbons, one gold satin cord, & two screwdrivers, may be worn as chokers or necklaces, one plaque w/brooch fitting, the set (ILLUS. of largest plaque) **$49,938**

Coral Floral-carved Pendant from Set

Pendant & earrings, bicolor coral, the pendant carved as a large finely-petaled flower blossom below a cluster of small carved flowers, matching earrings, gilt-metal mounts, 19th c., one flower bud detached, the set (ILLUS. of pendant) **$529**

Pendant-brooch & earrings, amethyst & 14k gold, the earrings w/two graduated gold rings, each set w/a facet-cut amethyst w/delicate wirework scrolls at the bottom suspending a foxtail gold fringe, the brooch w/an engraved center gold ring centering a large amethyst & flanked by smaller rings holding smaller amethysts, delicate wirework scrolls at the top & bottom w/a foxtail gold fringe at the bottom, brooch signed "W. & S.B.," boxed, second half 19th c., the set (earrings w/later screw-backs, evidence of solder) **$1,175**

Rare Blossom-form Diamond Slides

Slides, each designed as a Queen Anne's Lace blossom set w/rose-cut diamonds & demantoid garnets, circular-cut ruby blood spot, platinum-topped 18k gold mounts, w/Tiffany box, unsigned, minor

losses, pin stems added, Edwardian, England, early 20th c., pr. (ILLUS.) **$10,281**

American Painted Porcelain

American painted porcelain jewelry comprises a unique category. While the metallic settings and porcelain medallions were inexpensive, the painted decoration was a work of fine art. The finished piece possessed greater intrinsic value than costume jewelry of the same period because it was a one-of-a-kind creation, but one that was not as expensive as real gold and sterling silver settings and precious and semiprecious jewels. Note that signatures are rare, backstamps lacking.

Dorothy Kamm

Bar pin, decorated w/pink roses & greenery, brass-plated bezel, ca. 1880s, 7/16 x 1 1/2" **$30**

Bar pin, decorated w/pink roses on a pale green ground, burnished gold tips & brass-plated bezel, ca. 1900-1915, 2 5/8" w. **$50**

Belt Buckle Brooch with Portrait

Belt buckle brooch, oval, decorated w/a profile of a woman wearing a pink top & white shawl, pink roses in her curly brown hair, black choker at her neck, burnished gold rim, gold-plated bezel, signed "M.e.M.," 1900-17, 1 7/8 x 2 3/8" (ILLUS.) **$175**

Belt Buckle Brooch with Pansy

Belt buckle brooch, oval, decorated w/a white pansy, accented w/white enamel, on a burnished gold ground, gold-plated bezel, 1900-17, 1 11/16 x 2 1/4" (ILLUS., previous page) **$75**

Art Nouveau Florals on Belt Brooch

Belt buckle brooch, oval, decorated w/an Art Nouveau-style water lily design outlined w/raised paste, petals filled in w/lavender enamel, burnished green & gold background, gold-plated bezel, 1900-17, 1 7/8 x 2 5/8" (ILLUS.) **$150**

Bachelor Buttons on Belt Brooch

Belt buckle brooch, oval, decorated w/blue bachelor buttons & greenery on a polychrome ground, irregular burnished gold border outlined in black, gold-plate bezel, 1900-17, 1 7/8 x 2 5/8" (ILLUS.) **$115**

Belt buckle brooch, oval, decorated w/roses & greenery on a polychrome ground, burnished gold scalloped border outlined in black, gold-plated bezel, 1900-17, 1 15/16 x 2 11/16" **$125**

Brooch, decorated w/violets on a light yellow brown ground w/raised paste scrolled border covered w/burnished gold & burnished gold rims, gold-plated bezel, ca. 1890-1920, 1 1/2" d. **$65**

Brooch, oval, decorated w/a conventional-style Colonial dame in light blue & yellow w/opal lustre background & burnished gold rim, brass-plated bezel, ca. 1915-25, 1 5/8 x 2 1/8" **$60**

Brooch, oval, decorated w/a conventional-style lavender iris & green leaves outlined in black on a yellow lustre ground w/white enamel highlights on petal edges & yellow enamel highlights on flower centers, burnished gold rim, gold-plated bezel, ca. 1900-20, 1 5/8 x 2 1/8" **$80**

Pink Rose on Oval Brooch

Brooch, oval, decorated w/a large pink rose & green leaves on a light blue ground, burnished gold rim, gold-plated bezel, 1 1/8 x 1 3/8" (ILLUS.) **$45**

Brooch, oval, decorated w/a sunset landscape scene w/house by stream, trees in background, burnished gold rim, gold-plated bezel, 1 1/2 x 1 15/16" **$175**

Brooch, oval, decorated w/a tropical Florida scene, burnished gold border & brass-plated bezel, ca. 1920s, 1 1/2 x 2" **$85**

Florida River Landscape on Brooch

Brooch, oval, decorated w/a tropical river landscape in polychrome colors, signed on the lower left "OC" (Olive Commons, Coconut Grove, Florida), gold-plated bezel, ca. 1920s, 1 3/8 x 1 1/4" (ILLUS.) **$125**

Brooch, oval, decorated w/pink & white & ruby roses & green leaves on a rich blue ground w/white enamel highlights, burnished gold border & rim, gold-plated bezel, ca. 1940s, 1 1/2 x 2" **$65**

Brooch, rectangular, decorated w/a tropical scene of palm tree in white on a platinum ground, painted by Olive Commons, Miami, Florida, sterling silver bezel, ca. 1920s-1940s, 3/4 x 1" **$110**

Brooches with Pink & Ruby Roses

Brooches, round, decorated w/pink & ruby roses & green leaves on a polychrome ground, burnished gold rim, gold-plated bezel, 7 /8" d., pr. (ILLUS.)............................. **$75**

Cuff pin, rectangular, decorated w/a purple iris outlined & bordered in burnished gold, brass-plated bezel, ca. 1900-15, 1/4 x 1 1/16" **$25**

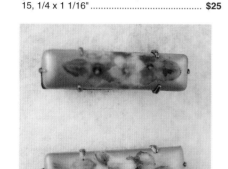

Cuff Pins with Forget-me-nots

Cuff pins, rectangular, decorated w/forget-me-nots on a burnished gold ground, gold-plated bezel, ca. 1900-15, 1/4 x 1 1/4", pr. (ILLUS.) **$45**

Flapper pin, oval, decorated w/a stylized, elegant red-haired woman wearing blue dress & fur stole, pink flower & large comb in her hair, white ground w/burnished gold border, gold-plated bezel, ca. 1922-30, 1 11/16 x 2 1/8" **$135**

Flapper pin, oval, decorated w/bust of stylized red-haired flapper on a pastel polychrome ground, burnished gold rim & brass-plated bezel, ca. 1924-28, 1 5/8 x 2 1/8"... **$125**

Handy pin, crescent shape, asymmetrically decorated w/a purple pansy on an ivory ground, burnished gold tip & brass-plated bezel, ca. 1880-1915, 2" w.......................... **$35**

Handy pin, crescent-shaped, decorated w/forget-me-nots & leaves on a burnished gold ground, gold-plated bezel, ca. 1890-1915, gold wear, 1 13/16" w. **$30**

Hatpin Head with Wild Roses

Hatpin, circular head, decorated w/pink wild roses & greenery on a yellow ground, burnished gold rim, gold-plated filigree setting, head 1 1/16" d., shaft 9" l. (ILLUS. of head).. **$125**

Pendant, decorated w/a purple pansy w/white enamel center accents & burnished gold border, gold-plated bezel, ca. 1880s-1914, 1" d. **$60**

Pendant, oval, decorated w/forget-me-nots on a pastel polychrome ground w/white enamel highlights & burnished gold rim, gold-plated bezel, ca. 1900-25, 1 1/4 x 1 3/4" **$65**

Scarf pin, medallion-shaped, decorated w/violets, brass-plated bezel & shank, ca. 1880-1920, medallion 1 1/4" d., shank 3" l. **$75**

Shirtwaist Button with Clover Leaf

Shirtwaist button, oval w/shank, decorated w/a three-leaf clover in green on a yellow & brown ground, burnished gold rim, 7/8 x 1 1/16" (ILLUS.) **$25**

Shirtwaist Button with Flower

Shirtwaist button, round w/eye, decorated w/a conventional stylized long blossom flanked by pointed oval leaves in pale yellow, dark blue & black on a burnished gold ground, 1 1/16" d. (ILLUS., previous page).. **$35**

Shirtwaist set: oval brooch & pr. of oval cuff links; decorated w/blue forget-me-nots on an ivory background w/white enamel highlights, brass-plated mounts, ca. 1900-10, brooch w/burnished gold freeform border & rim, 1 3/8 x 1 3/4", cuff links w/burnished gold rims, 13/16 x 1 1/16", the set.. **$250**

Brooch from Shirtwaist Set

Shirtwaist set: oval brooch & two round buttons w/shank; each decorated w/forget-me-nots & greenery on a pastel polychrome ground, burnished gold rim, gold-plated bezel, brooch 1 1/4 x 1 3/4", buttons 15/16" d., the set (ILLUS. of brooch) **$90**

Watch chatelaine, oval, decorated w/a woman wearing a rose-colored bodice, light shading to dark warm green ground, set in gold-plated rim w/twisted gold edge, ca. 1880s, 1 1/8 x 1 3/8" **$175**

Watches

Unusual Victorian Chatelaine Watch

Chatelaine watch, lady's, a silver-gilt waist clasp centered by a crystal orb & suspending gold bar links suspending the 18k gold round watch w/domed crystal over the white enamel dial w/Roman numerals, lever escapement movement, signed pin-set, display back, by Henry Capt, French import stamp on waist clasp, in original fitted box (ILLUS.) **$940**

Fine Marcus & Co. Lady's Lapel Watch

Lapel watch, open-faced, lady's, Marcus & Co., 14k gold, the rosetone metal dial w/Arabic numerals, the watch within a cage of openwork C-scrolls & tendrils & suspended from a matching bar-form lapel pin, the cage engraved front & back, watch replaced, signed, 2 1/8" l. (ILLUS.) **$2,468**

Antique Enameled Gold Pendant Watch

Pendant watch, lady's, enameled 18k gold, the red guilloche enamel case w/a central polychrome reserve painted w/three cherubs, black enamel accents, white enameled dial w/Arabic numerals, enclosing a jeweled damascened nickel Swiss movement, enamel loss to edge (ILLUS.)... **$1,175**

Agassiz Edwardian Pendant Watch

Pendant watch, open-faced, lady's, Agassiz, enamel, diamond & seed pearl, the silvertone engine-turned metal dial w/Arabic numerals & a subsidiary seconds dial, enclosing a 17-jewel nickel lever escapement movement, 18k gold, platinum & en plain enameled case in black centered by a ring of seed pearls w/rose-cut diamond accents, engraved border, Edwardian era, early 20th c. (ILLUS.) **$764**

Gem-set Gold Open-faced Pendant Watch

Pendant watch, open-faced, lady's, gem-set 18k gold, white enamel dial w/Roman numerals, enclosing a gilt jeweled movement, the back of the case centered by a bead-set cushion-cut sapphire surrounded by six rose-cut diamonds within another ring of sapphires, silver ground, suspended from a gold-plated chain mounted w/an old 14k gold tracery enamel & seed pearl slide (ILLUS.) **$470**

Pendant watch, open-faced, lady's, Longines Wittnauer, the silvertone round dial w/Arabic numerals, enclosing a 15-jewel three-adjustment nickel lever escapement movement, platinum & 14k gold case w/a central square on the back w/black enamel & diamond accents (ILLUS., top next column) **$499**

Longines Wittnauer Lady's Watch

Pretty Enameled Lady's Pendant Watch

Pendant watch, open-faced, lady's, enamel & diamond, the white enamel dial w/Arabic numerals, enclosing a jeweled bar lever escapement movement, the back of the case w/blue guillouché enameling outlined w/18k gold & platinum border scrolls & a central floret set w/small rose-cut diamonds, French guarantee stamps, Edwardian era, early 20th c. (ILLUS.) **$441**

Pocket watch, demi-hunting case, lady's, Tavannes, the goldtone metal dial w/Arabic numerals & a subsidiary seconds dial, enclosing a 15-jewel lever escapement movement, in a pale blue guillouché enameled case w/swag designs, Edwardian era, early 20th c. **$705**

Pocket watch, hunting case, lady's, 18k gold, enamel & diamond, the white enamel dial w/Roman numerals & subsidiary seconds dial, enclosing a Swiss lever escapement 15-jewel movement, black-enameled case w/rose-cut diamond flower designs **$705**

Lovely Lady's Hunting Case Watch

Pocket watch, hunting case, lady's, Jaques Rouleet, Locle, 18k gold & enamel, the white enameled dial w/Roman numerals & a subsidiary seconds dial, enclosing a signed key-wind & set 15-jewel lever escapement bar movement, the scalloped gold case centered on one side w/an oval enameled portrait of a pretty Victorian lady framed w/black tracery enamel & rose-cut diamond highlights, the other side centering a portrait of a cherub (ILLUS.) **$1,410**

Fine Enameled Gold Elgin Pocket Watch

Pocket watch, hunting case, man's, Elgin, white enamel dial w/Arabic numerals & a subsidiary seconds dial, enclosing an engraved 15-jewel movement, front of the 14k gold case centered by an oval reserve enameled w/blue forget-me-nots divided by a band set w/old mine-cut diamonds, a tiny red ribbon at the top, inscribed & dated 1897 (ILLUS.) **$499**

Swiss Man's Gold Hunting Case Watch

Pocket watch, hunting case, man's, Geneva, Switzerland, white enamel dial w/Roman numerals & a subsidiary seconds dial, enclosing a slide-activated 24-jewel movement, the gold case lightly engraved w/a Latin motto & book & sabre designs, cracks in dial, missing crystal (ILLUS.) **$1,293**

Rare Antique Gold Patek Philippe Watch

Pocket watch, hunting case, man's, Patek Philippe, white enamel dial w/Arabic numerals & a subsidiary seconds dial, enclosing a slide-activated movement, plain polished 18k gold case w/engraved cartouche, triple-signed, in a fitted box (ILLUS.) **$11,750**

Lady's Pocket Watch with Enameled Scene

Pocket watch, open-faced, lady's, 18k gold, enamel & seed pearl, white enamel dial w/Roman & Arabic numerals, enclosing a pin-set gilt lever escapement movement, the top of the case centered by a round reserve enameled w/a scene of a young shepherdess in a woodland, edged w/seed pearls, Swiss guarantee stamps (ILLUS.) **$705**

Fine English Open Face Pocket Watch

Pocket watch, open-faced, man's, R.H. Taylor, Manchester, England, the 18k gold case back engraved w/floral designs & a monogram, the white enamel dial w/Roman numerals, full-sweep seconds hand, a 13-jewel lever escapement movement, pin-set, England hallmarks, late 19th c. (ILLUS.) **$823**

Tiffany Man's 14k Gold Pocket Watch

Pocket watch, open-faced, man's, Tiffany & Co., white enamel dial w/Arabic numerals & subsidiary seconds dial, Agassiz 16-jewel movement w/five adjustments, plain polished case w/small dents on the back (ILLUS.) **$1,116**
Pocket watch, open-faced, man's, W.J. Cartier, Arctic, Rhode Island, sterling silver case, white enamel dial w/Roman numerals, sunken subsidiary seconds dial, enclosing an engraved adjustable 17-

jewel nickel lever escapement movement, engraved case **$705**

Early Open-faced Man's Pocket Watch

Pocket watch, open-faced, man's, enamel & gold, the enamel & goldtone dial w/Arabic numerals within arches centering an en grisaille painted scene of a classical kneeling woman greeting a sailing ship, quarter-hour repeating fusee movement, plain polished 18k gold case, w/watch key, early 19th c. (ILLUS.) **$1,645**

Very Fine French Enameled Pocket Watch

Pocket watch, open-faced, man's, J. Felix, B. Baillons, Paris, France, enameled gold, the white enamel dial w/Arabic numerals, a key-wind pin-set gilt verge fusee quarter hour repeating movement, the 18k gold case decorated on one side w/a colorful enamel bucolic landscape scene w/shepherd & maiden, engraved edges w/enameled flowers, ca. 1830 (ILLUS.) **$4,230**

Rare Late 18th Century Pocket Watch

Pocket watch, open-faced, man's, P. Jerrot, Paris, France, the white enamel dial w/Roman numerals, cylinder fusee two-bell quarter hour repeating movement, engraved 18k gold case decorated w/a colorful enamel scene of a lady paying homage to Amistad w/rose-cut diamond accents, a frame of tiny seed pearls, late 18th c. (ILLUS.) **$3,290**

Antique Patek Philippe Pocket Watch

Pocket watch, open-faced, man's, Patek Philippe, enameled 18k gold, the white enamel dial w/Arabic numerals, enclosing a jeweled lever escapement movement, the dial bezel engraved w/small triangular devices accented by black enamel, the back w/an engraved monogram, Swiss assay mark, triple-signed (ILLUS.)... **$3,290**

Pocket watch & chain, hunting case, man's, Waltham Riverside, white enamel dial w/Roman numerals & a subsidiary seconds dial, enclosing an adjusted gilt movement, the 14k gold case engraved on the front & back w/foliate & landscape designs, suspended from a gilt double curb link chain w/pencil, the set **$881**

Mixed Metal Watch & Chatelaine

Pocket watch & chatelaine open faced, lady's, the mixed-metal three-section chatelaine composed of rounded graduated plaques inlaid w/tricolor goldtone morning glories, the watch w/a matching design, the white enamel dial w/Roman numerals, a jeweled nickel movement, pin-set, ca. 1882, 2 pcs. (ILLUS.) **$470**

Wristwatch, platinum, 18k gold & diamond, the bezel w/alternating sections of engraved gold & diamond mélée bead-set in platinum, silvertone dial w/Arabic numerals, 17-jewel movement, black grosgrain ribbon adjustable strap, discolored dial, by Kennard & Co., early 20th c. **$294**

CHAPTER 2
Costume Jewelry (19th & 20th Century)

Costume jewelry, made of inexpensive, non-precious materials, was created to accessorize the current fashions of its time. Rhinestones and plated metals replaced diamonds and gold and became especially popular with the newly liberated Flappers of the 1920s.

Because it was originally inexpensive, costume jewelry was meant to be discarded as fashions changed but women often saved it because of its appealing beauty and design. Throughout the 20th century succeeding generations of women have relied on costume jewelry to enhance their clothing ensembles.

Designers and manufacturers of costume jewelry made original designs to suit every woman's budget. Some inexpensive pieces were sold in variety stores while higher priced pieces were offered through catalogs and local department stores. The most upscale department stores and boutiques sold the top of the line "fashion" jewelry.

The designs of costume jewelry could be very regal and beautiful, even imitating the precious gems used in high end jewelry, but other pieces were meant be worn for fun and often featured whimsical or comical designs. Even politics or popular movies and songs could be tied in to costume jewelry designs.

Just as pieces were originally offered in a range of prices, today vintage pieces will be priced according to the quality of the design and materials used. Many collectors today consider old costume jewelry a form of wearable art uniquely representing the era when it was produced but also appealing to modern tastes. Because the best pieces feature craftsmanship and designs that would be too expensive to replicate in today's world, these objects are especially appealing to 21st century collectors. In the current market, some unique signed pieces of older costume jewelry can sometimes sell for more than modern high quality jewelry featuring precious metals and gems.

Commercially produced and originally inexpensive jewelry from the late 19th and early 20th century has reached the century mark and is officially "antique," while pieces manufactured from World War I through the 1960s are certainly considered fine "collectibles." Whatever a person's interests or tastes there will be pieces of old costume jewelry for them to collect and enjoy. It can be worn today with just as much pride and enjoyment as it offered to women of past decades. Marion Cohen

Acknowledgments:

My sincere gratitude to those who not only generously allowed me to catalog and photograph pieces from their collections but also shared their expert knowledge: Davida Baron, Paula Beck, Mary Ann Bosshart, Shirley Dreyer, Joan Orlen and Doris Skarka. Also, special thanks must be given to my photographer, Robert Cohen.

I would like to dedicate the following to the memory of my late husband, Julius Cohen, whose love and devotion continues to inspire and encourage me in all my literary efforts.

Bakelite Bar Pin with Cherries

Bar pin, Bakelite, a red bar w/a red trace link chain suspending clusters of red cherries & green leaves (ILLUS.) **$294**

Bar pin, cloisonné on copper, design of blue flowers, ca. 1920, 2 3/4" w. **$45-65**

Bar pin, glass, oval shape, black, rectangular facets, Czechoslovakia, 7/8 x 1 7/8"
.... **$30-45**

Bar pin, goldplate, carnelian glass, Art Deco Chinese character writing w/center carved carnelian glass flower, 2 3/4" w.
.... **$55-75**

Bar pin, sterling, applied cats & kittens faces, 2 3/4" w., 1/2" h. **$65-85**

Sterling & Gemstone Sterling Bar Pin

Bar pin, sterling silver & gemstone, Edwardian-style, the oblong openwork ornate frame centered by a large chrysoprase cabochon w/smaller carnelian, amber & amethyst cabochons around the sides, 1 x 2 3/4" (ILLUS.) **$185-215**

Bar pin, white metal, three center emerald green square stones, clear rhinestone trim, 2 1/4" w. **$55-70**

Belt buckle, Bakelite, Art Deco style, two-part, black w/rayed design, 3 1/2" l., 2" h.
.... **$50-65**

Two Agate Bead Bracelets

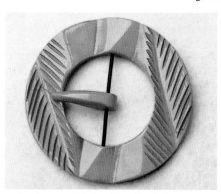

Leaf-carved Yellow Bakelite Belt Buckle

Belt buckle, Bakelite, round ring design w/stylized yellow carved leaves, 2 3/4" d. (ILLUS.)... **$40-55**

Black Celluloid & Rhinestone Belt Buckle

Belt buckle, black celluloid, two-piece, in the shape of an angular belt buckle pavé-set overall w/rhinestones, 2 1/2" l., 1 5/8" h. (ILLUS.) **$25-35**

Belt buckle, celluloid, two-piece, carved as red leaves, ca. 1935, 3 3/8" l., 1 1/2" h. **$30-40**

Belt buckle, silver plate, two-piece Art Nouveau design w/center fleur-de-lis, 3 1/4" w., 1" h. **$25-35**

Steel Belt Buckle

Belt buckle, steel made in marcasite style, 3 3/4" w., 1 3/4" h. (ILLUS.) **$25-35**

Belt buckle, steel made in marcasites style, two-piece, 1 1/2" h. **$25-35**

Bracelet, agate beads, pinkish orange marbleized beads on orange elastic, 3/8" w. (ILLUS. left with aventurine bracelet, top of page)... **$25-35**

Bracelet, aventurine beads, mottled green on matching elastic, 3/8" w. (ILLUS. right with agate bead bracelet, top of page) **$25-35**

Swirled Green & Yellow Bakelite Bracelet

Bracelet, Bakelite, bangle-type, a wide band in mottled green & yellow swirl carved w/deep angled grooves & large ovals, interior circumference 8" (ILLUS.) ... **$129**

Bracelet, Bakelite, bangle-type, carnelian orange, w/carved leaves & flowers, 5/8" w...................................... **$80-100**

Bracelet, Bakelite, bangle-type, chartreuse green/yellow marbled, no carving, 1/2" w.. **$35-50**

Black Bakelite Bracelet with Acorns

Bracelet, Bakelite, bangle-type, licorice black color carved w/large stylized acorns & oak leaves, interior circumference 7 3/4" (ILLUS.)................................... **$264**

Bracelet, Bakelite, bangle-type, plain, un-carved yellow, 1"w. **$45-70**

Bracelet, Bakelite, bangle-type, yellow, carved sun rays design, 3/4" w. **$55-75**

Bracelet, Bakelite, bangle-type, yellow, no carving, 7/8" w.. **$55-75**

Lime Green & Cream Bakelite Bangle

Bracelet, Bakelite, injected bangle-type, a narrow rounded lime green band injected w/oval cream dots, interior circumference 8" (ILLUS.) **$499**

Red & Yellow Dots Bakelite Bangle

Bracelet, Bakelite, laminated bangle-type, a narrow rounded deep red band inset w/yellow polka dots, interior circumfer-ence 7 3/4" (ILLUS.) **$499**

Bracelet, Bakelite, Philadelphia-style, the hinged butterscotch bangle terminating in raised multi-colored triangles, interior circumference 6 1/2" d. **$3,525**

Bracelet, Bakelite, stretch-type, reverse-carved design w/a central applejuice plaque w/carved floral design, completed by applejuice & butterscotch links, interi-or circumference 6 1/4" d. **$764**

Bracelet, Bakelite, the double-hinged piece in an applejuice color reverse-carved & painted w/a black floral design.................. **$764**

Bracelet, brass, link-type, w/six large figural brass rose charms, ca. 1900.................. **$45-65**

Bracelet, celluloid & goldplate, decorated w/five large royal blue celluloid flowers connected by goldplated links, 6 1/2" l. (ILLUS., bottom of page)........................ **$70-90**

Bracelet, copper, cuff-style, decorated w/raised Western-style designs w/or-ange glass bead accents, 1 1/4" w. **$40-55**

Bracelet with Blue Celluloid Flowers.
Courtesy of Joan Orlen

Bracelet with White Enameled Flowers.
Courtesy of Joan Orlen

Bracelet, enameled goldplate & faux pearls, composed of five oblong metal links each mounted w/three-dimensional white enameled flowers & green leaves w/faux pearl accents on a black enamel ground, w/safety chain, 3/4" w., 7" l. (ILLUS.) **$65-90**

Bracelet, enameled goldplate, hinged bangle-style, decorated w/black enamel, belt & buckle-style, 3/8" l. **$40-55**

Bracelet, enameled goldplate, multiple links in the damascene style, each one w/an enameled bull fighting scene, 1 1/4" w., 7" l. **$35-55**

Rare Haskell Floral Cuff Bracelet

Bracelet, engraved Russian gold-plated metal & faux gems, cuff-style, the wide metal band mounted w/an overall floral design composed of clusters of tiny faux seed pearls, roses montées & glass cabochons & beads imitating coral, unmarked Haskell, ca. 1950, 7" l. (ILLUS.) **$1,912**

Bracelet, glass, coral color molded glass flowers & leaves section threaded on elastic, unsigned Czechoslovakian components, 7/8" w. **$75-90**

Bracelet, glass, coral-colored glass molded w/flowers & leaf sections on two elastic bands, Czechoslovakia, 7/8" w. **$75-95**

Bracelet, glass & white metal, Art Deco style, green chrysoprase-color to glass square links alternating w/white metal filigree links, 1 1/2" w., 7 1/4" l. **$65-85**

Bracelet, gold filled, "bricks" style w/center rectangular amethyst 3/4 x 1/2" stone, bracelet is 7" l., 5/8" w. **$65-85**

Bracelet, gold filled, child's size, hinged bangle-type, initials, Victorian, 1/4"w. **$30-45**

Bracelet, gold filled, cobalt blue stones, alternating w/gold circles, 7" l., 3/4" w., 3/4" h. **$90-110**

Bracelet, gold-filled, link-type, five links w/oval shell cameos on scalloped center pieces, each link w/borders of cylinders & twisted metal, signed "Sammartino Bros. Providence," ca. 1910, 1" w. **$375-400**

Bracelet, goldplate, bangle-type, hinged, decorated w/raised oak leaf & acorn design on a brushed background w/safety chain, signed "Freirich," 5/8" w. **$80-100**

Bracelet, goldplate, bangle-type, hinged, top set w/clear rhinestones, 1" w. **$50-70**

Bracelet, goldplate, bangle-type, ribbed design, signed "Ciner," 3/4" w. **$50-75**

Bracelet, goldplate, composed of circular links alternating w/bars, signed "Goldette," 1/2" w. **$45-65**

Bracelet, goldplate, faux cultured pearl & rhinestone, the links centered by faux pearls w/rhinestones set in the connecting links, 3/8" w., 7" l. **$35-50**

Goldplate Bracelet

Bracelet, goldplate, glass, carved oval links in scarab style, each link a different color, 1/2" w. (ILLUS.) **$45-60**

Bracelet, goldplate, link-type, set w/individual multicolored carved glass scarabs, 1/2" w. **$55-70**

Bracelet, goldplate, linked chain w/ten varied charms decorated w/blue, green & turquoise enamel **$40-60**

Bracelet, goldplate & rhinestone, bangle-type, hinged, the overlapping front decorated w/large emerald-cut rhinestones & four rows of small rhinestones & gold rays, signed "Vargas," the front 2" w. **$150-175**

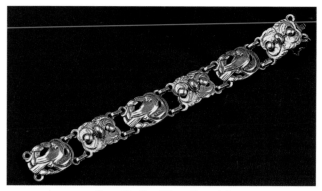

Coro Sterling Silver Bracelet

Bracelet, goldplate & rhinestone, multiple links in textured gold each centered by a large Aurora Borealis rhinestone, w/safety chain, signed "Coro," 1" w., 6 1/4" l. **$75-95**

Bracelet, goldplate & rhinestone, the links decorated w/brushed gold flowers each centered by a rhinestone, signed "Florenza," 5/8" w. **$70-90**

Bracelet, ivory & wood, rectangular ivory plaques mounted on wooden links, the ivory etched w/scenes of Eskimo, polar bears or seals, the links joined by ivory bead spacers on two rows of elastic, 1" w. **$55-75**

Bracelet, Lucite, bangle-type, double row of applied black cone-shaped designs around entire bracelet, ca. 1965, 2" w. **$40-60**

Bracelet, onyx & pearl, small black onyx beads & freshwater pearls w/gold spacers, 6 1/2" l. **$35-50**

Unsigned Chanel Faux Gem Bracelet

Bracelet, pate-de-verre faux gems & gold plated metal, the links in gilt metal cen-

tered by an oblong green glass cabochon imitating an emerald flanked by smaller squared red glass cabochons imitating rubies, unsigned Chanel, France, ca. 1955, 8" l. (ILLUS.) **$717**

Bracelet, rhinestone, a single row of emerald-cut clear rhinestones, signed "Weiss," 3/8" w. **$110-135**

Bracelet, rhinestone & glass, links w/large hand-set marquise-cut & round clear rhinestones w/dangling royal blue glass balls, signed "Kramer of New York," 1" w., 7" l. **$250-280**

Bracelet, rhinestone & metal, expansion-style, white metal bracelet completely covered w/large emerald-cut clear rhinestones, 1/2" w. **$85-100**

Bracelet, rhinestone & white metal, link-type, decorated w/clear stones & large marquise-shaped center stones, 5/8" w. **$50-70**

Bracelet, sterling, bangle-type, hinged w/safety chain, no decoration, Mexico, 1" w. **$65-80**

Bracelet, sterling, link-type, w/connected curved ribbed leaves, signed "Jewelart," 1/2" w. **$55-75**

Bracelet, sterling, link-type, w/enamel on sterling Pekinese dog charm, 1930s....... **$55-75**

Bracelet, sterling, link-type, w/matching sterling cat charm, 1950s, 1/4" w. **$45-65**

Bracelet, sterling silver & blown glass, long openwork silver links alternating w/citrine-colored bubbled glass cabochon links, 1/2" w. **$70-86**

Bracelet, sterling silver, composed of openwork links featuring a stylized bird alternating with openwork links w/scrolled leaves & buttons, signed by Coro, 7 1/2" l. (ILLUS., top of page) **$411**

Bracelet, sterling silver & glass stones, silver flower-form links each set w/a large red cabochon stone in the center, 3/4" w., 7" l. **$135-155**

Bracelet, sterling silver, hinged bangle-style, plain design, signed "Mexico JPH," 1 1/8" l. **$100-125**

Bracelet, sterling silver, hinged bangle-style, plain design w/pointed top, hallmarked & signed by DePercin **$100-125**

Sterling Bracelet with Rhinestones

Bracelet, sterling silver & rhinestone, late Retro style, openwork design of ribbons/scrolls in rectangular panels linked together, entirely set w/clear rhinestones, signed "Unicraft Sterling," 1 3/8" w. (ILLUS.) **$175-195**

Bracelet, turquoise & metal, assorted real turquoise nuggets strung on elastic w/white metal textured spacer beads, 1/2" w. **$70-90**

Bracelet, vermeil (gold over sterling) flexible links of amber triangular stones, hallmarked, 1/4" w................................ **$85-110**

Bracelet, vermeil (gold over sterling silver) & cubic zirconiums, tennis-style, the single strand set w/cubic zirconiums, 1/8" w., 7 1/4" l. **$110-135**

Unusual Geometric Cuff Bracelet

Bracelet, white leather, silver plated metal & plexiglass, cuff-style, a semi-rectangular metal cuff lined on the exterior w/a wide band of white leather, inset near the top w/a large rectangular block of plexiglass, attributed to Courrèges, France, 1965-68, unsigned, inside length 5 3/4" (ILLUS.).. **$717**

Bracelet, white metal & glass, ornate openwork metal links mounted w/four faux turquoise glass cabochon stones in raised settings, 7/8" w., 6 1/2" l.......................... **$35-55**

Bracelet, white metal & glass, the metal links set w/a turquoise glass carved scarab alternating w/white metal ancient Egyptian profiles, 5/8" w., 6 1/4" l............ **$50-75**

Bracelet, white metal & rhinestone, hinged bangle-style, the top pavé-set w/rhinestones, w/safety chain, 3/4" l................... **$45-60**

Bracelet, white metal & rhinestone, hinged bangle-style, the top pavé-set w/rhine-

stones w/curved metal spacers, openwork back, signed "Lisner," 1/2" l......... **$60-75**

White Metal & Glass Bracelet

Bracelet, white metal set w/multicolor agate style glass stones, links style, w/one link hanging as a charm, 6 1/2" l., 3/4" w. (ILLUS.)...................... **$45-65**

White Metal & Colored Stone Bracelet

Bracelet, white metal & stone, flat links each set w/a different colored semi-precious stone alternating w/loop links, 3/8" w., 5 3/4" l. (ILLUS.) **$30-45**

Bakelite Figural Boot Brooch

Brooch, Bakelite, a long rectangular licorice black bar carved w/pointed lines suspending a pair of butterscotch boots w/black soles, 2 x 3" (ILLUS., previous page) **$176**

Bakelite Brass-studded Fish Brooch

Brooch, Bakelite & brass, designed as a tropical fish in butterscotch accented by brass studs & a brass eye, 3" l. (ILLUS.) ... **$411**

Bakelite Oval Butterscotch Brooch

Brooch, Bakelite, butterscotch color, oval form carved w/a stylized floral design (ILLUS.) **$88**

Signed Dior Rhinestone Flower Brooch

Brooch, enameled cast silver & rhinestone, designed as a tiered flowering leafy branch w/the leaves set overall w/clear rhinestones, the lower branches suspending faceted red glass stones imitating rubies, the main stem enameled in green, probably designed by Roger Jean Pierre & made by Mitchel Maer, Wales, marked "Sterling - Chr. Dior - 1958," 3 1/8" l. (ILLUS.) **$657**

Brooch, enameled rhodium-plated metal & rhinestone, designed in the form of a realistic cyclamen flower enameled in pink on a green stem, accented w/clear rhinestones, Trifari mark, ca. 1941, 2 1/2 x 4" (ILLUS., top next column) **$1,076**

Fine Trifari Cyclamen Brooch

Very Rare Trifari Sailboat & Woman Brooch

Brooch, enameled rhodium-plated metal, rhinestone & faux glass gems, designed as a sailboat w/the sail enameled in gold, the deck in yellow & the flag in red, the bottom of the hull lined w/clear rhinestones & green glass stones, mounted w/the standing figure of a stylized woman w/one hand holding the mast & the other arm waving, her head, hands & legs enameled & her clothing composed of unfoiled faceted & baguette glass stones imitating emeralds, rubies & sapphires, signed by Trifari, ca. 1940, 2 3/8 x 2 3/4" (ILLUS.) **$2,988**

Faux Gem "Fruit Salad" Style Brooch

Brooch, faux glass gemstones, rhinestones & rhodium-plated metal,"fruit salad" style, the openwork oblong metal mount forming a rhinestone-set branch supporting flowers & leaves of stamped glass stones imitating rubies, emeralds & sapphires, American, unsigned, ca. 1936, 3 1/2" l. (ILLUS., previous page) **$896**

Trifari "Jelly Belly" Poodle Brooch

Brooch, gilt sterling silver, rhinestone & Lucite, "jelly belly" style, designed as a standing poodle trimmed in small clear rhinestones & w/a bulbous clear Lucite body, small red glass stone eye, marked by Trifari, ca. 1944, 1 3/4 x 2" (ILLUS.) **$448**

Rare Trifari "Jelly Belly" Sailfish Brooch

Brooch, gilt sterling silver, rhinestone & Lucite, "jelly belly" style, designed as a sailfish w/the wide back fin & tail lined w/clear rhinestones, the body & head formed by large pieces of clear Lucite, the head w/a green glass cabochon eye, signed by Trifari, ca. 1941, 2 1/2 x 3 1/4" (ILLUS.)... **$1,195**

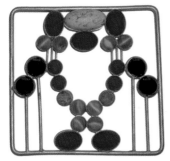

Hoffmann-inspired Brass & Glass Brooch

Brooch, gold-plated brass & glass stone, design inspired by Josef Hoffmann, an open rectangular bar frame enclosing vertical bars topped by dark glass cabochons flanking an openwork design composed of blue, red, purple & green glass cabochons, marked "Ugo Correani Per Chloe," designed by Karl Lagerfeld & Ugo Correani for Chloe, France, 1984, 4 1/4" sq. (ILLUS.) **$538**

Rare Unsigned Chanel Glass Stone Brooch

Brooch, pate-de-verre stone & rhinestone, the openwork oblong mount set w/a variety of large cabochon glass stones in red, purple, light & dark blue & dark green & accented around the center w/circular- and baguette-cut clear rhinestones, unsigned Chanel, France, ca. 1960, 2 x 2 1/4" (ILLUS.) **$1,673**

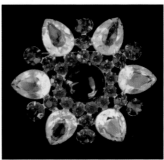

Blue & Pink Rhinestone Vendome Brooch

Brooch, rhinestone & goldplate, a stylized snowflake design w/an outer ring of large marquise-cut aqua rhinestones alternating w/pairs of smaller round deep blue rhinestones, a central ring of red rhinestones around a large dark blue cabochon in the middle, signed "Vendome," 1950s, 2 3/4" d. (ILLUS.) **$30-50**

Cameo pendant, sterling silver, glass & mother-of-pearl, a mother-of-pearl portrait cameo on a black glass ground within a sterling silver frame, Italy, pendant 1" l., sterling chain 24" l.......................... **$55-75**

Cameo pin, goldplate & plastic, the plastic cameo w/a real diamond chip on the side, mounted in a goldplate frame, on the original store card, 1 1/4 x 1 5/8" **$20-30**

Dior Faux Pearl & Rhinestone Choker

Lucite & Plastic Cameo Pin.
Author's Collection

Cameo pin, Lucite, a clear rectangular Lucite plaque w/carved angled lines in each corner, centering an oval black plastic cameo w/a profile of a Victorian lady, 1 3/4 x 2 1/4" (ILLUS.).............................. **$60-80**

Charm bracelet, enameled goldplate, decorated w/ten assorted charms in blue, turquoise or green enamel, 7" l. **$40-55**

Charm bracelet, gold-filled & agate, etched link chain w/a swivel charm & an oval coral agate on one side, grey agate on the other, ca. 1900, chain 3/8" w............... **$195-225**

Charm bracelet, sterling chain suspending charms in the shape of birds & hearts decorated w/turquoise & enamel, signed "Meka, Denmark," 7" l. **$50-65**

Chatelaine pins, silver plate & rhinestone, two clear rhinestone-set wishbones on two chains, ca. 1940, each wishbone 1 3/4" w. **$65-90**

Choker, faux pearl & rhinestone, composed of eight strands of faux pearls centered by a round mount set w/faceted rectangular & round rhinestones suspending a rhinestone drop w/a navette-cut stone, unsigned Dior, France, ca. 1952, 11" l. (ILLUS., top of page)............................. **$1,315**

Choker, silver plated metal, rhinestone & glass bead, composed of two graduated wide flat bands w/multiple strands of black alternating w/brown beads, decorated at the front w/a large beaded spearpoint device w/clusters of yellow, orange, green, dark blue & light blue glass beads, the clasp accented w/clear rhinestones, Italy, 1962, 15" l. (ILLUS., bottom of page)... **$1,195**

Clip, dress-type, 935 grade sterling & rhinestone, large clear baguettes & marquise stones in center, openwork sides set w/small clear rhinestones, 1 3/4" h. **$90-120**

Clip, dress-type, antiqued gold plate, leaf shape w/openwork flowers in center, each flower set w/blue, white or turquoise center, signed "NE," 1 7/8 x 2 1/2"......... **$40-50**

Clip, dress-type, antiqued gold plate & rhinestone, curved ribbon shape, openwork metal decorated w/four center handset large oval red rhinestones in graduated sizes, from large on top to small on bottom, each surrounded by clear rhinestone trim, 1 1/4 x 3 1/4" **$85-110**

Dramatic Multi-Strand Italian Beaded Choker

Clip, dress-type, copper-finish metal & glass, ornate filigree & etched design decorated w/large pink art glass oval stone on top, 2 x 2 1/2" **$50-75**

Amber Flower Dress Clip

Clip, dress-type, gold plate, glass & rhinestone, large spray of three gold bell-shaped flowers w/large center amber crystal centers & pavé clear rhinestone petals & stem, 2 x 3 1/2" (ILLUS.) **$75-100**

Dress Clip of Multicolored Rhinestones

Clip, dress-type, goldtone metal, openwork kite-shaped design studded w/large purple, pink, aqua, yellow, green & clear rhinestones, 1 3/4 x 2 1/4" (ILLUS.) **$55-75**

Multicolored Cabochon Dress Clip

Clip, dress-type, goldtone metal, oval openwork design w/large oval red cabochon stone in center surrounded by panel w/leaf decoration & four smaller round multicolored cabochon stones in ropetwist border, an outer panel decorated w/fleur-de-lis & 12 oval multicolored cabochon stones, 2 1/4 x 2 1/2" (ILLUS.) **$70-90**

Clip, dress-type, rhinestone, floral motif set w/large blue, red, green & yellow marquise stones around green domed center, 1 3/4" d. **$35-50**

Clip, dress-type, rhinestone, green crackle glass center stone inside frame of pink cabochons, upper bottom row of pink, green, yellow & blue rhinestones, lower bottom row of five ribbon-style designs set w/tiny blue, red & purple cabochons, three hanging blue glass cone shapes, 2 1/2 x 2 3/4" **$65-85**

Clip, dress-type, rhinestone, inverted triangle shape, large pink oval rhinestones in openwork design w/matching channel-set square rhinestone borders & accents, 1 5/8 x 2 3/4" **$65-85**

Clip, dress-type, rhinestone, openwork metal completely set w/clear rhinestones in Art Deco design, center large clear marquise stone w/red, emerald green & blue etched glass leaves above & below, small black enamel accents, 1 1/2 x 2" **$70-95**

Black & Clear Rhinestone Dress Clip

Clip, dress-type, rhinestone, three vertically stacked large round black stones framed by slightly smaller clear oval & marquise rhinestones, signed "Doctor Dress," 2 x 2 1/2" (ILLUS.) **$75-100**

Clip, dress-type, white metal & glass, openwork design completely set w/pale blue faux moonstones, clear rhinestone trim between stones, 1 3/4 x 2 1/4" **$70-90**

Clip, dress-type, white metal & rhinestone, ornate openwork rococo design w/double swag chains & large oval clear & pink rhinestones in center, signed "Doctor Dress," 2 1/4 x 3" **$75-100**

Clip, fur-type, gold plate, glass, enamel & pearl, floral spray design w/pink, green, blue & purple glass squares forming flowers, a single side spray of graduated pearls, a light pink enameled bow at bottom, 2 1/4 x 3 3/4" **$100-120**

Clip, fur-type, gold plate, glass & enamel, spray design of three flowers w/large amber rhinestone centers, small clear rhinestone trim, navy blue enamel ribbon at top, signed "Trifari," 2 5/8" h. **$125-150**

Clip, fur-type, gold plate, sword design w/fil-igreed hilt set w/large red cabochon on top, smaller red, green & blue cabochons on border & at center, signed "Monet," 2 x 3" **$125-150**

Clip, fur-type, rhinestone, spray design of pink etched glass leaves w/turquoise, pink & lavender oval rhinestone flowers w/blue-green enameled stems & pavé rhinestones, 1 1/2 x 2 1/4" **$80-100**

Clip, sweater-type, gold plate & pearl, chain of pearls hanging between gold-plated leaves.. **$25-35**

Clip, sweater-type, sterling, two circles connected by 3" chain, signed "Tiffany & Co." **$75-100**

Rare Ken Scott Wreath-style Collar

Collar, glass bead, faux pearl & leather, the wide graduating wreath-like band w/a wide pointed front, set overall w/a mixture of greenish blue & orange beads imitating coral & turquoise & small faux pearls, accented w/sewn on large gilt leather leaves, Ken Scott, Italy, 1965, 15" l. (ILLUS.) **$1,793**

Comb, celluloid, amber color, a plain top above 21 teeth, ca. 1880, 4 5/8" w., 4" h. **$70-95**

Fine Carved Art Nouveau Comb.
Author's Collection

Comb, tortoiseshell, Art Nouveau style, painted matte dark brown, the arched top carved w/ornate openwork scrolls & leafy scrolls, two long flat teeth, 5" l. (ILLUS.) **$65-85**

Dress clip, antiqued white metal & rhinestone, an ornate swirled openwork metal mount set w/two large oval clear rhinestones accented by smaller round clear rhinestones, two hanging swag chains at the bottom, signed "Doctor Dress," 2" w., 3" h. **$150-175**

Art Glass & Clear Stone Deco Dress Clip

Dress clip, art glass, Art Deco style, a long pointed mount decorated w/two vertical rows of three oval red glass cabochons w/blue veining, the top, center band & base set w/clear emerald-cut stones & round rhinestones, attributed to Eisenberg, 1 1/2" w., 3" h. (ILLUS.) **$300-325**

Dress clip, Bakelite, black, densely carved leaves, vines design, 2" h. **$45-70**

Dress clip, Bakelite, designed as an emerald green carved flower in a twisted metal frame above carved leaves, 2 1/4" l........ **$75-95**

Triangular Bakelite Dress Clip with Flower

Dress clip, Bakelite, long narrow black triangle decorated w/an applied gilt-metal flower & leaf sprig centered by a pearl, 2" l. (ILLUS.) **$40-60**

Dress clip, brass & celluloid, the entire brass clip covered w/white celluloid flowers w/red centers, 2" l. **$30-50**

Dress clip, brass, Victorian-style design w/acorns & oak leaves, 1 7/8" h............. **$40-65**

Dress clip, celluloid, a pink leaf w/a knot design at the top, 2 x 2" **$30-50**

Dress clip, celluloid, designed as pink flowers & leaves w/two dangling flowers, 2 x 2 1/2".. **$30-50**

Dress clip, celluloid & rhinestone, a gold leaf design w/a textured surface, decorated w/a rhinestone-set flower & central strip, 3 1/4 x 3 1/2" **$55-70**

Dress clip, crystal, rhinestone & white metal, Art Deco style, the metal mount decorated w/a design of square clear crystals, the top centered by a large red dome w/red marquise-cut rhinestone accents &

square, rectangular & marquise-cut clear rhinestones, 1 x 2 1/2" **$65-90**

Goldplated Insect Dress Clip

Dress clip, fur-type, goldplated insect motif, green rhinestones eyes, purple center diamond-shaped stone on body, 1 1/2 x 1" (ILLUS.)... **$40-55**

Dress clip, goldplate, an overall ornate medieval design, 2" l. **$40-65**

Dress clip, goldplate & crystal, a background of goldplate leaves set w/three lavender marquise-cut crystals, 2 3/4 x 3" **$200-250**

Clip with Gold Flowers & Blue Stones

Dress clip, goldplate, crystal & rhinestone, shield-shaped, centered by bold-relief goldplate flowers centered by a blue rhinestone, the border composed of large emerald-cut royal blue crystals, signed "Czechoslovakia," 1 1/2 x 2 1/2" (ILLUS.)
.... **$85-115**

Dress clip, goldplate & glass, designed as a flowerpot w/three forest green inverted teardrop glass flowers, rhinestone trim on the pot, 1 3/4 x 2 1/2" **$50-65**

Dress clip, goldplate & rhinestone, an ornate openwork goldplate mount set w/pink, purple, green, yellow, light blue & clear large round rhinestones, 1 3/4" w., 2 1/2" h. **$100-125**

Dress clip, goldplate & rhinestone, decorated w/metal flowers, each w/a pink or green rhinestone center, scalloped borders, 2 1/2" l. **$45-65**

Dress clip, metal & rhinestone, Art Deco style, the metal mount decorated w/rows of green & clear baguette rhinestones in graduated sizes, 2"h. **$40-60**

Shield-shaped Clip with Ornate Design. Courtesy of Davida Baron.

Dress clip, metal, rhinestone & glass, Art Deco style, shield-shaped, the openwork mount w/geometric banding set w/clear rhinestones & small sections of black enamel trim, the bottom center w/a navette-shaped design w/a group of large green, red & blue marquise-cut stones at the top & bottom centered by a large horizontal clear marquise-cut stone, 1 1/2" w., 2" h. (ILLUS.)........... **$125-150**

Dress clip, moonstone & rhinestone, the openwork mount decorated w/four rows of oval moonstones accented w/clear rhinestones, resembles a Mazer design, 1 3/4" w., 2 1/4" h............................... **$150-175**

Dress clip, plastic yellow iridescent bubbles design, 2" **$35-45**

Dress clip, red cinnabar & goldplate, the goldplate oval decorated w/carved cinnabar flowers in the center, China, 2" l. **$55-75**

Dress clip, rhinestone, Art Deco style, openwork shield shape, 1 7/8" h............. **$30-45**

Dress clip, rhinestone, leaf-shaped & pavé-set w/rhinestones, 1 3/8" h...................... **$25-40**

Blue Marquise Dress Clip

Dress clip, rhinestones, all deep blue marquise stones in openwork design, 2" x 2 3/4" (ILLUS.) **$55-65**

Ornate French Dress Clip with Rhinestones & Molded Blue Glass Plaques.
Courtesy of Davida Baron

Round Flower Design Dress Clip

Dress clip, rhinestones, round flower design set w/red, blue, green, amber petals, 1 3/4" d. (ILLUS.) **$30-45**

Dress clip, white metal, glass & rhinestone, Art Deco style, a long openwork shield-shaped mount composed of scrolls & stylized leaf designs, set overall w/round & baguette clear rhinestones & accented near the top w/a pair of curved blue glass bands molded w/flowers & a larger half-round pale blue glass plaque also molded w/flowers, French, 3 1/4" w., 2" h. (ILLUS., top of page) **$200-225**

Dress clip, white metal & plastic, Art Deco style, a white metal shield-shaped mount decorated w/dark green vertical plastic bars, 1 x 2" **$55-75**

Dress clip, white metal & rhinestone, the filigree metal mount overlaid w/solid & filigree metal flowers each centered by a blue rhinestone, 1 1/2 x 1 3/4" **$40-60**

Dress clip-pendant, metal, crystal & rhinestone, the mount designed as a central flower arrangement of oval & diamond-shaped purple crystals w/an ornate border of large round purple crystals & tiny purple rhinestones, the back w/a loop for wearing on a chain as a pendant, 1930s, 2 1/4" w., 2 3/4" h. **$125-150**

Art Deco Green Bakelite & Rhinestone Dress Clips.
Courtesy of Joan Orlen

Dress clips, Bakelite & rhinestone, Art Deco style, carved Bakelite mottled dark green fluted spearheads decorated near the top w/a pair of large rectangular-cut clear rhinestones below a row of small round clear rhinestones, the back carved w/a yellow plaid design, 2" w., 1 1/2" h., pr. (ILLUS.) **$125-150**

Dress clips, cabochon set, blue, red, green stones in open design, 2 1/4" h., pr. **$65-85**

Dress clips, duette-type, red enamel Art Deco motif, rhinestones trim, signed Coro, 2 3/4" w. **$90-120**

Rare Clear & Colored Rhinestone Duette Dress Clips.
Courtesy of Davida Baron

Dress clips, goldplate & rhinestone, duette-type, each openwork mount in a half-round fanned design, the flat bottom edge band w/a loop & issuing spokes all set w/small clear round rhinestones, the center also set w/an arched band of alternating oval turquoise & grape purple large stones, the outer border band composed of the same large stones, signed "Joseph Weisner NY," each half 1 1/2 x 2", the attached pair 3" w., pr. (ILLUS.).. **$500-550**

Dress clips, rhinestone, Art Deco duette-type, converts to a pair of clips when removed from the pin frame, 2 5/8" w. **$65-85**

Dress clips, rhinestone, white metal bows set w/triangular & baguette rhinestone accents, 1 x 1", pr. **$35-50**

Dress clips, three rows of faux moonstones in inverted pyramid style rows, Art Deco, 1 1/2 x 1 1/2" l., pr. **$60-80**

Dress clips, white metal, glass stone & rhinestone, the metal mount decorated w/a row of clear carved baguette & round rhinestones above a group of five blue glass faux gems, signed "Artisan NY," 1 1/4 x 1 1/2", pr. **$60-85**

Coro Duette Dress Clips-Brooch

Dress clips-brooch, sterling silver & multicolored faceted stones, duette-style, designed as a comical silver monkey w/the body set w/a large facet-cut oval pink stones, green glass bead eyes, clips can be joined to form a brooch, signed "Coro Duet," each 1 1/4 x 2" (ILLUS.) **$235**

Earrings, art glass, millefiore-style mauve drops, gold ear wires, 1 5/8" l., pr. **$25-35**

Earrings, ceramic, designed as a black & grey wing-like design w/a black oval cabochon stone in the center, 2 1/2" l., pr. ... **$30-50**

One of Two Versace Earrings

Earrings, enameled silver plate, clip-on type, each designed as a long swag of small rose blossoms & leaves enameled in shades of red, orange & chartreuse, marked "Gianni Versace - Made in Italy," 1991, each 6" l., pr. (ILLUS. of one) **$657**

Earrings, enameled sterling silver, screw-on pendant-type, designed as a sterling triangle enameled w/a black triangle, signed "AAR" & hallmarked, Mexico, 1 5/8" l., pr.. **$65-85**

Earrings, glass, hanging teardrop style, green Peking glass, screwback-type, ca. 1925, 2 1/4" l., pr...................................... **$65-85**

Earrings, glass stone, rhinestone & enameled metal, clip-on type, the oval metal mount in bright green w/a large green art glass cabochon stone center, double rows of small rhinestones on the four sides, 1 1/2 x 1 5/8", pr. **$35-55**

Gold Plate & Cabochon Earrings

Earrings, goldplate & cabochon, hoop top w/double circle drop w/blue oval cabochon set stones, drop can be removed so hoop top can be worn alone, signed "Agatha," 2" l., pr. (ILLUS.) **$45-60**

Earrings, goldplate, designed as flowers, clip-on type, signed "Jomaz," 1 1/4" d., pr... **$60-75**

Dramatic Enameled Leaves & Rhinestone Pendant Earrings.
Courtesy of Joan Orlen

Earrings, goldplate, enameled goldplate & rhinestone, clip-on pendant-type, the top clip designed as a spray of greenish blue enameled long pointed leaves around a five-petaled flower centered by a milky opalecent rhinestone, the large rounded openwork goldplate pendant mounted w/several additional enameled leaf sprigs accented by scattered turquoise blue & milky opalescent rhinestones, 1 1/2" 2., 3 1/4" l., pr. (ILLUS.) **$50-75**

Earrings, goldplate & glass bead, pendant-type, a goldplated oval framed set w/large green, blue & red glass cabochons, 2" l., pr. **$25-40**

Earrings, goldplate & pearl, flower-shaped w/the center set w/a 1/4" d. cultured pearl, signed "Kramer N.Y.," pr. **$45-60**

Unusual Goldplate Concentric Ring Earrings. Courtesy of Joan Orlen

Earrings, goldplate, plastic & rhinestone, designed as openwork concentric undulating goldplate circles centered by a large domed black plastic cabochon, scattered clear rhinestone accents, 2" d., pr. (ILLUS.)... **$45-70**

Earrings, goldplate & rhinestone, clip-on pendant-type, designed as three graduated diamond shapes set w/royal blue & yellowish green rhinestones, a blue glass cabochon on the clip, signed "Kramer," 3" l., pr. **$90-120**

Spiral Bead-decorated Earrings. Courtesy of Joan Orlen

Earrings, goldplate, rhinestone & glass bead, pendant-type, a long metal spiral set w/small clear faceted Aurora Borealis rhinestones accented w/larger hanging Aurora Borealis crystal beads, 2 1/2" l., pr. (ILLUS.)... **$70-95**

Earrings, goldplate, three-dimensional flower motif w/striped gold finish, signed "Jomaz," 1 1/2" d., pr............................. **$50-70**

Earrings, metal & rhinestone, clip-on type, the mount designed as a butterly set w/lavender & blue pear-shaped rhinestones, signed "Weiss," 1 x 1", pr. **$90-120**

Earrings, pearl, large 1/2" d. cultured pearl ball drops, clip-on type, signed "Richelieu," 1" l., pr. **$45-65**

Earrings, pearl & rhinestone, round rhinestone-set form accented w/pearls, clip-on type, on original card marked "Metaphor," 3/4" d., pr........................... **$20-30**

Earrings, pearls, large 3/8" d. ball pearl drop w/smaller pearl on top, clip-ons, signed "Richelieu," 1" h., pr.................... **$40-60**

Green Peking Glass Earrings

Earrings, Peking glass, mottled light & dark green drops, screw-backs, ca. 1925, 2 1/4" l., pr. (ILLUS.) **$65-80**

1950s Loop Rhinestone Earrings

Earrings, rhinestone, hoop-type, the ring & clip set w/rhinestones, clip-on type, ca. 1955, 1 7/8" d., 2 1/4" h., pr. (ILLUS.)..... **$65-80**

Earrings, rhinestone & pearl, a baguette rhinestone-set feather-shaped mount centered by a pearl, screw-on type, ca. 1955, 3/8" w., 7/8" h., pr......................... **$30-40**

Red & Clear Rhinestone Earrings

Earrings, rhinestone, slightly curved design w/horizontal rows of red baguette stones inside bordering clear round rhinestones, clip-on style, 1" l., pr. (ILLUS.) **$40-55**

Earrings, sterling & enamel, fan design in blue & green enamel, signed "Siam," 1 1/4" w., pr. **$50-70**

Earrings, sterling silver, clip-on type, designed as a folded silver ribbon, signed "Paloma Picasso - Tiffany & Co.," 1 3/8" h., pr. **$90-120**

Earrings, sterling silver, pierced ear-type, a curved oval shape w/three graceful curved stems, Mexico, 1 1/4 x 1 1/2", pr. **$45-65**

Earrings, white metal, round, center black enamel flower w/cultured pearl centers, screw-on type, 5/8" d., pr. **$25-35**

Fur clip, goldplate, crystal & rhinestone, the goldplate mount designed as an iverted spray of red & pink crystal flowers, trimmed w/a ribbon set w/blue baguette stones & pavé-set w/clear rhinestones, signed "Trifari," 1 3/8" w., 3" h. **$300-325**

Rare Fur Clip Attributed to Eisenberg. Courtesy of Davida Baron

Fur clip, goldplate, glass stone & rhinestone, the mount designed as graceful branches trimmed w/large blue pear-shaped stone flowers trimmed w/small opaque coral glass stones, attributed to Eisenberg, ca. 1935, 2 1/4 x 3 3/4" (ILLUS.) **$700-725**

Fur clip, rhinestone & enamel, a white enameled flower set w/red & clear square rhinestone trim, "trembling" center w/rhinestones, 2 1/4" h. **$60-85**

Fur clip, rhinestone, Retro style, large marquise & emerald-shaped clear stones set in an openwork white metal mount, signed "Eisenberg Original," 3 1/8" h. **$275-300**

Fur clip, white metal & glass stone, the openwork metal mount w/leaves centered by oval cabochon blue glass faux gems, signed "Napier," 2" h. **$45-65**

Hatpin, goldplate, head of cat, yellow rhinestone eyes, head is 1" w., overall 9" **$110-125**

Hatpin, sterling, Art Nouveau head of woman w/long flowing hair, three purple stone accents, head is 1 1/4 x 3/4", overall 7" l. **$150-175**

Handpainted Hatpins

Hatpins, plastic, black flat large heads with h.p. multicolor dots, heads 3 3/8" l. x 1" w., overall 7 1/2" h., pr. (ILLUS.) **$70-90**

Necklace, 950 grade sterling silver & onyx, composed of hinged silver links designed as flat circles each centered by a round black onyx, handmade, unsigned, 16 1/2" l. **$150-175**

Necklace, amber, composed of graduated oval amber beads in shades of yellow alternating w/marbleized brown, 29" l. **$150-175**

Necklace, art glass beads, a long rope strand composed of blue, green & turquoise glass beads, 52" l. **$50-70**

Necklace, art glass beads, composed of large green beads w/red marbleizing & red, green & textured gold spacers, a matching filigree clasp, signed "Miriam Haskell," 30" l. **$285-310**

Necklace, art glass beads, four-strand style, each strand composed of coral-colored glass beads w/golden flecks, gold spacers, adjusts to 16" **$65-90**

Necklace with Bicolor Art Glass Beads

Necklace, art glass, bicolored oblong flattened beads in shades of red, yellow, green & blue, beads alternate w/silvered metal chains, 36" l. (ILLUS.) **$35-50**

Necklace, Aurora Borealis crystal beads, graduated strand, 21" l. w/3" extensioin chain **$60-80**

Bakelite Necklace with Various Fruits

Necklace, Bakelite, a red trace link chain suspending a carved strawberry, pear, orange, lemon, apple & peach in various colors, minor paint loss, overall 16 1/2" l. (ILLUS.)... **$999**

Necklace, Bakelite, composed of butterscotch, black, green & red geometric fringe, completed by large red trace links, metal clasp w/losses, ca. 1930s, 14 1/2" l. **$646**

Necklace, Bakelite, the red trace link chain suspending a strawberry, pear, orange, lemon, apple & peach, minor paint losses, 16" l. **$499**

Necklace, beads, crystal, yellow, graduated, ca. 1925, 28" l. **$100-125**

Necklace, beads, garnets, graduated sizes, faceted, self bead clasp, 16" l. **$125-150**

Necklace, ceramic beads, composed of large pink & mauve beads w/gold metal spacers, 18" l. **$30-55**

Necklace, crystal Aurora Borealis beads, composed of bronze-colored, beige & clear beads, some clear beads w/gold enamel on half the bead, 22" l. **$45-65**

Necklace, crystal beads, composed of clear graduated Aurora Borealis beads, adjusts from 21" to 23"............................... **$40-60**

Necklace, crystal beads, composed of clear graduated crystal beads strung on a chain, Czechoslovakian, 1930s, 16" l. **$50-75**

Necklace, crystal & goldplate, the goldplate mounts designed at the lower front as a cluster of three five-petal flowers flanked by three graduated flowers connected to diamond-shaped links, all set w/small green crystals & a center yellow crystal, the cluster w/slender metal stems each ending in multicolored pear-shaped crystal beads, attributed to Countess Cis, France, 16" l. (ILLUS., bottom of page)
.... **$1,500-2,000**

Rare Designer Crystal Flower Necklace. Courtesy of Davida Baron

Necklace, enameled brass & carnelian, Art Deco style, designed as a flat chain w/a center carved carnelian stone & four enameled brass plaques w/Chinese designs in yellow, black & orange, two smaller carnelian stone accents, 15" l. **$145-175**

Necklace, enameled copper, composed of turquoise-enameled links w/a copper overlay design, signed "Matisse," adjusts from 16" to 18" **$60-80**

Necklace, faux cultured pearl, double strand w/two different sizes of pearls, 25" l. **$35-55**

Fine Faux Pearl & Glass Bead Tassel Necklace. Courtesy of Davida Baron

Necklace, faux cultured pearls, glass bead & goldtone, a strand composed of three faux pearls alternating w/a red, blue or green beads & small gold metal bead spacers, suspending a large tassel w/a large domed goldplate top above the 12 strands also featuring the faux pearls & glass beads, signed "de Lillo," tassel 4" l., overall 18" l. (ILLUS.) **$750-1,000**

Necklace, faux pearl, choker-style, double-strand cultured-type, a large faux pearl centering the rhinestone-set round clasp, signed "Ciner," 14" l. **$50-75**

Necklace, gemstone beads, designed w/sections of twisted small onyx beads, oval freshwater pearls & long coral beads w/gold metal spacers, 22" l. **$95-120**

Necklace, glass beads, composed of blue glass beads w/gold metal spacers, signed "Monet," 14 1/2" l. **$40-60**

Necklace, glass beads, composed of coral-colored graduated beads strung on a sterling silver chain, ca. 1940, 16" l. **$80-96**

Necklace, glass, beads of various colors & shapes accented w/long cylindrical art glass beads, 38" l. (ILLUS., top next column) **$65-85**

Necklace, glass beads, sections of coral- and turquoise-colored beads alternating w/smaller black beads, 37" l. **$45-60**

Multicolored Glass Bead Necklace

Necklace, glass, bright multicolored beads w/large flat bright orange accents, 39" l. **$50-65**

Necklace, goldplate chain, composed of two snake chains & two large-link chains w/a large ring clasp, unsigned but designer quality, 15" l. **$40-65**

French Goldplate & Green Glass Flower Necklace. Courtesy of Davida Baron

Necklace, goldplate & glass, a double swag metal link chain suspending small poured-glass green balls, suspending a large stylized five-petal flower w/goldtone petals & center accented by green glass additional petals, France, ca. 1930, flower 2 1/4" w., overall 14" l. (ILLUS.) **$250-275**

Necklace, goldplate & glass bead, composed of multiple chains of large apple green twisted glass beads alternating w/sections of chain, signed "Kramer," adjusts to 17" l. **$50-70**

Necklace, goldplate & glass beads, metal chain set w/five glass beads in purple & yellow each ending in fringe, signed "LCI," 42" l. **$55-75**

Necklace, goldplate & glass, composed of faux ancient Roman goldplate coins each w/a yellow glass insert, goldplate & glass beads, metal chain set w/five glass beads in purple & yellow each ending in fringe, signed "LCI," 42" l. **$95-110**

Necklace, goldplate, glass & pearl, multiple chains w/large 6 1/2" pendant & pink, fuchsia & moss-green rhinestones around pink/blue center cabochon, w/hanging clusters of pearl teardrops, the pearl clusters repeated along chains, signed "Florenza," about 17" l. **$175-190**

Necklace, goldplate & glass stone, composed of four rows of ornate openwork metal links in a bib style, each row w/a center cabochon emerald green stone, snake chains lead to the clasp, signed "Sandor," 14" l. **$175-200**

Necklace, goldplate & glass stone, composed of seven chains fitted w/framed colored glass round, square & oval red, blue, purple & green stones, Korea, 24" l. **$35-55**

Necklace, goldplate, library chain style, copy of Medieval design, 31" l. **$25-40**

Goldplate & Rhinestone Retro Necklace

Ornate Filigree Goldplate & Rhinestone Necklace.
Courtesy of Davida Baron

Necklace, goldplate & rhinestone, the wide curved ornate filigree goldplate center plaque centered by a stylized floral goldplate mount accented by clusters of red rhinestones w/loops of red rhinestones at each end, suspended on a heavy goldplate link chain leading to a matching clasp, signed "Karu," overall 17" l. (ILLUS.) **$250-275**

Necklace, goldplate & rhinestone, three graduated chains w/large links decorated w/large gold-plated beads cabochon set w/large blue, red & green marquise rhinestones, the center chain w/large medallion-style star pendant, unsigned, 27" l. **$75-95**

Necklace, goldplated chain, w/thirteen assorted hanging goldplated charms, some moveable, 30" l. **$30-45**

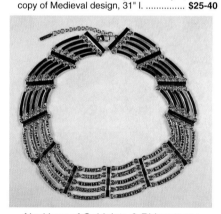

Necklace of Goldplate & Rhinestones

Necklace, goldplate & rhinestone, collar-style, six front panels, each made up of five horizontal rows of pink & red rhinestones, the panels separated by vertical bars of pink & red baguettes; six back panels, each w/six horizontal goldplate bars separated by vertical goldplate bars, all without rhinestones, signed "Napier," 14" adjusts to 16 1/2" (ILLUS.) **$75-100**

Necklace, goldplate & rhinestone, Retro-style small stylized flowers & leaves w/rhinestone centers & joined by rhinestone-set links, signed "Trifari," 12" l. w/3" extender chain (ILLUS., top next column) **$55-75**

Necklace, goldplated chains, five strands alternating w/green glass beads, signed "Kramer," adjusts to 16" **$55-75**

Necklace, green malachite beads in graduated sizes w/green bead spacers, 23" l. **$85-100**

Necklace, mother-of-pearl beads, graduated white oval beads, w/a 14k white goldfilled clasp, 18" **$40-60**

Necklace, pale blue agate beads w/silver metal spacers, 23" l. **$30-45**

Necklace, plastic bead, composed of large plastic beads in pebble shapes in brown, black, amber & tan w/gold metal spacers, 68" l. **$40-60**

Necklace, plastic, beads, African style ridged large silver beads w/faux carved ivory accent beads, 16 1/2" l. **$25-35**

Necklace, plastic & rhinestone, amber-colored beads marbled to look genuine, set w/black rhinestones, black faceted glass spacers, 12" adjusts to 15"...................... **$35-50**

Necklace, quartz beads, translucent white beads, sterling silver clasp, 26" l. **$45-60**

Necklace, rhinestone, a clear single strand w/a center w/five graduated rows, signed "H.," 15" l. w/3 1/4" extender chain......... **$35-50**

Necklace, rhinestone, composed of large individually set multi-colored stones, 14" l. w/3" extension chain **$45-60**

Choker-style Looping Rhinestone Necklace.
Author's Collection

Necklace, rhinestone & white metal, choker-style, the white metal mount composed of repeating large loops set overall w/clear rhinestones, signed "Bogoff," 13" l. (ILLUS.)..................................... **$115-135**

Necklace, rhinestones, Aurora Borealis, individually set 3/8" d. stones, adjusts to 16".. **$35-50**

Necklace, silver plated metal & iridescent glass bead, composed of silver plate pretzel-shaped links suspending across the front five drops composed of small glass bead links supporting a large round iridescent glass bead, marked "Paco Rabanne - Paris," France, ca. 1970, 18" l. (ILLUS., top next column) **$359**

Rabanne Silver Plate & Bead Necklace

Necklace, sterling & amethyst, sterling chain decorated w/center flower design of pear-shaped amethysts w/matching drop, three pear-shaped amethysts on either side, 18" l. **$140-165**

Necklace, sterling silver, composed of double-leaf links alternating a smooth finish & striped finish, signed "Van Dell," 14" l. w/2" extender chain **$75-95**

Necklace, sterling silver, designed w/heavy double twisted link chain, 28" l. **$55-75**

Necklace, sterling silver, gemstone & marcasite, the silver chain suspending four ornate designs each set w/three dark blue cabochon gems, ca. 1935, 16" l. **$165-185**

Necklace, sterling silver & rhinestone, choker-type, the flat chain w/center domed design set w/square rhinestones, unfastens at either end of the center design, signed "EB," 14" l. **$80-100**

Necklace, white metal & rhinestone, composed of five raised textured metal circles each hand-set w/multicolored marquise-cut rhinestones, signed "Schiaparelli," 14" l. **$275-320**

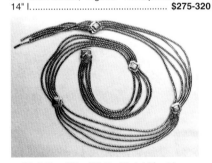

Christian Dior White Metal Necklace

Necklace-belt, white metal, composed of sections of five slender flat chains in a festoon style separated w/diamond-shaped floral mounts, hook closure w/tassel, can be used as a belt for a small waist, signed "Christian Dior," 26" l. (ILLUS.) **$65-85**

Necklace-pendant, gold-filled chain & gemstone, the chain suspending an openwork oval pendant w/an amethyst flower & leaves w/three cultured pearl drops, overall 20" l. **$135-160**

Pendant, carnelian, heart-shaped, 1" (no chain) **$35-50**

Pendant, chrome & glass perfume bottle-form, the small round glass bottle w/a black glass center set w/a diamond-shaped clear rhinestone, on double chains, screw-on cap w/dauber, 1 1/2" l. **$50-75**

Pendant, copper, abstract design on 21" copper chain, signed "Bell," 1 1/2" x 2" ... **$35-50**

Pendant, copper, embossed 1960s Art Nouveau revival motif, woman in profile wearing a headdress over long flowing hair, 1 3/4 x 2 1/4", chain 24" l. **$35-50**

Egyptian Green Pendant

Pendant, glass, molded Egyptian green 3" scarab on 24" chain w/green beads between chain segments (ILLUS.) **$55-75**

Winard Gold-filled & Stone Pendant

Pendant, gold-filled & stone, a chain composed of 12k gold-filled round links alternating w/long slender pierced links, suspending a large octagonal mount in brushed gold set w/a large translucent black emerald-cut stone, signed "Winard," pendant 1 1/2" l., chain 21" l. (ILLUS.)... **$95-120**

Pendant, goldplate & glass, the long goldplate chain suspending a circular drop w/a hanging carnelian-colored glass cabochon drop, overall 16" l. **$40-65**

Pendant, goldplate & rhinestone, a Victorian Revival style ornate openwork design w/a large black glass stone in the center flanked by rows of small black rhinestones on each side, no chain, 2" h. w/bail.. **$40-65**

Kitten Pendant in Goldplate

Pendant, goldplate & rhinestone, three dimensional model of kitten w/green rhinestones eyes sitting in rope-twist circle hanging from 24" chain, 2" d. (ILLUS.) ... **$55-75**

Pendant, goldplate, sterling & shell cameo, oval shape w/Three Graces motif, 1 1/8" (no chain).. **$125-150**

Pendant, green jade, a circular design carved w/Chinese letters, on a black cord w/adjustable slide w/a center rhinestone, ca. 1925, cord 32" l. **$95-125**

Pendant, jade, pale green 2 1/4" d. pendant w/embossed Chinese characters on black cord w/slide adjuster, ca. 1925, 32" l. **$95-120**

Pendant, sterling, 1 1/2" pendant of 1920s-style girl wearing locket, 16" l............. **$125-145**

Pendant, sterling & garnet, birds in nest pendant w/single garnet accent, 21" l. **$50-70**

Pendant, sterling, openwork 1" pendant w/heart motif & leaf & vine design, 16" l. **$45-65**

Pendant, sterling silver, designed as an ornate heart w/a solid silver heart in the center, heart 1 3/8 x 1 1/2", on a 24" l. chain **$60-85**

Pendant, sterling silver, glass bead, rhinestone & marcasite, Art Deco style, an ornate silver framed centered by a large beveled red glass stone, the frame accented w/marcasites & a red rhinestone at the top, pendant 1 3/4" l., sterling chain 18" l. **$50-70**

Pendant, sterling silver, the oval shape molded w/the profile of a helmeted woman, Victorian, no chain, 2" h **$60-85**

Pendant, white metal, marcasite & stone, Art Deco style, the metal pendant set w/marcasites & black stones, ca. 1935, pendant 2" l., on a 17" chain **$55-75**

Pendant, white metal & rhinestone, designed as a metal butterfly set w/Aurora Borealis rhinestones, black rhinestone eyes, pendant 1 x 1 1/4", on a 17" l. chain... **$25-35**

Pendant, white metal & stone, metal chain w/an openwork drop enclosing a large oval black stone that changes colors to green, yellow, blue or black depending on wearer's mood, chain 16" l. **$20-35**

German Enameled Brass Pendant/Box

Pendant-box, enamel & brass, the oval brass box enameled on the top w/pink enamel against a guilloché ground h.p. w/small pink roses & green leaves, signed "Germany," 1 x 1 1/2" (ILLUS.).... **$70-95**

Pendant-locket, gold-filled, Art Nouveau style, the front w/a female face in high-relief, rhinestone trim, initials on the back, no chain, 1 1/2" l. **$80-110**

Pendant-locket, sterling silver, Art Deco style, octagonal silver case 1 1/8" w., on a 24" l. chain **$85-110**

Unusual Beaded Pendant-Necklace

Pendant-necklace, polychrome glass & plastic bead, composed of open rounded links set w/clear glass beads, suspending a large flower-form pendant w/the petals hand-set w/bright red alternating w/dark blue plastic beads around a green plastic bead center, marked "Coppola Toppo," for Emilio Pucci, Italy, 1967, pendant 6" d., necklace 27" l. (ILLUS.)................. **$1,135**

Pin, 830 grade silver, designed as flowers arranged in a snowflake design, Victorian, 2" d... **$85-115**

Pin, agate in ornate goldplate frame, oval, brown, 1 3/8" white center stone, ca. 1910, overall 1 1/2 x 1 3/4" **$125-150**

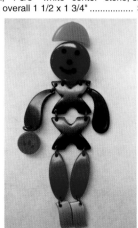

Bakelite Articular Man Pin. Courtesy of Paula Beck

Pin, Bakelite, designed as a comical articulated figure of a man holding a round circle embedded w/flowers, composed of red, purple, orange, black & brown segments, 2" l., 6" h. (ILLUS.) **$165-185**

Pin, Bakelite & goldplate, an openwork floral-carved coral-colored Bakelite plaque w/white marbleizing, set in a plain goldplate frame, 1 1/4 x 1 3/4" **$125-155**

Wood & Bakelite Cherry Cluster Pin

Pin, Bakelite & wood, an oval wooden disk suspending a bunch of red cherries on green stems (ILLUS.)................................. **$176**

Brass Floral Design Pin

Pin, brass openwork floral design w/large 1 1/4" oval turquoise stone, used to hold sashes in place, ca. 1910, 2 1/4 x 3" (ILLUS.) **$55-75**

Pin, celluloid, designed as a red bow dangling a red on white lacy heart inscribed "To My Valentine," ca. 1940, 2" h............ **$25-35**

Purple Crystal & Goldplate Pin. Courtesy of Davida Baron

Pin, crystal & goldplate, the openwork beaded goldplate rounded mount designed as a stylized blossom set w/large faceted oval & round purple crystals w/three drops set w/four additional crystals, signed "Leo Glass," 2" w., 3 1/2" h. (ILLUS.) **$175-200**

Joan Rivers Orchid Pin

Pin, enamel, model of an orchid in deep and light pink, small aurora borealis rhinestone accents, pearl center, signed "Joan Rivers," 2 1/2" h., 2 1/4" w. (ILLUS.) **$65-80**

Pin, enamel on brass, in the shape of three Dutch girls running, in red, blue, green & white enamel, 1 3/8" w., 3/4" h............... **$30-45**

Enamel Stop Sign Pin

Pin, enamel, red "Stop" sign w/dangling charms of traffic light and traffic signs, 4" h. (ILLUS.) **$25-35**

Pin, enamel & rhinestone, contemporary design of parrot in flight, its wings & tail of red, blue & green enamel, its body & wings trimmed w/clear pavé rhinestones, unsigned, 5 x 5 1/4" **$125-150**

Pin, enamel & rhinestone, dragonfly design w/black & turquoise enamel body w/blue rhinestones set in head, signed "Hattie Carnegie," 2 1/4 x 3" **$85-110**

Pin, enamel, rhinestone & goldplate, a large center flower in black enamel, the openwork border w/black rhinestones, signed "Florenza," 2" d. **$65-80**

Pin, enameled goldplate & faux pearl, designed as a Bonsai tree w/pink & blue enameled flowers & large faux pearls, 2 3/4" w., 2 1/4" h................................ **$250-275**

Rhinestone-set Moth Pin. Courtesy of Davida Baron

Pin, enameled goldplate & rhinestone, designed as a large moth w/the open wings outlined in black enamel & set w/large pink, lavender & pale blue marquise-cut stones, the body set w/a large emerald-cut yellow stone & a purple & pink marquise-cut stone, 1930s, 4" w., 2" h. (ILLUS.)...................................... **$125-150**

Pin, enameled goldplate & rhinestone, designed as an orchid flower enameled in fuschia & pink, Aurora Borealis rhinestones on the stems, a large faux pearl center & goldplate trim, signed "Joan Rivers," 2 1/4 x 2 1/4"................................. **$75-100**

Fancy Lily Flower Coro Pin.
Author's Collection

Pin, enameled goldplate & rhinestone, Retro style, designed as a large stylized lily-form blossom enameled in deep pink, the center issuing tall scrolling stamens set w/clear rhinestones, the curled leaves below the blossom also set w/clear rhinestones above the goldplate stems, signed "Coro," 1 3/4" w., 3 3/8" h. (ILLUS.)...... **$150-175**

Pin, enameled metal, designed as layered leaves enameled in blue & green, signed "Sandor," 1 3/4" h. **$40-65**

Pin, enameled metal, glass stone & rhinestone, designed as a parrot perched on a branch, a large red glass cabochon body, an enameled green head w/tiny rhinestones set in the comb, a yellow cabochon glass eye, blue enameled wings & metallic green tail feathers, signed "Art," 1 x 3 1/4" **$145-165**

Pin, enameled metal & rhinestone, designed as a bouquet of flowers completely set w/small clear rhinestones, large oval turquoise rhinestone centers & oval pink rhinestone buds, enameled stems, 2" w., 2 3/4" h. **$125-150**

Pin, enameled metal & rhinestone, designed as a parrot w/topaz rhinestones set in the head & neck, bronze & topaz-enameled feathers, signed "Ciner," 1" w., 3 3/4" h. **$150-175**

Pin, enameled metal & rhinestone, model of a dragonfly in turquoise enamel w/a blue rhinestone head, signed "Hattie Carnegie," 2 1/4 x 3" **$70-95**

Pin, enameled, model of a Christmas wreath in green holly w/red berries, signed "Zentall," 1 3/4" d. **$25-35**

Pin, enameled sterling silver, designed as a figure of a 1920s couple dancing, the lady wearing a short purple dress & shoes & white beads, the man wears a black suit, English silver hallmarks, a Butler & Wilsons copy of an Art Deco era original, 1 1/4" w., 3 1/8" h. (ILLUS., top next column)....................................... **$175-200**

Copy of an Art Deco Pin.
Courtey of Paula Beck

Pin, enameled sterling silver & rhinestone, model of a butterfly w/enameling & four yellow rhinestone accents, signed "WB," 1 1/2".. **$75-95**

Metal Basket Pin

Pin, glass & goldplated metal, coral, green, light blue, dark blue blown glass flowers in openwork gilt metal basket, signed "Jeanne," 2 x 2" (ILLUS.) **$95-120**

Pretty Stone-set Floral Vase Pin.
Courtesy of Davida Baron

Pin, glass stone, rhinestone & metal, the delicate metal openwork mount designed as a footed urn-form vase filled w/flowers within an open ring, the vase formed by a ribbed pale blue stone, the flowers composed of rounded faceted stones in shades of red, blue, amber & green, the ring & vase foot set w/small clear rhinestones, signed "Sorrell Originals," 2 1/2" w., 3 3/4" h. (ILLUS.)................ **$300-350**

Pin, goldplate, brushed & smooth gold-finished moving design w/small hanging diamond shapes, signed "Monet," 2 x 3 5/8"... **$85-110**

Pin, goldplate & crystal, designed as a flower spray w/four emerald-cut red crystals on swirled petals & a ribbon-style base w/a blue crescent-shaped stone accent, signed "R. DeRosa," 1 3/4" w., 3 1/2" h. **$300-325**

Fine Corocraft Floral Spray Pin.
Courtesy of Davida Baron

Pin, goldplate, crystal & rhinestone, designed as a large stylized flower spray w/long goldplate leaves & stems set w/clear rhinestones, each flower w/a hand-set emerald-cut crystal in lavender, green, topaz or red, signed "Corocraft," 4" w., 3 1/3" l. (ILLUS.)........................ **$400-425**

Pin, goldplate, designed as a circle of open-mouthed tiger heads, 3" d. **$35-50**

Pin, goldplate & enamel, circle design w/iridescent green Christmas tree w/white enamel star attached, 1 3/8" d. **$30-45**

Pin, goldplate, enamel & pearl, elephant w/red & green enamel saddle, a large cultured pearl on trunk, signed "Monet," 1 3/4 x 3"... **$60-80**

Pin, goldplate, enamel & plastic, large & small white daisies w/raised yellow plastic centers, green leaf, signed "Weiss," 2 3/4" h. **$50-75**

Pin, goldplate, faux pearl & glass bead, a design of four large goldplate leaves each set in the center w/grey marquise-cut rhinestones, suspending nine dangling chains ending in a large grey baroque faux pearls & grey Aurora Borealis beads resembling grapes, 2" w., 4" l. **$175-200**

Pin, goldplate, faux pearl & glass stone, the mount w/a scalloped edge, decorated w/cabochon glass stones w/foil inclusions & goldtone flowers w/a pearl center, 1 7/8" d.. **$50-75**

Goldplate & Glass Bead Pin

Pin, goldplate & glass beads, circle entirely covered w/Aurora Borealis hanging glass drops, 1 3/4 x 2 1/2" (ILLUS.) **$60-85**

Pin, goldplate & glass, large elongated trapezoid-shaped olive green glass stones arranged in flower style, separated by citrine-colored stones, a hexagon-shaped yellow/green center stone, unsigned, 2 1/4" d.. **$75-100**

Pin, goldplate & glass, snail design w/ribbed jade green glass body, pavé rhinestone trim, signed "Panetta," 1 1/2" **$55-75**

Pin, goldplate & glass stone, Art Deco style, a large octagonal purple center glass stone framed by goldtone flowers w/faux pearl centers, made in Czechoslovakia, 1 x 2 1/4" **$70-95**

Pin, goldplate, glass stone & rhinestone, a model of a tulip flower centered by purple marquise-cut stones, purple rhinestone buds & a gold bow at the base, clear rhinestone trim, unsigned Mazer, 2 1/2 x 3 3/4"..................................... **$250-300**

Pin, goldplate, glass stone & rhinestone, a snowflake design set w/orange, pink & purple rhinestones & marquise cabochon pink stones on an openwork goldplate ground, 2 x 2 1/4"................................... **$35-55**

Pin, goldplate, glass stone & rhinestone, designed as a scarecrow w/snake chain arms & gold, his gold jacket set w/rhinestones, a jade green glass stone face & a top hat set w/rhinestones, signed "Pauline Rader," 2 1/2" h. **$55-85**

Four-swag Chain Pin

Pin, goldplate & large cabochon purple & blue glass stones, four swag chains on bottom, signed "Christian Dior-Germany," dated "1965," 1 1/2 x 2 1/2" (ILLUS.) **$75-90**

Pin, goldplate & rhinestone, a heart-shaped frame enclosing the word "Mother," multicolored rhinestone trim, 1 1/2" **$25-40**

Pin, goldplate & rhinestone, an oval openwork goldplate design of branches w/leaves & flowers w/a purple rhinestone center, all centered by a large oval purple stone, Victorian, 1 1/2 x 2" **$60-85**

Pin, goldplate & rhinestone, Christmas tree set w/red, green, blue & clear rhinestones, 2" **$40-60**

Rhinestone-set Bow Pin.
Courtesy of Shirley Dreyer

Pin, goldplate & rhinestone, designed as a large goldplate filigree bow set overall w/scattered lavender rhinestones, signed "Sweet Romance U.S.A.," 2 1/4 x 2 3/4" (ILLUS.)... **$65-85**

Pin, goldplate & rhinestone, designed as an open fan set w/rows of pink & Aurora Borealis rhinestones, signed "Givenchy," 3" w., 2 1/2" h. **$125-150**

Pin, goldplate, rhinestone & enamel, bird w/long tail on branch, red, blue & green enamel feathers, two rows of tiny clear rhinestones between wing & tail feathers, green rhinestone eye, 2" **$40-60**

Sunburst Pin with Rhinestones

Pin, goldplate & rhinestone, medal-style, three-dimensional sunburst design w/four pear-shaped amber stones & four smaller pear-shaped black stones radiating from large amber center stone framed by eight smaller clear rhinestones, signed "Joan Rivers," 2 1/2" d. (ILLUS.) **$125-150**

Pin, goldplate & rhinestone, model of a Christmas tree set w/red, clear & green rhinestones, signed "Art," 1 5/8 x 2 1/2" **$45-70**

Pin, goldplate & rhinestone, model of a turtle w/a trembling head, decorated w/red, green & clear rhinestones, signed "Lewis Ltd.," 2" **$70-90**

Pin, goldplate, rhinestone, pearl & enamel, bird on branch w/iridescent blue & green enamel head & tail feathers, blue, green & red wings, the body set w/clear pavé rhinestones, green rhinestone eye, pearls & green enamel leaves on branch, signed "DJV Taiwan," 2" **$35-50**

Pin, goldplate & rhinestone, three-dimensional flower w/brushed gold petals & center rhinestones, in original box, signed "Coro" in block letters, ca. 1970, 2 1/4" d... **$65-80**

Christmas Ball Pin

Pin, goldplate, rhinestones, Christmas ball design set w/multicolored large & small rhinestones, goldplated holly leaves top, 1 1/2" w., 2 1/4" h. (ILLUS.) **$25-35**

Christmas Joy Pin

Pin, goldplate, rhinestones, enamel, Christmas motif, word "JOY" w/red enamel on the "J" & "Y," center "O" in form of a wreath w/red rhinestones, green enamel, w/original box, 1 1/2 x 2" (ILLUS.) **$15-25**

Pin, goldplate, scarecrow motif w/green stone face, rhinestone trim, hanging chains forming arms & body, signed "Pauline Rader," 2 1/4" h......... **$55-75**
Pin, goldplate & stone, designed as an arrangement of bamboo canes mounted w/a large oval pink glass cabochon stone, signed "Pauline Rader," 1 1/2" h. **$75-95**

Lea Stein Flapper Head Pin.
Courtesy of Paula Beck

Pin, laminated celluloid, Art Deco Revival style, a geometric fanned back in mottled dark blue w/a fine latticework design, mounted w/the profile head of a Flapper wearing a white cloche hat & a raised C-form stepped blue earring, the creamy face inset w/a black star-shaped eye, signed "Lea Stein," 2 1/4" w., 2" h. (ILLUS.) **$85-110**

Letter "E" Pin

Pin, mahogany, letter "E" carved inside center oval, 2 1/2 x 2" (ILLUS.) **$25-40**
Pin, matte finish goldplate, onyx & faux cultured pearl, Retro style, designed as leaves inside a circle decorated w/black onyx & faux pearl flowers, ca. 1950, 1 1/4" d. **$40-65**
Pin, mother-of-pearl & goldplate, butterfly motif w/etched mother-of-pearl wings, unsigned, designer quality, 3 1/4" w., 2" h. (ILLUS., top next column) **$55-75**

Butterfly Pin

Pin, pewter & rhinestone, designed as a floral spray featuring multicolored oval clear rhinestone blossoms, 2" w., 4" h........ **$135-155**
Pin, rhinestone, a circle of clear rhinestone leaves w/small purple rhinestone accents, signed "Eisenberg," 1 1/2" d..... **$125-150**
Pin, rhinestone, Art Deco style, composed of large emerald green marquise-cut rhinestones w/clear rhinestone trim, French, 2 x 3" **$175-195**
Pin, rhinestone, circle-in-circle design, individually set large square pink stones, pearls & moss green marquise-cut stones, signed "Schreiner NY," 2 3/8" d. **$225-250**
Pin, rhinestone, designed as a large flower in two layers, one layer in clear round rhinestones & a marquise-cut rhinestone center, atop a tier of large marquise-cut rhinestone petals, signed "Weiss," 2 3/4" d... **$165-185**

Coach & Horse Pin

Pin, rhinestone, enamel & antiqued white metal, model of a coach w/enameled coachman driving four horses, coach & horses set w/blue, green, pink, & clear rhinestones, wheels on coach spin, unsigned, designer quality, 3" w., 1 1/2" h. (ILLUS.)... **$75-95**

Garnet-colored Rhinestone Pin

Pin, rhinestone, garnet colored marquise stones set in snowflake-style design, unsigned, 1 1/2 x 2" (ILLUS.)..................... **$60-85**

Pin, rhinestone, glass stone & white metal, a three-dimensional flower-form metal mount decorated w/fuschia marquise-cut rhinestones & deep purple marquise-shaped cabochon stones, also hand-set w/small lavender rhinestones, unsigned, attributed to Schreiner **$150-175**

Pin, rhinestone & goldplate, basket of flowers motif w/clear stones, flowers in larger red, blue, purple rhinestones, 1 3/4" h., 2" w. **$35-50**

Pin, rhinestone & goldplate, the openwork mount centered by a large square purple stone, the background set w/clear baguettes & clear round rhinestones w/purple marquise-cut rhinestones at the ends, signed "Sorrell Originals," 3 1/2" w., 1 3/4" h. **$300-325**

Pin, rhinestone & goldplate, the openwork star design mount hand-set w/pink marquise-cut rhinestones w/clear round rhinestone accents, a clear faceted large rhinestone at the center, a border of pink round rhinestones, attributed to Vogue, 3 1/2 x 3 1/2" **$150-200**

Pin, rhinestone, large handset Aurora Borealis stones in emerald, square & kite shapes w/large amber rhinestones in round, marquise & emerald cuts, Austria, 1 1/2 x 2 5/8" **$75-100**

Pin, rhinestone & white metal, modeled as a white metal sword completely pavé-set w/clear rhinestones, 1940s, 4 1/2" l. **$55-80**

Pin, sterling silver & agate, the narrow sterling frame set w/a mottled orange & black oval agate, Victorian, 1 x 1 1/4" **$135-155**

Pin, sterling silver & cairngorm stone, designed as a silver thistle w/a large amber cairngorm stone at the top, English hallmarks, 1 1/2" h. **$95-125**

Pin, sterling silver, designed as a long-tailed bird on a cut & etched octagonal ground w/scalloped edges, ca. 1915, 1 3/8 x 1 3/4" **$125-150**

Sterling Silver Pin with Color Enameling

Pin, sterling silver & enamel, a rectangular frame w/abstract silver scrolls highlighted w/segments of red, blue, green, white or yellow enamel, signed "Balle," 1 1/4 x 1 5/8" (ILLUS.)......................... **$150-175**

Pin, sterling silver, figure of Asian man w/yoke across his shoulders, w/two balls attached to yoke, 2 1/2" h., 2 1/4" w........ **$60-85**

Pin, sterling silver, marcasite & amethyst, a silver ribbon shape set w/marcasites &

two small heart-shaped amethysts on the side, 2" w., 3/4" h. **$75-95**

Pin, sterling silver, marcasite & glass stone, the oval mount centered by a large green oval glass stone, trimmed w/marcasites, ca. 1930, 1 1/2" **$95-125**

Pin, sterling silver, model of a flamingo w/a turquoise eye, Mexico, 2 1/4" h............... **$50-65**

Pin, sterling silver, model of a horseshoe w/raised rectangular design, English hallmarks, Victorian, 1 1/8" **$75-100**

Pin, sterling silver, open circle w/two stylized flowers in center overlapping the outer rim of the circle, 1 1/2" d. **$55-75**

Pin, sterling silver & rhinestone, figure of a female water skier wearing a pink rhinestone bathing suit, waves trimmed w/clear rhinestones, 2" w., 3" h............. **$90-120**

Pin, vermeil (pink gold over sterling), large flower, curved petals, made in Mexico, unknown hallmark, center 3/4" faux blue topaz, 2 3/4" d. flower **$125-150**

Pin, white metal, Art Deco revival style, model of a lady's head wearing a hat w/a hanging tassel, 3 1/2" h. **$50-70**

Fine Signed Red Crystal & Rhinestone Flower Pin. Courtesy of Davida Baron

Pin, white metal, crystal & rhinestone, modeled as a large flower composed of an outer ring of large half-round crystal petals around openwork pointed inner petal set w/clear rhinestones, the three openwork leaves further set w/clear rhinestones, signed "Reinard," 2" w., 3 1/2" h. (ILLUS.).. **$350-375**

Pin in the Form of a Snake

Pin, white metal & glass, in the form of a snake, large oval purple stones & smaller round light blue stones set as flexible body of snake, fasteners w/antique finish forming its head & tail, unsigned, 7 3/4" l. (ILLUS., previous page) **$95-120**

Pin, white metal & glass stone, Art Deco style, a starfish-like white metal frame centered by a large octagonal mauve art glass stone, 1 x 1 1/4" **$45-70**

Pin, white metal, marcasite & hematite, swirled design w/large hematite oval stone, smaller matching black rhinestones & two marcasite set swirls, West Germany, 1 x 1 1/2" **$40-55**

Pin, white metal & rhinestone, center emerald-cut purple stone in frame of clear rhinestones w/side trim of pear-shaped purple stones, clear rhinestone accents, signed "McClelland Barclay," 1 1/4 x 2 1/2" **$200-225**

Pin, white metal, rhinestone & crystal, the openwork metal mount design composed of oval aqua crystals, a green oval rhinestone center & large marquise-cut fuschia rhinestones w/clear marquise-cut rhinestone accents, 3 1/4" w., 1 3/4" h. **$150-175**

Pin, white metal, rhinestone & opaline stones, floral spray set w/white opaline pear-shaped stones, trimmed w/round clear rhinestones, signed "Kramer," 2 1/2" **$65-85**

Pin, white metal & rhinestone, snowflake design set w/large emerald green marquise stones in small clear round rhinestone borders, signed "Weiss," 2 1/2" d. **$80-110**

Pewter & Glass Bead Pin-Box

Pin-box, pewter & glass bead, round metal top w/a latticework design centered by a large black glass cabochon, plain round box base, signed "Seagull Pinwash NS Canada," comes w/black cloth drawstring bag, 1 3/4" d., 3/4" h. (ILLUS. open) **$60-80**

Pin-pendant, goldplate, glass, plastic, rhinestones, raised pink glass center w/purple & pink rhinestones, fancy metal folds w/purple plastic centers, ca. 1943-1948, 3" d. **$55-75**

Pin-pendant, goldplate & glass stone, the full-relief goldplate mount w/an outer border of royal blue pear-shaped stones

w/oval turquoise blue glass stones in the center, purple cabochon stone accents, unsigned but designer quality, 1 1/4" deep, 3 3/4" d. **$200-225**

Goldplate Lion Head & Scroll Pin

Pin-pendant, goldplate & rhinestone, designed as a large lion head mask w/green rhinestone eyes surrounded by large tight scrolls, signed "Goldette," 3 1/4" w., 3 3/4" h. (ILLUS.) **$85-110**

Heart Pin-Pendant

Pin-pendant, red enamel stylized heart, made in France, signed "YSL" (Yves St. Laurent), 1 1/2 x 1 1/2" (ILLUS.) **$45-65**

Pin-pendant, sterling silver, Art Nouveau style, designed as the head of an Art Nouveau maiden w/long hair amid swirling flowers & vines, early 20th c., 1 1/2" **$95-120**

Ring, beadwork, hand-made, silver beads w/blue Aurora Borealis flower front **$20-30**

Goldplate & Red Stone Adjustable Ring

Ring, goldplate, rhinestone & colored stone, ornate goldplate mount w/a deep scrolling sides highlighted w/small rhinestones & centering a large red cabochon stone, opens on a hinge, adjustable size, signed "Art" (ILLUS.)... **$35-50**

Miram Haskell Rhinestone & Glass Bead Tiara

An Amethyst & Silver Ring & A Silver Ring with Blue Crystals.
Left Courtesy of Shirley Dreyer; right from the Author's Collection

Ring, sterling silver & amethyst, the silver mount w/ridged sides, centering a raised oval amethyst (ILLUS. left with domed ring with blue crystals)........................ **$100-125**

Ring, sterling silver, goldplate & crystal, the domed mount w/looped sides set w/three rows of deep blue crystals centered by a clear crystal, size 6 1/2 (ILLUS. right with the silver & amethyst ring).................... **$75-100**

Scarf clip, goldplate, a textured seashell design, signed "Pauline Rader," 2 1/2" w., 1 1/2" h. **$60-75**

Tiara, rhinestone, green glass beads & Russian gold-plated metal, the round metal wire frame mounted w/a wreath of repeating rhinestone-set leaves accented w/faceted green glass leaves, unsigned M. Haskell, 1950s, 12 5/8" l. (ILLUS., top of page).. **$956**

Watch & pin, lady's, lapel-type, a goldfilled bar pin decorated w/flowers w/purple center stones, suspending the open-faced watch signed "Gotham," 2 pcs. **$150-175**

Sets

Carved & Painted Bakelite Bangle Bracelet & Earring Suite

Bracelet & earrings, Bakelite, engraved & painted, the bangle bracelet in a creamed corn color carved w/bands of diamond-like designs painted in bluish green, the domed rounded stud-type earrings w/a matching decoration, earrings 1" d., bracelet interior circumference 8" (ILLUS.)....................................... **$294**

Schreiner Faux Gem Flower Brooch & Earring Suite

Brooch & earrings, brass & glass stone, the openwork five-petal brass frame set around the sides w/long yellow glass stones imitating citrines centered by a large faceted green glass stone imitating an emerald, each earring set w/four long yellow glass stones, Schreiner, ca. 1960, earrings w/replaced clips, earrings 1 x 1", brooch 3 x 3 1/4", the suite (ILLUS., bottom previous page) **$956**

*Set of Three Bakelite & Rhinestone Clips.
Courtesy of Joan Orlen*

Clips, Bakelite & rhinestone, each a tapering rectangular shape in mottled apple juice color centered w/a thin band set w/clear rhinestones, small clip, 1 1/2" h. larger clips 2" h., set of 3 (ILLUS.) **$175-200**

Necklace & bracelet, goldplate, Retro-style openwork leaf-shaped links form each piece, signed "Monet Jewelers," bracelet, 7/8" w., 7" l., necklace 14" l. , 2 pcs **$75-95**

Goldplate & Rhinestone Necklace

Necklace & bracelet, goldplate w/rhinestone trim, flexible brickwork design, necklace made like a collar, adjustable length, matching bracelet, both pieces signed "Denbe," necklace adjusts to 14", matching bracelet is 6" l., 1" w., the set (ILLUS. of necklace) **$120-145**

Necklace & bracelet, rhinestone, each designed as a single row of clear emerald-cut rhinestones, signed "Weiss," necklace adjusts to 14" l., bracelet 6" l., the set **$225-250**

Enameled Goldplate Saint Laurent Set

Necklace, bracelet & earrings, enameled goldplate, the necklace a tapering band decorated w/large gold crosses alternating w/bright red enameled panels, matching hinged bangle bracelet & round clip-on earrings, signed "YSL" (Yves Saint Laurent), the set (ILLUS.) **$125-150**

Necklace, bracelet & pin, rhinestone, the necklace in a twisted rope designed w/rows of fuchsia rhinestones alternating w/rows of tiny grey rhinestones, the bracelet w/shaped links centered by two rows of fuchsia rhinestones flanked by borders of tiny grey rhinestones, the large flower-form pin w/the swirled petals set overall w/small grey rhinestones around the large center set w/fuchsia rhinestones, signed "Trifari," necklace adjusts to 14", bracelet 7" l., pin 2 1/2" d., the set (ILLUS., top next page) **$1,500-1750**

Necklace & dress clips, goldplated sterling silver & faux gems; the festoon-style necklace w/a gilt silver chain mounted w/graduated rounded & oblong clusters of corded filigree wire forming clover designs & bezel-set w/faceted glass stones imitating citrines, amethysts, rubies, emeralds & diamonds, the inverted teardrop-shaped clips of matching design, Hobé, clip marked "Sterling Pat 1052188," ca. 1942, clips 1 1/4 x 1 3/4", necklace 15" l., the suite (ILLUS. of necklace, bottom next page) **$1,195**

Rare Three-piece Trifari Rhinestone Set.
Courtesy of Davida Baron

Hobé Festoon Necklace from Rare Jewelry Suite

Cabochon & Marcasite Necklace & Earring Set

Necklace & earrings, French iridescent glass, marcasite & goldplate, the 16 1/2" necklace made of nine green oval mold-formed cabochons, each w/pontil mark on back, in ornate goldplated settings filling front half of necklace, the back half of necklace a link chain w/18 large marcasites in cup settings; the matching 2 1/8" l. drop earrings each made of two green oval cabochons in ornate settings connected by goldplated links, the set (ILLUS.).. **$250-275**

Necklace & earrings, goldplate & cabochon glass stones, the necklace composed of links in matte finish goldplate set w/a green, blue, amber or black cabochon glass stone, Alice Caviness, matching clip-on earrings, earrings 1 3/4" l., necklace 15" l., the set **$180-210**

Necklace & earrings, rhinestone, 16" l. necklace w/three-dimensional squares set w/clear, citrine & grey rhinestones & clear baguette centers, 5/8" each, grey rhinestone chain; matching 3/4" sq. earrings, all signed "Hobé," the set **$150-175**

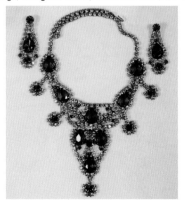

Dramatic Bib-style Necklace & Earrings

Necklace & earrings, rhinestone, the 16" bib-style necklace w/eight large 3/4" roy-

al blue crystal pear-shaped stones in descending design w/clear floral accents w/matching blue centers, all on chain made of clear rhinestones; the matching 2 1/4" l. drop earrings w/blue pear-shaped & smaller blue round stones set in frame of clear rhinestones, unsigned, the set (ILLUS.).................................... **$325-350**

Necklace & earrings, sterling silver & rhinestone, Retro-style design set w/clear round & baguette stones, on a chain set w/round rhinestones, screw-on earrings, signed "Carl-Art," earrings 1 1/4" l., necklace 13" l, the set........... **$135-155**

Venetian Necklace & Earring Set

Necklace & earrings, Venetian art glass, the 17" necklace made of 13 large flat red circular beads w/gold flecks & much smaller cylindrical matching spacers; simple matching 1" d. earrings, the set (ILLUS.)... **$75-100**

White Metal & Green Art Glass Set

Necklace & earrings, white metal & art glass, the chain necklace w/oval metal oval spacers & filigree beads alternating w/swirled green glass beads ending in a double drop, matching teardrop-shaped screw-on earrings, earrings 1 1/8" l., necklace 25" l. w/a 4 1/2" l. double drop, the set (ILLUS.)...................................... **$70-95**

Goldplate & Faux Opal Set

Rare Renaissance Style Goldplate & Rhinestone Set.
Courtesy of Davida Baron

Pendant & earrings, goldplate & faux opal center stones, flower motif on chain, center opal stone in clear rhinestone frame, 1/2" d., 16" fine chain, matching screw-on earrings, 12" d., the set (ILLUS., previous page) **$50-75**

Pendant-necklace, pin & dress clip, goldplate & rhinestone, Renaissance style, the pendant-necklace w/a long fine baton-link chain suspending the ornate oblong filigree goldplate pendant accented w/blue & red rhinestones, the pin in a horizontal goldplate design matching the pendant, the clip also of matching design, unsigned Czechoslovakian, 1930s, pendant-necklace overall 23 3/4" l., the pin 2 x 3 1/4" & clip 2 1/4" x 2 3/4", the set (ILLUS., top of page)... **$1,500-2,000**

Pin & earrings, crystal, rhinestone & goldplate, the pin composed of three goldplate flowers each w/a central blue crystal drop & five smaller blue crystal drops, matching clip-on earrings, unsigned but designer quality, pin 1 3/4 x 2 3/4", the set **$125-150**

Pin & earrings, enamel w/rhinestone trim, curved blue enamel feather motif, matching earrings, signed "Kramer," pin 1 3/4" x 2, mint in original gift box, the set (ILLUS., top next column) **$150-175**

Pin & Earrings, goldplate, w/black, tan & white fur, pin w/two fur-set circles on S-shaped design, 3 1/4" w., clip-on earrings 1" d., the set (ILLUS., bottom next column) **$35-50**

Rhinestone Trim Pin & Earrings

Black, Tan & White Fur Pin & Earrings

Ice Blue Snowflake Pin & Earrings

Pin & earrings, rhinestone, ice blue baguettes, ovals in snowflake motif, pin 2" d., screw-on earrings, 3/4" h., the set (ILLUS.)... **$65-80**

Red & Blue Pin & Earring Set

Pin & earrings, rhinestone, the 3" d. pin w/large round red crystal center stone surrounded by/row of smaller red rhinestones, a third row made up of blue baguettes radiating from center w/red pear-shaped stones at ends, resembling candles; the matching 1 1/4" d. earrings w/blue center stones & alternating blue & red baguettes radiating from center, the set (ILLUS.) **$125-150**

Chatelaine-style Pin & Earring Set

Pin & earrings, white metal, faux turquoise, the 5" l. chatelaine-style pin w/two chains

ending in white metal blackamoor heads w/filigree trim & round turquoise stones; the matching 1" d. earrings in floral design w/turquoise stone centers, the set (ILLUS.).. **$65-85**

Pin & necklace, enamel on gold plate, the 2 5/8 x 3" pin w/three open iridescent purple & gold flowers w/clear rhinestone trim on petals in three-dimensional design; the 16" l. necklace w/single row of conforming flowers, chain ends, 1 1/4" w., unsigned, the set................. **$145-170**

Set of Three Comical Fruit Pins.
Courtesy of Paula Beck

Pins, enameled metal, each cast as a different comical fruit, a pineapple, an apple & a strawberry, each w/moving eyes, enameled in shades of yellow, red, green & brown, 1 1/2" to 1 3/4", the set (ILLUS.) **$60-80**

Pins, sterling, pair of seated tall cats, signed "Beau Sterling," 2 1/2" h., the set............ **$75-95**

Scarf tacs, rhinestone & goldplate, each in the shape of a goldplate flying bird set w/clear rhinestones w/a green rhinestone head, signed "Ballou," each 3/4 x 1", the set of 3 .... **$25-40**

CHAPTER 3
Mod Jewelry (1960s-1980s)

Fun and funky, the inexpensive and colorful jewelry from the age of Flower Power and new political awareness, often represented a break from the traditional designs of the past. Flower-shaped pins and bright beads of the Hippie era were a visible statement of the ideas and ideals that were evolving during the Dawning of the Age of Aquarius. - Dana Cain

Bracelet, P.O.W. (prisoner of war), chrome-plated brass alloy w/black etched lettering showing the name of a P.O.W. or M.I.A. in Viet Nam & date reported missing, VIVA, 1970s **$35-75**

Late 1960s Sterling "Love" Bracelet

Bracelet, sterling silver, a center rectangular pierced plaque w/the word "Love" flanked by heart-shaped ends joined two snake chains to the clasp that suspending a pierced Peace symbol charm, marked "Sterling USA," late 1960s (ILLUS.) **$25-35**

1960s Choker with Pendant Daisy

Choker, a thin metal ring suspending an enameled metal daisy, 1960s, band 5 1/2" d. (ILLUS.) **$15-25**

Mod Triple-Strand Purple Bead Necklace

Necklace, plastic, a triple strand of plastic opaque & transparent purple beads, 1960s, 52" l. (ILLUS.)............................. **$15-25**

Plastic 1960s Black-Light Necklace

Necklace, plastic black-light type, a triple strand of plastic beads in yellow, green & orange joined by a gilt metal clasp, glows under black light, 1960s, 50" l. (ILLUS., bottom previous page) **$25-38**

Necklace, plastic, composed of almond-shaped lime green beads alternating w/tiny green beads, metal clasp, 1960s, 48" l. (ILLUS.) **$12-18**

Mod Plastic Scarab Beetle Necklace

Necklace, plastic, composed of links molded in the shape of an Egyptian scarab beetle, in various colors, joined by gilt-metal links & w/a chain clasp, 14 1/2" l. (ILLUS.) **$12-20**

Necklace, plastic, "Love Beads," composed of multiple slender strands of small lime green, aqua & yellow beads, gilt metal clasp, 1960s, 54" l. (ILLUS., bottom of page) **$18-30**

Mod Lime Green Plastic Bead Necklace

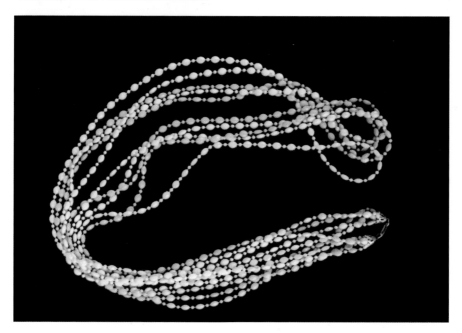

1960s "Love Beads" Necklace

1960s "Equality Necklace" in Pewter

Pendant-necklace, pewter, a stylized flower-shape medallion w/two rows of tapering shaped petals, suspending on a chain w/large wire links, "Equality Necklace," Metzke, 1960s (ILLUS.) **$10-15**

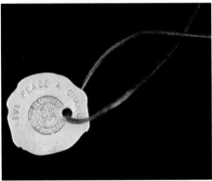

Unusual Disneyland "Give Peace A Chance" Pendant

Pendant-necklace, pewter, souvenir-type, designed as a stylized Spanish doubloon w/a center circle stamped w/a skull & crossbones & "Pirates of the Caribbean - Disneyland," the outer edge stamped "Give Peace A Chance," on a black leather cord, 1970, pendant 1 1/2" w. (ILLUS.)..... **$50-65**

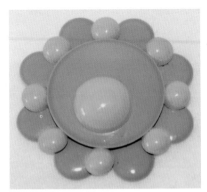

Abstract Flower-form Colorful Pin

Pin, enameled metal, designed as an abstract flower w/an outer band of bright blue petals alternating w/chartreuse buttons around a wide blue disk center mounted w/a large chartreuse button, 1960s, 2 1/2" d. (ILLUS.) **$14-20**

Red Five-Petaled Flower Pin

Pin, flower-shaped, enameled metal blossom w/five red heart-shaped petals around a yellow center w/pink buttons, gold back, 1960s, 1 3/4" w. (ILLUS.) **$10-15**

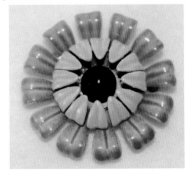

Flower Pin with Pink & Yellow Petals

Pin, flower-shaped, enameled metal large blossom w/an outer ring of outward scrolled pink petals around a ring of inward curved yellow petals & a black center button, 1960s, 1 3/4" d. (ILLUS.) **$10-15**

Flower Pin with Fanned Orange Petals

Pin, flower-shaped, enameled metal large blossom w/fanned, scallop-edged orange petals around a large chartreuse button center, 1960s, 2 1/4" d. (ILLUS.).... **$8-12**

Flower Pin with Serrated Petals

Pin, flower-shaped, enameled metal large blossom w/serrated orange & deep yellow petals around a yellow center knob, on a green leafy stem, 1960s, 3" h. (ILLUS.) ... **$10-15**

Yellow-petaled 1960s Flower Pin

Pin, flower-shaped, enameled metal large blossom w/spaced pale yellow petals around an orange button center, 1960s, 2 3/4" d. (ILLUS.) **$10-15**

Red, White & Blue 1960s Flower Pin

Pin, flower-shaped, enameled metal large daisy-like blossom w/blue & white petals & a large red center, 1960s, 3" d. (ILLUS.) **$10-15**

Daisy-like Pin in Red, White & Blue

Pin, flower-shaped, enameled metal large daisy-like blossom w/red & white petals & a large blue button center, 1960s, 2 1/2" d. (ILLUS.) **$8-12**

1960s Yellow Flower on Stem Pin

Pin, flower-shaped, enameled metal large daisy-like bright yellow blossom on a chartreuse leafy stem, 1960s, 4" h. (ILLUS., previous page).. **$10-15**

1960s Shasta Daisy Flower Pin

Lavender & Pink 1960s Flower Pin

Pin, flower-shaped, enameled metal large lavender & pink blossom w/inwardly curled petals, on a slender green leafy stem, 1960s, 4" h. (ILLUS.)...................... **$12-16**

Stylized Flower Pin in Yellow, White & Black

Bright Pink 1960s Flower Pin

Pin, flower-shaped, enameled metal large pink daisy-like blossom, 1960s, 3" w. (ILLUS.) **$10-15**

Pin, flower-shaped, enameled metal large Shasta daisy blossom w/a large yellow center, on a green stem w/two long leaves, 1960s, 3" h. (ILLUS., top next column) **$8-12**

Pin, flower-shaped, enameled metal large stylized blossom w/graduated tiers of petals in yellow, white & black w/a black center, 1960s, 3" d. (ILLUS., middle next column) **$8-10**

White Flower Pin with Two Tiers of Petals

Pin, flower-shaped, enameled metal large white daisy-like blossom w/two tiers of long petals around a round center knob, 1960s, 3 1/2" d. (ILLUS.) **$12-18**

White Flower Pin with Notch-tipped Petals

Pin, flower-shaped, enameled metal large white daisy-like blossom w/long petals w/notched tips, white center button, 1960s, 2 3/4" d. (ILLUS.)........................ **$10-15**

Colorful Tin Bird Pin

Pin, lithographed tin, a flattened colorful bird, Japan, 1980s, 2" l. (ILLUS.).............. **$5-10**

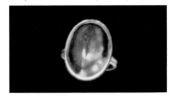

A 1970s "Mood Ring"

Ring, "Mood Ring," the domed "stone" changes colors depending on mood of the wearer, found in various styles, 1970s (ILLUS.).. **$35-60**

1960s Cluster Bead Ring

Ring, plastic & gilt-metal, mounted w/a cluster of dark green & chartreuse beads w/gilt metal center beads, adjustable band, 1960s (ILLUS.).............................. **$15-25**

CHAPTER 4
Modern (1920-1950s)

Art Deco

Very Fine Art Deco Sapphire, Diamond & Black Opal Bar Pin

Bar pin, black opal, sapphire, diamond & platinum, the long central band centered by a row of chanel-set sapphires flanked by bands of full-cut diamonds w/larger rectangular step-cut sapphires at the ends, all flanked by large hexagonal black opals, engraved open gallery, signed by Marcus & Co. (ILLUS., top of page).. **$11,750**

Art Deco Bar Pin with Large Diamonds

Bar pin, diamond & platinum, wide bar sent down the center w/five large circular-cut old European-cut diamonds surrounded by small diamond mélée & millegrain accents, diamonds weighing about 3.80 cts., 14k gold pin stem, 2 3/4" l. (ILLUS.)......... **$2,350**

Art Deco Pearl & Diamond Bar Pin

Bar pin, pearl, diamond & platinum, the narrow band centered by a small black pearl, the side bands each set w/three white pearls separated by groups of old European-cut diamonds, millegrain accents, 2 1/8" l. (ILLUS.).. **$470**

Platinum, Diamond & Sapphire Bar Pin

Bar pin, platinum, diamond & sapphire, the oblong middle section centered by a large circular-cut diamond surrounded by six baguette-cut diamonds, the narrow tapering pointed side sections set w/full- and princess-cut diamonds & small double bands of buff-top sapphire accents, diamonds weighing about 2.45 cts., 2 1/8" l. (ILLUS.)..................................... **$1,175**

Deco Bar Pin with Diamonds in Rings

Bar pin, platinum & diamond, the long openwork bar w/pointed ends, set across the center w/rings each enclosing 13 old European-cut diamonds weighing about 1.65 cts. (ILLUS.)................................... **$1,175**

Art Deco Sapphire Bar Pin

Bar pin, platinum, pink star sapphire & diamond, the narrow mount bezel-set w/six sapphire cabochons alternating w/seven full-cut diamonds (ILLUS.) **$1,528**

Platinum, Sapphire and Diamond Bar Pin

Bar pin, platinum, sapphire & diamond, Art Deco bezel, bead-set throughout w/sixty-six old European, French, baguette & single-cut diamonds, approx. total wt. 1.98 cts., rectangular and triangular-cut sapphire accents, millegrain accents & pierced gallery (ILLUS.).......................... **$3,055**

Bar pin, sapphire, diamond & platinum, the long open gallery centered by a bezel-set circular-cut blue sapphire surrounded by leaf-like designs & narrow oblong side bands set overall w/old European- and single-cut diamonds weighing about 1.38 cts., millegrain accents, original box from The Goldsmith & Silversmiths Co., London, England **$2,233**

Carnelian & Enameled Gold Art Deco Bracelet

Diamond and Diamond & Ruby Art Deco Bracelets

Rare Diamond & Emerald Art Deco Line Bracelet

Unique Art Deco Diamond, Emerald & Onyx Bracelet from Van Cleef & Arpels

Bracelet, carnelian & enameled 14k gold, composed of large oblong carnelian links alternating w/smaller oblong flat plaques decorated w/red & green geometric designs & centered by a red stone, 7 1/4" l. (ILLUS., top of page)............................. **$2,233**

Bracelet, diamond & 14k white gold, composed of box- and bezel-set old European- and mine-cut diamonds weighing about 3.38 cts., blue stone highlights & engraved accents, missing one blue stone, 6 3/8" l. **$1,763**

Bracelet, diamond & 18k white gold, composed of 18 openwork articulated links w/geometric designs set overall w/372 round-cut diamonds weighing about 9.50 cts., each hinge set w/a single blue sapphire tip, 7" l. (ILLUS. top with narrow Art Deco diamond & ruby bracelet, second from top)... **$5,520**

Bracelet, diamond & emerald, line-type, the narrow band centered by a row of 43 box-set old European-cut diamonds, flanked by thin rows of channel-set square-cut emeralds, diamonds weighing about 4.55 cts., platinum mount, missing one emerald, 7 1/2" l. (ILLUS., third from top)
.... **$7,344**

Bracelet, diamond, emerald, onyx & platinum, the flat band decorated w/twelve full hexagonal rings set w/old single-cut diamonds enclosing a larger European-cut diamond, alternating w/geometric narrow panels decorated w/buff-top onyx flanked channel-set step-cut small emeralds, millegrain accents, open gallery, diamonds weighing about 6.11 cts., No. 20681, marked by Van Cleef & Arpels, Paris (ILLUS., fourth from top)
.... **$30,550**

Art Deco Diamond & Platinum Bracelet with Emerald Highlights

Rare Art Deco Diamond Bracelet with Rectangular & Diamond-form links & Onyx Accents

Very Rare Caldwell Art Deco Diamond & Platinum Bracelet

Two Very Fine Art Deco Diamond & Gem-set Bracelets

Bracelet, diamond, emerald & platinum, long rectangular plaques alternating w/round links, set overall w/old European-, transitional-, single- and marquise-cut diamonds weighing about 6.72 cts., w/triangular-cut small emerald highlights & millegrain accents, 7" l. (ILLUS., bottom previous page) **$8,225**

Bracelet, diamond & gold, centering three old European-cut diamonds flanked by two diamond mélée, completed by platinum-topped 14k gold bar links, No. 1843, 7" l. **$764**

Bracelet, diamond, onyx & platinum, composed of slightly arched rectangular links centered by a diamond-shaped frame w/a full-cut diamond surrounded by smaller old mine-cut diamonds w/bands at each end, joined by single-line diamond-set links flanked by thin French-cut onyx-set lines, engraved edges, diamonds weighing about 7.54 cts., missing seven onyx pieces, break in the mount, 6 3/4" l. (ILLUS., top of page) **$11,750**

Bracelet, diamond & platinum, a long narrow form w/double bands divided by three oval segments, set overall w/162 old European-, single-cut & baguette diamonds w/millegrain accents, signed by J. E. Caldwell, ca. 1930s, 7 1/4" l. (ILLUS., second from top) **$16,450**

Bracelet, diamond & platinum, a long straight form w/an openwork mount composed of various geometric links bead- and bezel-set overall w/old European-cut diamonds weighing about 5.75 cts., millegrain accents, 7 1/2" l. (ILLUS. bottom with other Art Deco diamond bracelet with swelled links, bottom of page) **$8,225**

Bracelet, diamond & platinum, a long thin design composed of long double parallel links joined by octagonal links, decorated overall w/bezel- and bead-set marquise, baguette, full- and single-cut diamonds, diamonds weighing about 3.81 cts., ca. 1930, 7" l. (ILLUS. top with flat sapphire, diamond & platinum bracelet, third from top) **$6,463**

Two Fine Art Deco Diamond Bracelets

Bracelet, diamond & platinum, composed of long swelled links composed of three bands joined by small oblong links centered by an old European-cut diamond, set overall w/other European- and single-cut diamonds, diamonds weighing about 6.80 cts., millegrain accents, 7 1/2" l. (ILLUS., top, above) **$12,925**

Art Deco Swelled-center Diamond & Sapphire Bracelet

Rare Art Deco Diamond, Sapphire & Platinum Bracelet

Art Deco Line Bracelet with Diamonds & Synthetic Sapphires

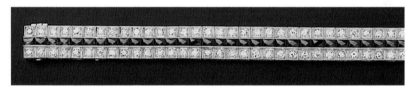

Fine Art Deco Diamond & Synthetic Sapphire Bracelet

Bracelet, diamond, ruby & 18k white gold, composed of long narrow links alternating w/circular open links, the long links centered by a band of square-cut rubies flanked by small diamonds, circular links further set w/diamonds, rubies weighing about 3.60 cts., the diamonds weighing about 4.00 cts., 7" l. (ILLUS., with diamond & white gold bracelet, second from top, page 151).. **$2,530**

Bracelet, diamond, sapphire & 18k white gold, the narrow side bands composed of geometric links set w/diamonds, the swelled serpentine central section further set w/diamonds accented w/small French-cut sapphires w/further bands of French-cut sapphires down the sides, diamonds weighing about 3.5 cts., the sapphires weighing about 2.0 cts. (ILLUS., top of page)... **$2,760**

Bracelet, diamond, sapphire & platinum, long flat form set overall w/old European- and single-cut diamonds w/a total weight of about 8.43 cts., further channel-set w/blue sapphire highlights, millegrain accents & engraved sides, 7" l. (ILLUS., second from top)................................... **$12,925**

Bracelet, diamond, synthetic sapphire & 18k white gold, line-type, box-set w/20 full-cut diamonds weighing about 1.10 cts. alternating w/channel-set synthetic blue sapphires, millegrain accents, engraved mount, 7 1/2"l. (ILLUS., third from top)... **$3,173**

Bracelet, diamond & synthetic sapphire, a long narrow band centered by a line of French-cut synthetic sapphires flanked by lines of bead-set old European-cut diamonds & millegrain accents, platinum mount, ca. 1930s, 7" l. (ILLUS. of part, fourth from top) **$4,700**

Art Deco Bracelet with Alternating Rectangular & Round Emerald & Diamond Links

Bracelet, emerald & diamond, composed of alternating openwork rectangular & circular links each centered by a bezel-set emerald cabochon framed by bead-set single-cut diamonds, diamonds weighing about 5.00 cts., French guarantee stamps & partially worn hallmark, 7 3/8" l. (ILLUS.)..................................... **$7,050**

Two Art Deco Enameled Gold Bracelets

Bracelet, enamel & 14k yellow gold, composed of oblong links decorated in green & black champlevé enamel w/a dragon, hallmark of Enos Richardson & Co., ca. 1930, 7 1/2" l. (ILLUS. of part, bottom with other Art Deco enameled bracelet, top of page) **$823**

Bracelet, enamel & 14k yellow gold, composed of slightly arched white & navy blue striped champlevé enamel links joined by ribbed spacers, hallmark of Wordley, Allsopp & Bliss, ca. 1930, 7 1/4" l. (ILLUS. of part, top with other Art Deco enameled bracelet, top of page) **$999**

Gem-set & Diamond 1930s Indian Bracelet

Bracelet, gem-set & diamond, composed of links prong-set w/various cabochons including a ruby, emerald, moonstone, garnet, synthetic yellow & blue sapphire, citrine & a cat's-eye chrysoberyl, alternating w/floret-style open links set w/small diamonds, silver & gold mount, India, ca. 1930, 6 1/2" l. (ILLUS.) **$1,175**

Fine Pearl Bracelet with Diamond Clasp

Bracelet, natural pearl, diamond & platinum, composed of five strands of 89 off-white pearls w/rose overtones measuring about 5.85 to 7.20 mm, completed by a large oblong openwork Art Deco clasp bead- and bezel-set w/old mine-, European- & rose-cut diamonds weighing about 6.84 cts., w/23 loose pearls, 6 1/4" l. (ILLUS.) **$8,519**

Bracelet, platinum & black onyx, the thin band channel-set w/French-cut onyx, millegrain accents & foliate-engraved mount edges, No. 12339, 7 1/8" l. (ILLUS. bottom with other narrow Art Deco onyx & diamond bracelet, page 156) **$2,820**

Art Deco Diamond & Carved Sapphire & Ruby Bracelet

Bracelet, platinum, diamond & carved sapphire & ruby, composed of sapphire & ruby leaves interspersed w/eight old marquise, 16 old mine-cut & 75 single-cut diamonds, completed by interlocking circular single-cut diamond links, approx. 2.28 cts., one diamond & two colored stones missing, 7" l. (ILLUS.)..... **$7,050**

Rare Platinum and Diamond Bracelet

Bracelet, platinum & diamond, composed of articulated geometric-form plaques set w/three marquise, four half-moon, ninety baguette, & 394 full- and single-cut diamonds, approx. total wt. 11 cts., 7 1/4" l. (ILLUS.) **$22,913**

Rare Geometric-link Art Deco Diamond Bracelet

Bracelet, platinum & diamond, composed of three large openwork rectangular links centered by a row of three large marquise-cut diamonds surrounded by stepped openwork designs & border bands set w/further baguette & full-cut diamonds, each long link joined by wide bars & narrow oblong diamond-set open links, diamonds weighing about 20.70 cts., millegrain accents, 7 1/4" l. (ILLUS.) **$38,775**

Rare Art Deco Platinum, Diamond, Emerald & Onyx Bracelet

Bracelet, platinum, diamond, emerald & onyx, composed of three long flexible plaques spaced by pairs of oblong links, set throughout w/318 old European- and single-cut diamonds, approx. 8.40 cts., highlighted by carved emerald leaves & cabochon onyx, millegrain accents & open gallery, a few nicks & abrasions to emeralds, 7" l. (ILLUS.) **$14,100**

Art Deco Diamond Bracelet with Ring & Long Bar Links

Bracelet, platinum & diamond, long links alternating w/ring links joined by a bar, bead- and channel-set overall w/15 baguette, 15 square step-cut & 162 full-cut diamonds weighing about 3.65 cts., 7" l. (ILLUS.) **$9,988**

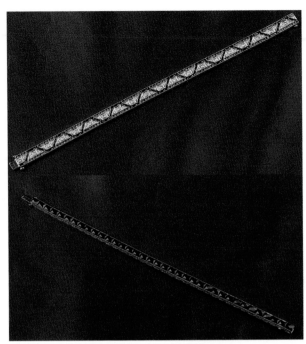

Two Narrow Art Deco Bracelets

Bracelet, platinum, diamond, onyx & emerald, the narrow band bead-set w/a center band of full-cut diamonds flanked by thin channel-set borders of French-cut emeralds, an undulating band of inset black onyx down the center, millegrain accents, 7" l. (ILLUS. top with onyx & platinum bracelet, top of page) **$4,700**

Fine Art Deco Platinum & Diamond Link Bracelet

Very Fine Art Deco Bracelet with Various Diamonds & Emeralds

Bracelet, platinum & diamond, rectangular links w/an open cross center each joined by a shaped bar link, bead-set overall w/264 full-cut diamond mélée, diamonds weighing about 4.83 cts., 6 3/4" l. (ILLUS., middle of page) **$4,700**

Bracelet, platinum, diamond & synthetic sapphire, the flat band box-set w/42 old European- and single-cut diamonds bisected by a thin zigzag band of calibre-cut synthetic sapphires, diamonds weighing about 2.94 cts., millegrain accents, foliate-engraved edges, 7 1/2" l. **$4,700**

Bracelet, platinum, emerald & diamond, the slender side links composed of single bezel-set old European diamonds, the swelled central section further set w/smaller bezel-set diamond & old European- and single-cut diamonds, a central navette-cut diamond & two sheild-shaped diamonds, accented w/calibré-cut emeralds, millegrain accents, engraved edges, diamonds weighing about 6.00 cts., 6 3/4" l. (ILLUS., third on the page) **$15,275**

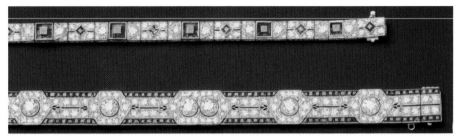

Two Rare Art Deco Ruby & Diamond Bracelets

Bracelet, platinum, ruby & diamond, a narrow band bezel-set w/14 square step-cut rubies alternating w/blocks of bead-set & single-cut diamonds w/some blocks centered by small square-cut sapphires, diamonds weighing about 4.90 cts., millegrain accents, engraved edges, partial signature of Black, Starr & Frost, New York, New York, 7" l. (ILLUS. top with other rare ruby and diamond Art Deco bracelet, top of page) **$21,150**

Bracelet, platinum, ruby & diamond, a wide strap composed of sections w/double narrow bands of bezel- and bead-set old European-cut diamonds flanked by bands of step-cut & calibré-cut rubies, alternating w/large hexagonal panels w/a border of diamonds framing a large central diamond, millegrain accents, diamonds weighing about 13.16 cts., 7 1/8" l. (ILLUS. bottom with other rare Art Deco ruby & diamond bracelet, top of page) **$42,300**

Bracelet, platinum, sapphire & diamond, a long flat design bead-set overall w/old European- and single-cut diamonds highlighted w/thin bands of channel-set French-cut sapphires, millegrain accents, diamonds weighing about 6.40 cts., added safety catch, 7" l. (ILLUS. bottom with thin open link diamond bracelet, on page 152) **$10,575**

Elaborate Art Deco Strap Bracelet with Diamonds & Sapphire Accents

Bracelet, platinum, sapphire & diamond, a wide flat band composed of sections w/rows of bezel- and bead-set old European & single-cut diamonds alternating w/openwork sections w/a geometric arrangement of further diamonds & calibré-cut sapphire highlights all centered by a large round diamond, diamonds weighing about 8.65 cts., millegrain accents, engraved sides, 6 3/4" l. (ILLUS., above) **$17,625**

Art Deco Platinum, Sapphire & Diamond Bracelet

Bracelet, platinum, sapphire, & diamond, articulated links w/channel-set calibré & square step-cut sapphires & bead-set old European-, rose- and single-cut diamonds, approx. total wt. 3.34 cts., 7 1/4" l. (ILLUS., above) **$11,163**

French Art Deco Silver & Rhinestone Bracelet

Bracelet, silver & rhinestone, the flat side straps set down the sides w/three rows of circular-cut rhinestones flanked by outer rows of baguette rhinestones, the swelled central section composed of arched links set overall w/small circular-cut & larger baguette rhinestones w/a large circular-cut rhinestone in the center, France, ca. 1930, mark of maker & French assay mark for silver, 7" l. (ILLUS.) **$1,016**

Fine Deco Black Opal & Diamond Brooch

Brooch, black opal, diamond & platinum, centered by a large round black opal framed by a ring of rose-cut diamonds flanked by long slender diamond-set bars, millegrain accents (ILLUS.) **$5,053**

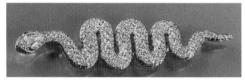

Fine Art Deco Diamond Snake Brooch

Brooch, diamond & gem-set platinum, designed as an undulating snake, set overall w/about 350 pavé-set old mine- and European-cut diamonds, the head set w/a pear-cut diamond weighing about .50 cts., marquise-cut ruby eyes (ILLUS.) **$7,050**

Austrian Art Deco Diamond Brooch

Brooch, diamond & gold, the oval openwork mount centered by an oblong blossom design centered by a row of three large old European-cut diamonds, small diamonds form the background, diamonds weighing about 1.50 cts., millegrain accents, 14k white gold mount, hallmarks of Vienna, Austria, 1 1/2" l. (ILLUS.) **$1,645**

Art Deco Pearl-centered Diamond Brooch

Brooch, diamond & pearl, long openwork rectangular mount w/a center band centered by a white pearl flanked by two large circular-cut diamonds, the rest of the banded mount bezel- and bead-set w/old European- & mine-cut diamonds, platinum-topped 14k gold mount (ILLUS.) **$705**

Brooch, diamond & platinum, a long open oval frame centered by a large old European-cut diamond weighing 1.29 cts., the outer frame set w/78 French-, baguette- and round-cut diamonds, millegrain accents, signed by Raymond Yard, ca. 1930 .... **$5,640**

Rare Tiffany Art Deco Diamond Brooch

Brooch, diamond & platinum, elongated oval openwork mount decorated w/bands containing 66 large & small old European-cut diamonds weighing about 7.51 cts., millegrain accents, signed by Tiffany & Co. (ILLUS.) **$11,163**

Very Fine Cartier Diamond Bow Brooch

Brooch, diamond & platinum, model of a long bow set w/about 500 old European, mine- and transitional-cut diamonds, signed by Cartier, ca. 1930s (ILLUS.)... **$47,000**

Brooch, diamond & platinum, oblong filigree mount w/a rounded central section flanked by pointed end sections, the openwork mount set overall w/navette bead & bezel-set old European-cut diamonds, millegrain accents, gold pin, approximate weight 2.33 cts., ca. 1930 ...... **$1,528**

Brooch, diamond & platinum, oblong mount w/a rectangular center flanked by fanned end sections joined by ringed side sections, set in the center w/two round diamonds each approximately .69 cts., together w/162 bead & collet-set old European & single-cut diamonds, highlighted by eight straight baguette-cut diamonds, approximate total weight 10.44 cts., ca. 1930... **$4,700**

Navette-shaped Fine Deco Diamond Brooch

Brooch, diamond & platinum, the openwork navette-shaped mount bead-set w/a band of larger old European-cut diamonds flanked by smaller diamonds, signed by Dreicer, diamonds weighing about 1.70 cts., 1 3/4" l. (ILLUS.) **$3,290**

Deco Rectangular Diamond & Ruby Brooch

Brooch, diamond, ruby, onyx & platinum, a long narrow rectangular design bead-set overall w/transitional-cut diamonds weighing about 3.25 cts., bezel-set near one end w/a single step-cut ruby, the top & bottom edges offset by two lines of onyx, 1 7/8" l. (ILLUS.) **$4,935**

Diamond and Sapphire Bow Brooch

Brooch, diamond & sapphire, bow design, bead-set w/seventy-two old European & old single-cut diamonds weighing approx. 1.60 cts., edged by channel-set rectangular step-cut and calibre-cut sapphires, millegrain accents, platinum mount (ILLUS.)....................................... **$6,463**

Brooch, diamond, sapphire & platinum, a wide rectangular openwork mount swelled in the center, decorated w/rows & geometric panels set overall w/small single-cut diamonds accented w/by 14 larger old European-cut diamonds, cen-

Fancy Art Deco Diamond & Sapphire Brooch

tered by a large bezel-set oval-cut sapphire, millegrain accents, engraved gallery, diamonds weighing about 4.61 cts. (ILLUS.)... **$4,700**

Rare Art Deco Diamond & Sapphire Brooch

Brooch, diamond, sapphire & platinum, oval slender openwork scrolling frame set w/old European- and rose-cut diamonds centering a large oval double cabochon sapphire, French guarantee stamp, ca. 1930s, 1 x 1 3/4" (ILLUS.)..... **$9,988**

Unique Winged Scarab Brooch

Brooch, gem-set 14k gold, Egyptian Revival style, designed as a winged scarab w/the body formed by an oval amazonite cabochon enclosed by thin diamond-set bands & flanked by small S-scroll snakes & tall curved feathered gold wings bezel-set w/old European-cut diamonds & step-cut rubies, European assay marks, possibly Austrian (ILLUS.)............................... **$4,230**

Art Deco Gold & Enamel Bar Brooch

Brooch, gold (18k yellow) & enamel, a narrow slightly swelled rectangular gold bar centered by a long openwork section of roses among blue enameled & counter-enamel leaves, French & Austrian guarantee stamps & hallmarks, ca. 1930 (ILLUS.) .. **$940**

Unusual Art Deco Chalcedony Brooch

Brooch, green chalcedony, enamel & 14k gold, an oblong open ring of chalcedony carved w/stylized floral designs, each end mounted w/an openwork pierced gold tapering bar highlighted w/orange & black enamel, mark of Carter, Howe & Gough, Newark, New Jersey, 3" l. (ILLUS.) **$1,880**

Brooch, jade, diamond & platinum, the jade carved w/exotic foliage, the mount accented w/full-cut & baguette diamonds, millegrain highlights, red stone accent, white gold pin stem, 1 1/2" l. **$617**

Brooch, jade, platinum & diamond, a long rectangular central plaque of green jade carved w/scrolling openwork vines & gourds, two opposing corners w/two squared & stepped brackets set w/a total of 22 single-cut diamonds, French guarantee stamps & hallmark, ca. 1930........ **$2,585**

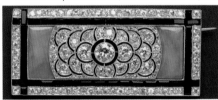

Rare Jadeite, Onyx & Diamond Brooch

Brooch, jadeite, onyx, diamond & gold, rectangular openwork plaque centered by a design of overlapping circles each set w/an old European-cut diamond & trimmed w/rose-cut diamonds all flanked by green jadeite panels, within a rectangular border of calibré-cut onyx & an outer border band of small rose-cut diamonds, French guarantee stamps, 7/8 x 1 7/8" (ILLUS.) **$9,988**

Brooch, Lalique glass, blue foil-backed glass molded w/chrysanthemums, gilt mount, signed, evidence of lead solder at pin stem, ca. 1920s **$588**

Art Deco Coral & Diamond Brooch

Brooch, platinum, coral & diamond, centered by a long oval floral & scroll pierce-carved coral plaque framed by baguette & single-cut diamond mélée, onyx highlights (ILLUS.) **$2,233**

Fine Art Deco Diamond & Pearl Brooch

Brooch, platinum, diamond & cultured pearl, rectangular openwork mount w/cut corners, set down the center w/three large pearls, openwork Greek key narrow bands flanked by bands set w/old European-, rose- and single-cut diamonds weighing about 3.00 cts., millegrain accents, 2 9/16" l. (ILLUS.) **$2,585**

Fancy Art Deco Bow Brooch

Brooch, platinum, diamond & onyx, bow-shaped, bead-set w/110 old European & single-cut diamonds, channel-set French-cut onyx & millegrain accents, pierced gallery (ILLUS.) **$4,230**

Art Deco Round Diamond Brooch

Unique & Extraordinary Art Deco Emerald & Sapphire Brooch

Brooch, platinum & diamond, round shape bead-set w/156 old European- and mine-cut diamonds, approx. 7.80 cts., millegrain accents (ILLUS., previous page). **$8,813**

Art Deco Buckle-shaped Diamond Brooch

Brooch, platinum & diamond, stylized open-work buckle shape, bead- bezel- and prong-set w/old European-cut & baguette diamonds weighing about 5.42 cts., 1 5/8" l. (ILLUS.)..................................... **$3,525**

Brooch, platinum, emerald & diamond, designed as two slender overlapping rings bead-set w/old European- and single-cut diamonds & centering a bezel-set large rectangular step-cut emerald, millegrain accents (missing one diamond) **$940**

Brooch, platinum, emerald & sapphire, Mughal-style, designed as a large diamond-form floral-carved emerald tablet within a scrolling narrow frame channel-set w/calibré-cut emeralds & sapphires, cabochon sapphire highlights, w/pendant hook, signed "Cartier N.Y.," evidence of solder at pin stem (ILLUS., top of page) **$270,000**

Unusual Art Deco Jade & Diamond Brooch

Brooch, platinum, jadeite & diamond, composed of three green jadeite cylinders each capped at both ends w/diamond-set pointed arches, convertible into three pins, designed & signed by Raymond Yard (ILLUS.)... **$6,756**

Art Deco Rock Crystal & Diamond Brooch

Extremely Rare Sapphire, Diamond & Platinum Art Deco Brooch

Brooch, platinum, rock crystal & diamond, a large open diamond composed of rock crystal sections capped by a geometric band set w/three large old European-cut diamonds & small full- and single-cut diamonds, the bottom tip set w/a floret device further set w/diamonds, originally a dress clip, diamonds weighing about 3.50 cts. (ILLUS., previous page)............ **$3,525**

Brooch, platinum, synthetic emerald & diamond, a central oval ring set w/old European-cut, single-cut & baguette diamonds enclosing a large prong-set emerald-cut synthetic emerald, diamond-set oblong side rings centered by a diamond-set leaftip, gold pin stem, approximate weight 1.52 cts. **$1,998**

Art Deco Decorated Rock Crystal Brooch

Brooch, rock crystal, coral & marcasite, a rectangular rock crystal plaque mount-

ed w/coral bead & marcasite florettes, marcasite & blue chalcedony accents, hallmark of Theodor Fahrner, ca. 1930 (ILLUS.) **$1,763**

Oval & Bar Sapphire & Diamond Brooch

Brooch, sapphire, diamond & platinum, designed as a long narrow open oval set overall w/old single-, European- and full-cut diamonds, centered at the top & bottom by French-cut sapphires, the middle crossed by a long band set w/alternating French-cut sapphires & European-cut diamonds, diamonds weighing about 1.72 cts., millegrain accents, 2" l. (ILLUS.)
.... **$2,468**

Brooch, sapphire, diamond & platinum, oblong bow-shaped mount set w/border bands of 98 full-cut diamond mélée & small sapphires, the center band w/five large old European-cut diamonds bordered by four large circular-cut sapphires, ca. 1930 (ILLUS., top of page)
.... **$32,900**

Rare Art Deco Gem-set Platinum Charm Bracelet

Long Art Deco Sapphire & Diamond Brooch

Brooch, sapphire, diamond & platinum, the long narrow oblong openwork frame centered by a step-cut blue sapphire framed by looping & arched bands bead-set overall w/single-cut diamonds weighing about 4.30 cts., millegrain accents, w/partial European hallmark (ILLUS.)
.... **$4,500-5,500**

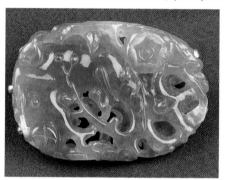

Finely Carved Jadeite Brooch-Pendant

Brooch-pendant, jadeite, a large pierce-carved oval green jadeite plaque w/overall vines, flowers & a bird, platinum fittings, 7/8 x 1 3/4" (ILLUS.) **$2,115**
Cameo pendant, platinum & blue chalcedony cameo, the oval cameo carved w/the head of a lady, a pendant bail set w/rose-cut diamonds, 1 1/2" l............................. **$7,640**
Charm bracelet, gem-set platinum, the converted platinum chain w/fine chain & bar links spaced by seed pearls suspending eight figural charms including a carved gem parrot, airplane, figure of a man & a horseshoe, 6 1/2" l. (ILLUS., bottom previous page) **$5,875**

Enameled Gold Art Deco Cuff Links

Cuff links, enameled 14k gold, each double oval link w/line-engraving & a band of blue enamel, American-made, pr. (ILLUS.) **$470**

French Art Deco Gem-set Cuff Links

Cuff links, gold (18k), sapphire & diamond, each long oval double link set in the center w/a large sugarloaf cabochon sapphire flanked by small star-set old mine-cut diamonds, French guarantee stamps, pr. (ILLUS.) **$3,643**

Wing-like Art Deco Diamond Dress Clips

Dress clips, diamond & platinum, each in a stylized wing-like form w/a large scroll tip, the scroll ending in a large full-cut diamond w/the bands in the wing further bead-set w/old single-cut diamonds, reverse w/evidence of solder, diamonds weighing about 5.64 cts., 2 1/4" l., pr. (ILLUS.) **$4,113**

Bold Scrolled Diamond Dress Clips

Dress clips, platinum & diamond, each designed in a swirling cornucopia-like form beside banded & fan-like sections, set overall w/full- and single-cut diamonds weighing about 6.75 cts., white gold frame for conversion to a brooch, pr. (ILLUS., previous page) **$4,700**

One of Two Very Rare Dress Clips

Dress clips, platinum & diamond, each of palmette form set throughout w/54 old European-cut diamonds, approx. 20.00 cts., further set w/32 French-cut, two baquette & 102 single-cut diamonds, approx. 29.00 cts., 14k white gold findings, ca. 1930 (ILLUS. of one) **$48,175**

Art Deco Geometric Diamond Dress Clips

Dress clips, platinum & diamonds, openwork trapezoidal mounts set along the bottom edge w/a cluster of three old European-cut diamonds, the tapering sides & geometric accents bead-set overall w/baguette, transitional- and single-cut diamonds, diamonds weighing about 6.54 cts., French guarantee stamps, numbered 10536 & 10007, w/18k white gold frame for brooch conversion, 1 x 2", pr. (ILLUS.) **$7,050**

Art Deco Sapphire and Diamond Dress Clips

Dress clips, sapphire & diamond, bead-set w/seventy-two full- and single-cut diamonds, channel-set, square-, step- and calibré-cut highlights, millegrain accents, platinum mount, w/brooch conversion, pr. (ILLUS.) **$3,173**

Art Deco Man's Onyx Dress Set

Dress set, gentleman's, designed as shaped square onyx tablets framed by tiny rose-cut diamonds, hallmark of Lartere Brothers, in a fitted box marked by Dreicer & Co., the set (ILLUS.) **$5,288**

Art Deco Diamond & Aquamarine Earrings

Earrings, aquamarine, diamond & platinum, pendant-type, a three-leaf top suspending angular open loops set overall w/single- and old European-cut diamonds & baguettes & centered by a rectangular step-cut aquamarine, millegrain accents, diamonds weighing about 3.10 cts., pr. (ILLUS.) **$3,408**

Fine Hardstone Art Deco Earrings

Earrings, chalcedony, coral, marcasite & onyx, each designed as a shaped blue chalcedony tablet suspended from a marcasite pagoda form w/coral bead accents, cabochon onyx tops, silver mounts, hallmark of Theodor Fahrner, ca. 1930, pr. (ILLUS.) **$2,938**

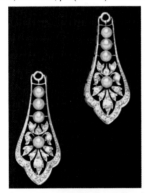

Art Deco Diamond & Pearl Earrings

Earrings, diamond, cultured pearl & platinum, pendant-type, the long openwork teardrop-shaped mount framed by a tapering band of small bezel-set old European-cut diamonds, the top set w/a row of three cultured pearls above a leaf-form design further set w/small diamonds & centered by another pearl, missing tops, 1 1/2 " l., pr. (ILLUS.) **$2,585**

Art Deco Diamond & Jadeite Earrings

Earrings, diamond, jadeite & platinum, pendant-style, designed as a cascade of three full-cut diamonds suspending a green jadeite pi ring, platinum mounts, 1 1/4" l., pr. (ILLUS.) **$2,703**

Fine Hexagonal Diamond Drop Earrings

Earrings, diamond & platinum, pendant-type, a three-section diamond-set link suspending a hexagonal frame centered by a large full-cut diamond framed by a band of small rose-cut diamonds, diamonds weighing about 2.85 cts., 18k gold findings, 1" l., pr. (ILLUS.)...................... **$4,700**

Art Deco Coral, Diamond & Platinum Jabot

Art Deco Onyx & Diamond Earrings

Art Deco Sapphire & Diamond Jabot

Earrings, platinum, onyx & diamond, pendant-style, flattened tear-form onyx drops w/rose-cut diamond floral surmounts, suspeneded from single-cut diamond tops, millegrain accents, later 14k gold posts, pr. (ILLUS.) **$940**

Jabot, coral, diamond & platinum, the narrow pin set at each end w/a scalloped openwork mount centered by a cabochon coral framed by full- and single-cut diamonds weighing about 1.16 cts., 3" l. (ILLUS., top of page).............................. **$1,880**

Jabot, platinum, 18k gold & diamond, designed as a small arrow bead-set at the flared top & pointed base w/old European- and single-cut diamonds, millegrain accents, signed by Cartier, numbered & w/a French guarantee stamp, ca. 1930... **$1,293**

Jabot, sapphire, diamond & platinum, a slender pin mounted at each end w/an arched mount, one set w/three cushion-cut sapphires surrounded by old mine- and European-cut diamonds, the other end set w/a single cushion-cut sapphire surrounded by further diamonds, diamonds weighing about 1.06 cts., closure needs adjustment (ILLUS.) **$1,763**

Locket, gold (14k), diamond & enamel, centered exotic bird in flight w/bead-set single-cut diamond body & ruby eye, black enamel background w/delicate white enamel border, opening to reveal two interior compartments, platinum bail.......... **$2,350**

Fancy Art Deco Diamond Lorgnette

Lorgnette, diamond, platinum & seed pearl, the oblong pierced & engraved frame w/a pointed top bead- and bezel-set overall w/99 old mine-, European- and rose-cut diamonds accented w/three triple pearl clusters, suspended from a fancy chain w/filigree diamond-shaped links highlighted by seed pearls & one bezel-set diamond accent, 32" l. (ILLUS., previous page) **$6,169**

Lorgnette & chain, platinum, diamond & seed pearl, oblong lorgnette w/engraved accents suspended from a chain w/baton links w/alternating full-cut diamond mélée & seed pearl spacers, lorgnette 2 3/4" l., the set **$881**

Extraordinary Mauboussin Diamond, Emerald, Sapphire & Ruby Art Deco Necklace

Necklace, gem-set platinum & diamond, the wide front section composed of leaf-carved, disk-form & cabochon rubies, sapphires & emerald leaves attached to a diamond-set band & w/geometric diamond-set links, finished w/a narrow link chain of diamonds, diamonds weighing about 8.96 cts., signed "Mauboussin - France," No. X1024, 16 1/2" l. (ILLUS.) **$149,000**

Rock Crystal & Amethyst Deco Necklace

Necklace, amethyst & etched rock crystal, composed of tapering leaf-engraved rock crystal beads w/faceted caps spaced by tiny faceted amethyst spheres, 18" l. (ILLUS.) **$353**

Carnelian & Enamel Necklace

Necklace, carnelian & enamel, five graduating floral carved & pierced carnelian plaques joined by bow-form celadon green & black enamel links, seed pearl accents, 14k gold mount, partially obliterated hallmark for "Carter Howe & Gough," 16 1/2" l. (ILLUS.)..................... **$4,700**

Art Deco Jadeite, Onyx & Gold Necklace

Necklace, jadeite, onyx & 10k gold, composed of bezel-set oval jadeite cabochon links joined by onyx-set flat bars & wire-wrapped links, suspending a green jadeite pi ring, 16" l. (ILLUS.) **$823**

Art Deco Opal & Rock Crystal Necklace

Necklace, opal & rock crystal, composed of white opal beads graduating in size from about 4.79 to 9.44 mm, interspersed w/faceted rock crystal disks, completed by a platinum & rose-cut diamond clasp, 16 1/2" l. (ILLUS.)..................................... **$1,880**

Necklace, pearl, platinum & diamond, composed of 79 ivory pearls graduating in size from 4.30 to 8.81 mm, completed by a box clasp set w/a cushion-cut diamond weighing 1.22 cts. framed by a ring of small calibré-cut rubies, ca. 1930, 23 1/2" l. **$3,173**

Art Deco Emerald & Diamond Pendant

Pendant, emerald, diamond & 14k yellow gold, teardrop-shaped lacy mount mounted in the center w/a large 14 ct. pear-shaped emerald surrounded by round-cut diamonds, 4.5 cts., gold mount (ILLUS.).. **$10,350**

Art Deco Black Opal & Diamond Pendant

Pendant, black opal, diamond & platinum, suspended from a earlier Edwardian diamond-set floral & ribbon swag pin, the oval pendant centered by a large black opal cabochon framed by old European- and single-cut diamonds, ca. 1930s (ILLUS.) **$4,818**

French Cast Silver Art Deco Pendant

Pendant, enameled cast silver, a rhomboid shape w/cast draping edged in bands of green & black enamel above a panel cast w/stylized flowerheads, the pointed base w/bands of green & black enamel, designed by Etienne David, France, ca. 1925, w/French assay mark for silver, 1 1/2 x 3" (ILLUS.) **$1,793**

Unique Egyptian Goddess Gold Pendant

Pendant, enameled & gem-set gold, Egyptian Revival style, designed as the standing figure of an Egyptian goddess w/champlevé enamel accents & holding one arm aloft w/a green cabochon in her hand raised, on an square amazonite pedestal, further decorated w/green chalcedony, garnet, carnelian & emeralds, suspended from a bar pin & fancy link gold chain w/lotus designs, French import stamps & European assay marks (ILLUS.) **$3,290**

Large Art Deco Aquamarine & Diamond Pendant

Pendant, platinum, aquamarine & diamond, a large long rectangular aquamarine framed by a geometric band set w/eight baguette, four bullet, one triangular & 58 full- and 12 single-cut diamonds, diamonds weighing about 2.95 cts., open gallery, overall 16 1/2" l. (ILLUS. of pendant) **$12,925**

Art Deco Carved Jade Pendant

Pendant, platinum, jadeite & diamond, the rectangular green jade plaque pierced & carved w/stylized florals, the openwork bail set w/diamond mélée, suspended from a delicate trace link chain, 17" l. (ILLUS.) **$2,938**

Pendant, silver & enamel, square plaque w/clipped corners surmounted by an urn & flower design on a green & black enamel ground, hallmark for David **$1,725**

Pendant, sterling silver & enamel, rectangular plaque design, divided into four rectangular panels, two corner ones w/small squares diagonally divided & decorated w/coral & black enamel, the other two corner squares set w/faceted black stone panels, probably onyx, gilt chain marked "935," pendant stamped w/initial mark of Theodor Fahrner & "935," Europe, ca. 1930 .... **$1,880**

Rare Art Deco Pendant-Brooch

Pendant-brooch, diamond, emerald & platinum, the long oval openwork mount set overall w/old European- and single-cut diamonds weighing about 6.93 cts., accented w/very thin bands of calibré-cut emeralds, millegrain accents, retractable diamond-set bail, 3/4" x 2" (ILLUS., previous page)... **$7,638**

Dramatic Diamond Art Deco Bow

Pendant-brooch, diamond, sapphire & platinum, model of a long, wide bow, centered by a large old European-cut diamond w/the box ornately set w/117 old European-, transitional- and single-cut diamonds totaling about 4 cts., highlighted w/narrow bands of small French-cut blue sapphires & millegrain accents (ILLUS.)................... **$7,050**

Pendant-brooch, platinum, diamond & emerald, openwork plaque set w/twenty-three old European- & single-cut diamonds & eighteen emerald & green stone accents, millegrain accents, deployant bail... **$2,938**

Pendant-brooch, platinum & diamond, oblong openwork form bead-set w/fifty-seven old European & full-cut diamonds, total wt. 2.20 cts., detachable bail.............. **$2,468**

Pendant-brooch & chain, diamond & platinum, the oblong pendant w/an openwork mount centered by an almond-shaped central section, bead- and bezel-set w/old mine-, European- and single-cut diamonds & millegrain accents, suspended from a delicate baton link chain w/bezel-set old European- and mine-cut diamond spacers, diamonds weighing about 6.11 cts., pendant 2 1/4" l. (ILLUS. of part, top next column).. **$7,050**

Dramatic Art Deco Diamond Pendant

Pendant-locket, platinum, diamond & faux green jade enamel, oval locket w/millegrain platinum mount set w/three circular-cut diamonds, faux green jade "en plein" enamel surface................................. **$920**

Art Deco Diamond & Platinum Pendant

Pendant-necklace diamond & platinum, detachable pendant centering a flexibly set faceted pear-shaped yellow diamond weighing approx. 9 cts., frame, bail & necklace further bezel & bead-set w/one marquise & 164 old mine- and old European-cut diamonds weighing approx. 5.25 cts., millegrain accents, platinum mount, 16" l. (ILLUS.) **$193,000**

Fine Chanel Rhinestone Pendant-Necklace

Pendant-necklace, silver plated metal & rhinestone, the necklace composed of open hexagonal links set w/small rhinestones & alternating w/oblong links centered by a green emerald-cut glass stone framed by small rhinestones, the pendant composed of a long open rectangle trimmed w/emerald-cut clear rhinestones & framing a large rectangular green emerald-cut glass stone, a Chanel design marked "Déposé," France, ca. 1935, necklace 30" l., pendant 4" l. (ILLUS.) **$1,554**

Pendant-necklace, sterling silver, marcasite & glass baguettes, pierced rectangular pendant set w/carved blue & pink flowerheads over a row of clear glass baguettes, set throughout w/marcasites, completed by a baton-link chain, one marcasite missing, chain not silver, 32" l. .. **$489**

Fine Art Deco Diamond & Pearl Pin

Pin, diamond, pearl & platinum, circle-style, the scrolling ring joined by two three-leaf clusters, bead-set overall w/old European-

and mine-cut diamond mélée & centered by a white pearl, ca. 1930s (ILLUS.) **$2,115**

Fine Art Deco Diamond-set Circle Pin

Pin, diamond & platinum, circle-style, the open circle bead-set w/37 old European, transitional- and full-cut diamonds weighing about 3.70 cts., 1 5/8" d. (ILLUS.) **$3,408**

Deco Diamond Bow Pin with Sapphires

Pin, diamond, sapphire & platinum, modeled as a large wide ribbon bow, bead-set throughout w/98 old European-, mine- and single-cut diamonds weighing about 1.73 cts., accented w/tiny diamond & leaf designs set w/French- and fancy-cut sapphires, millegrain accents, 2" l. (ILLUS.)... **$4,406**

Pin, jadeite & enamel, black, green & yellow enamel pagoda framing a pierced jadeite plaque depicting a bird among flowers, 14k gold mount, hallmark for Sloan & Co. **$3,055**

Pin, platinum & diamond, circle-style, designed as a circle containing scrolling script bead-set w/rose-cut diamonds, signed "Cartier - New York" **$3,173**

Deco Long Double-Ribbon Bow Pin

Pin, platinum & diamond, designed as a long open bow w/double ribbons at each end, bead-set w/old European-cut diamonds weighing about 1.60 cts., millegrain accents, open gallery (ILLUS.) **$1,998**

Cartier Art Deco Diamond & Onyx Pin

Pin, platinum, diamond & onyx, a long open oval ring, bead-set w/72 old European- and single-cut diamonds, centered by an undulating thin band of channel-set onyx, signed "Cartier Paris Londres" (ILLUS.) **$7,050**

Rare Cartier Mughal-design Pin

Pin, platinum, diamond & ruby, Mughal design w/a central leaf-carved ruby framed by old mine- and single-cut diamonds on a diamond-set stem accented w/emerald & ruby cabochons, signed by Cartier (ILLUS.) **$11,750**

Art Deco Sapphire and Diamond Pin

Pin, sapphire & diamond, bezel-set w/one faceted oval & two cushion-cut sapphires, w/forty-six old European- and old mine-cut diamonds, approx. total wt. 1.88 cts., millegrain accents, platinum mount, French hallmark & guarantee stamps (ILLUS.)...................................... **$4,700**

Art Deco Aquamarine Ring

Ring, aquamarine, diamond & enameled gold, the top prong-set w/a large oval-cut aquamarine, rose-cut diamond shoulders & black enamel accents, platinum & 18k gold mount, size 7 (ILLUS.) **$705**

Art Deco Black Opal & Diamond Ring

Ring, black opal & diamond, the top set w/an opal tablet flanked by the narrow shank set w/single-cut diamonds, open scrolling gallery, 18k white gold & platinum mount, dated 1934, English karat mark, in a Garrard & Co. box (ILLUS.).... **$1,998**

Very Rare Colored Diamond Deco Ring

Ring, colored diamond, colorless diamond & platinum, the wide domed top centered by a large bezel-set old European-cut yellow diamond weighing about 3.22 cts., the scrolling openwork mount bead-set overall w/24 old European-cut colorless diamonds, size 5 (ILLUS.)..................... **$15,275**

Art Deco Coral, Diamond & Enameled Ring

Ring, coral, diamond & enameled 14k gold, centered by a large bezel-set oval orangish red coral cabochon within a black enameled gold foliate frame w/single-cut diamond highlights, the shoulders w/a foliate design, size 7 1/4 (ILLUS.) **$1,528**

Ring, diamond & 14k gold, the top set w/a row of three old European-cut diamonds, the central one in a square mount, diamonds weighing about 1.15 cts., openwork mount, size 5 1/4 .... **$2,350**

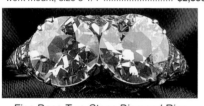

Fine Deco Two-Stone Diamond Ring

Ring, diamond & 18k white gold, twin-stone style, the top prong-set w/two old European-cut diamonds weighing about 1.16 and 1.28 cts., openwork gallery & shoulders, size 8 1/4 (ILLUS.) **$7,931**

Ring, diamond, box-set w/three old European-cut diamonds, gallery & shoulders pierced in a scroll design, platinum mount, size 6 .... **$8,338**

Deco Ring with Oval Emerald & Diamonds

Ring, diamond, emerald & platinum, the oval top centered by a faceted cushion-shape emerald framed by two rings of old mine- and European-cut diamonds, openwork diamond-set shoulders, diamonds weighing about 2.00 cts., millegrain accents, size 5 3/4 (ILLUS.) **$3,055**

Ring, diamond & gold, 14k white gold filigree mount w/one marquise diamond, ca. 1920 .... **$11,200**

Ring, diamond & onyx, navette-shaped onyx tablet bezel-set w/old European-cut diamond weighing approx. 2.89 cts., platinum & 18k gold mount, size 1 1/2 (evidence of solder) **$6,169**

Ring, diamond & platinum, bezel-set cushion-shaped old mine-cut diamond weighing approx. .81 cts., framed by 18 old mine-cut diamonds, platinum openwork mount w/millegrain accents, size 5 3/4 ... **$1,528**

Ring, diamond & platinum, solitaire-type, prong-set w/a transitional-cut diamond weighing about 1.30 cts. flanked by two bezel-set baguettes & a bead-set circular-cut diamond, together w/a wedding band, ca. 1935, size 7 .... **$4,818**

Art Deco Geometric Diamond Ring

Ring, diamond & platinum, the diamond-form top centered by a transitional-cut diamond weighing about .81 cts. & surrounded by a pierced cross-design & geometric panels set overall w/single- and full-cut diamonds, millegrain trim, size 7 1/4 (ILLUS.) **$1,528**

Ring, diamond & platinum, the filigree navette mount set w/nine old European-cut diamonds, millegrain accents, size 4 1/2 .... **$646**

Unusual Art Deco Diamond Ring

Ring, diamond & platinum, the long geometric top bead-set w/old European-, mine- and old single-cut diamonds weighing about 1.34 cts., millegrain accents, size 7 (ILLUS.) **$1,645**

Rectangular-topped Deco Diamond Ring

Ring, diamond & platinum, the long rectangular top centered by a large bead-set old European-cut diamond weighing about 1.12 cts., surrounded by other old mine- and European-cut diamonds weighing about 3.82 cts., open gallery, size 5 (ILLUS.) **$2,350**

Art Deco Ring with Large Sapphire & Diamonds

Ring, diamond, sapphire & platinum, the oblong top centered by a large bezel-set cushion-cut sapphire flanked by two large old mine-cut diamonds, the openwork mount further set w/thirty full-cut diamonds & millegrain accents, size 6 3/4 (ILLUS.).. **$2,468**

Art Deco Sapphire & Diamond Ring

Ring, diamond, sapphire & platinum, the rounded almond-shaped top centered by a bezel-set cushion-cut sapphire within an openwork frame bead-set w/ten old European-cut diamonds, millegrain accents (ILLUS.) **$6,463**

Art Deco Squared Sapphire & Diamond Ring

Ring, diamond & sapphire, the square top w/beveled corners, centered by a square-cut diamond surrounded by narrow bands of French-cut sapphires & full-cut diamond mélée, open gallery, size 6 (ILLUS.)... **$3,525**

Art Deco Diamond Ring

Ring, diamond, set w/a pear-shaped solitaire diamond weighing approx. 2.35 cts. further set w/six straight baguettes, nine single- & six transitional-cut diamonds, platinum mount signed "Shreve & Co., no. B9550," size 8 (ILLUS.).................. **$17,625**

Ring, diamond, set w/three old European-cut diamonds, approx. total wt. .60 cts., within a pierced & engraved platinum mount set w/four single-cut diamonds, millegrain accents, size 6 3/4..................... **$881**

Ring, diamond, transitional-cut solitaire diamond weighing approx. .94 cts. framed by 12 circular-cut diamonds, shoulders set w/six circular-cut diamonds, millegrain accents, incised shank, size 5 1/4 .... **$2,350**

Ring, emerald & diamond, 18k yellow gold silver washed crown centering an oval cabochon emerald surrounded by two rows of round diamonds flanked on each side by round diamonds, ca. 1930 .... **$896**

Emerald & Diamond Art Deco Ring

Ring, emerald, diamond & gold, the oval top centered by a bezel-set oval-cut emerald surrounded by a ring of 13 old European-cut diamonds weighing about 1.30 cts., platinum & 18k white gold mount, size 5 (ILLUS.)... **$1,645**

Deco Emerald & Diamond Ring

Ring, emerald, diamond & platinum, centering a large step-cut emerald flanked by graduating diamond baguettes, size 7 (ILLUS.)... **$3,819**

Very Fine Art Deco Emerald & Diamond Ring

Ring, emerald, diamond & platinum, the rectangular top centered by a step-cut emerald flanked by step-cut diamonds weighing about 1.12 & 1.20 cts., floral gallery & shoulders w/bead-set diamonds, millegrain accents, emerald w/nicks, size 4 1/2 (ILLUS.)................... **$16,450**

Art Deco Ring with Pear-shaped Gems

Ring, emerald, diamond & platinum, two-stone, set w/a large pear-cut emerald & an old pear-cut diamond weighing about 1.58 cts., shoulders set w/an oval-cut diamond & a heart-shaped emerald, 12 single-cut diamond accents, signed by Gattle, size 6 1/2 (ILLUS.)...................... **$5,875**

Gold Quartz, Diamond & Gold Ring

Ring, gold quartz, diamond & 18k white gold, the top set w/a rectangular gold quatrz tablet & shoulders, rose-cut diamond accents, French guarantee stamps, size 6 3/4 (ILLUS.)....................... **$940**

Green Jadeite Cabochon & Diamond Ring

Ring, jade, diamond & 14k white gold, set w/an oval green jadeite cabochon, the shoulders set w/small diamonds, size 7 1/4 (ILLUS.)... **$646**

Orange Tourmaline & Diamond Ring

Ring, orange tourmaline, diamond & 18k white gold, the oval top centered by a large prong-set oval-cut orange tourmaline weighing 2.79 cts., framed by a narrow ring of diamonds & w/full-cut diamonds on the shoulders, size 6 1/2 (ILLUS.) **$2,820**

Pink Sapphire & Diamond Art Deco Ring

Ring, pink sapphire, diamond & platinum, the square top centered by a bezel-set octagonal pink sapphire framed by bands of old European- and transitional-cut diamonds, the shoulders w/oval pink sapphire highlights, millegrain accents, ca. 1930s, size 6 (ILLUS.) **$5,288**

Ring, platinum, 14k gold & diamond, bead-set w/an old European-cut diamond weighing about .42 cts. in a scrolling foliate engraved mount, millegrain accents, size 8 3/4.. **$940**

Unusual Art Deco Green Stone Ring

Ring, platinum, carved stone & diamond, the top set w/a large domed carved cloudy green stone w/herringbone bands & a rosette center, the openwork mount accented w/54 tiny diamonds, size 6 1/2 (ILLUS.) .. **$715**

Ring, platinum & diamond, bead-set w/26 full-cut diamonds & two blue stone highlights, millegrain accents, size 5 1/4 .... **$529**

Cartier Diamond & Platinum Ring

Ring, platinum & diamond, bezel-set w/an old mine-cut diamond approx. 1.00 cts., surrounded by 12 old mine- and European-cut diamonds, approx. 2.34 cts., worn signature of Cartier, ca. 1930s, size 8 3/4 (ILLUS.)... **$8,225**

Dated Art Deco Sapphire & Diamond Ring

Ring, platinum, sapphire & diamond, the rounded top centered by a large cushion-cut sapphire weighing about 1.50 cts., surrounded by bead-set old single-cut diamond mélée, interior dated 1931, size 5 3/4 (ILLUS.)... **$2,350**

Extraordinary Art Deco Ruby Ring

Ring, ruby, diamond & 18k white gold, centered by a large prong-set cushion-cut ruby flanked by triangular panels w/diamond trillions, size 6 1/4 (ILLUS.) **$23,500**

Two-stone Ruby & Diamond Ring

Ring, ruby & diamond, two-stone style, the oblong top centered by two cabochon rubies flanked down the shaft by bands of calibré-cut rubies, all outlined by bands of full-cut diamonds weighing about 1.20 cts., open scrolling gallery, silver & gold mount, No. 0724, India, ca. 1930, size 4 (ILLUS.).. **$1,880**

Choice Domed Deco Sapphire & Diamond Ring

Ring, sapphire, diamond & 18k gold, the large rounded dome centered by a large old European-cut diamond weighing about 2.24 cts. framed by rays set w/smaller old European- and full-cut diamonds alternating w/panels of circular-cut blue sapphires, other diamonds weighing about 4.85 cts., size 6 (ILLUS.) **$7,344**

Ring, sapphire & diamond, openwork pierced platinum mount w/millegrain accents centered by a collet-set circular-cut sapphire, framed by eight old mine-cut diamonds, size 6 1/2..................................... **$863**

Rare Caldwell Sapphire & Diamond Ring

Ring, sapphire, diamond & platinum, the arched top centered by a large rectangular step-cut blue sapphire, flanked by large French-cut diamonds & further bead-set w/small diamonds, diamonds weighing about 1.72 cts., scrolling gallery, millegrain accents, engraved mount, marked by J.E. Caldwell & Co., Philadephia, size 7 1/4 (ILLUS.) **$11,750**

Art Deco Ring with Large Sapphire

Ring, sapphire, diamond & platinum, the square top centered by a large table-cut sapphire, the shoulders channel-set w/Swiss-cut diamonds & sapphires, several small sapphires chipped, ca. 1935 (ILLUS., previous page) **$1,880**

Rare Sapphire & Diamond Deco Ring

Ring, sapphire, diamond & platinum, the top centered by a large bezel-set oval sapphire surrounded by old European- and square-cut diamonds weighing about 1.80 cts., size 7 (ILLUS.) **$12,925**

Art Deco Turquoise & Diamond Ring

Ring, turquoise, diamond & platinum, the oval top set w/a gadrooned & domed turquoise plaque centered by a bezel-set transitional-cut round diamond, foliate shoulders w/diamond, black enamel & cabochon jadeite highlights, millegrain accents, signed by Black, Starr & Frost, New York, New York, size 5 1/4 (ILLUS.) **$4,113**

Art Deco Turquoise & Ivory Ring

Ring, turquoise, ivory & gold, bezel-set w/a turquoise-in-matrix cabochon framed by an ivory band, shoulders w/interlocking circle motifs, silver & gold mount, ivory band w/breaks, size 6 1/4 (ILLUS.) **$588**

Art Deco White Opal & Diamond Ring

Ring, white opal, diamond & platinum, the top prong-set w/a large oval opal framed by a narrow band of small diamonds, size 8 1/4 (ILLUS.) **$999**

Sets

Art Deco Gentleman's Cuff Link & Shirt Stud Suite

Cuff links & shirt studs, mother-of-pearl, diamond & gold; each cuff link w/a double round mother-of-pearl link centering a bezel-set old European-cut diamond & edged w/small rose-cut diamonds, platinum-topped 14k gold mount, three matching shirt studs, unsigned, in a Dreicer & Co. fitted box, the suite (ILLUS., bottom previous page).. **$2,468**

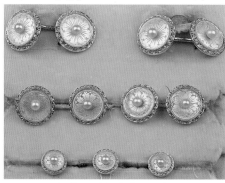

Art Deco Man's Dress Set

Dress set: cuff links & seven shirt studs; mother-of-pearl & seed pearl, each set w/an engraved mother-of-pearl round tablet centered by a seed pearl, in a narrow scrolling frame, platinum-topped 18k gold mount, mark of maker Larter & Sons, in a Shreve, Crump & Low fitted box, the set (ILLUS.).............................. **$1,880**

Necklace & earrings, pearl & diamond, composed of 58 ivory pearls w/rose overtones completed by a platinum & diamond clasp, the pendant-style earrings each set w/a pearl suspending a cascade of bezel-set old mine-cut diamonds ending in faux pearl drops, platinum-topped 18k gold mounts, earrings need repair, one diamond missing, the suite **$3,525**

Retro Style

Bracelet, amethyst & 14k yellow gold, composed of pairs of step-cut amethysts joined by arched gold bar links, 7 1/4" l. (ILLUS. of part, first bottom of page)
.... **$2,233**

Bracelet, bicolor 14k gold, composed of small arched links arranged in groups of three alternating w/pairs, 7" l. (ILLUS., second bottom of page) **$823**

Bracelet, bicolor 14k gold, ruby & diamond, the wide band composed of small hexagonal honeycomb links centered by a large undulating ribbon device centered by a thin band of channel-set rubies flanked in the center by bands of bead-set diamonds, deployant clasp, 7" l. (ILLUS., bottom of page)... **$3,643**

Retro Style Amethyst & Gold Bracelet

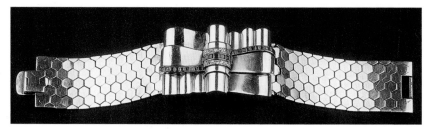

Bicolor Gold Arched Link Retro Bracelet

Retro Bicolor Gold Honeycomb & Ribbon Bracelet

Rare Retro Diamond & Platinum Bracelet, ca. 1950

Rare Retro Citrine-mounted Bracelet

Bracelet, citrine, diamond & 14k white gold, bangle-type, the tapering wide band prong-set at the top by a large rectangular fancy-cut citrine flanked by tapering panels of fancy pierced leafy scrolls set w/full-cut diamond mélée, diamonds weighing about 4.57 cts., two diamonds missing, interior circumference 6 1/2" (ILLUS.) **$4,994**

Bracelet, gem-set 18k bicolor gold, bangle-type, the hinged ring w/applied ribbon bow design set w/cabochon rubies, marquise- and single-cut diamonds & a navette-shaped jadeite, missing one diamond & one ruby, interior circumference 7" **$764**

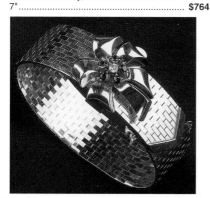

Gold Brickwork Bracelet with Ribbon Cluster Buckle

Bracelet, gold (14k), sapphire & diamond, buckle-style, the wide band composed of brickwork links joined by a ribbon cluster centered by a single full-cut diamond surrounded by a ring of small circular-cut sapphires, signed by Cartier, boxed, 6 3/4" l. (ILLUS.) **$3,055**

Bracelet, gold (14k), yellow gold oval links connected by domed half links alternating w/gadrooned pink gold links, European hallmark, 8 1/4" l. **$489**

Bracelet, gold (18k bicolor) & diamond, interlocking hexagonal links, clasp w/radiating elements, bead-set w/single-cut diamond highlights, 33.0 dwt., 7" l. **$705**

Bracelet, platinum & diamond, the strap centered by a raised scroll matching the band design composed of two outer bands set w/152 channel-set baguettes, the open center row prong-set w/85 full-cut diamonds, diamonds weighing about 35.00 cts., ca. 1950, 7" l. (ILLUS., top of page)... **$32,900**

Fine Gold, Ruby & Diamond Bracelet

Bracelet, ruby, diamond & 14k gold, buckle-style, wide gold brickwork band set w/mounts decorated w/four baguette & 26 old European-, full- and transitional-cut diamond weighing about 2.73 cts. & 24 circular-cut, 10 cabochon & three calibré-cut rubies, 7" l. (ILLUS.).................. **$2,468**

Fine Retro Style Gem-set Gold Bracelet

Bracelet, sapphire, diamond & 14k gold, composed of trapezoidal solid gold links w/a line of channel-set baguette sapphires along one end & centered by short pairs of bands set w/single-cut diamonds, No. 2328, mark of an American maker, retailed by Cartier, New York (ILLUS., bottom previous page) **$11,163**

Stylized Floral Retro Style Brooch

Brooch, diamond, synthetic rubies & 14k rose gold, a swirled styled leafy floral design, the center set w/an old European-cut diamond flanked by 38 small diamonds & synthetic rubies, 14k rose gold mount, mid-20th c. (ILLUS.)...................... **$275**

Retro Style Bicolor Gold Bow Brooch

Brooch, bicolor 14k gold, in the shape of a large bow, 2 3/4" l. (ILLUS.) **$470**

Gem-set 18k Gold Floral Sprig Brooch

Brooch, gem-set 18k gold, designed as a floral sprig set w/pear-cut blue & purplish red spinels, pink topaz, pink & pale purple sapphires & green chrysoberyl, highlighted w/small old European- and mine-cut diamonds, France, 2 1/4" l. (ILLUS.). **$3,525**

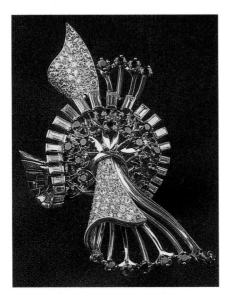

Fancy Retro Style Brooch

Brooch, diamond, ruby, 18k gold & platinum, designed w/a wide central openwork scroll set w/baguette-cut diamonds around circular-cut rubies, the scroll bisecting an openwork bow further set w/full- and single-cut diamonds & circular-cut rubies, French guarantee stamps, 3" l. (ILLUS.)... **$2,802**

Retro Four-Ribbon Gold Brooch

Brooch, gold (14k), designed as a fanned arrangement of four ribbed & curled open ribbons atop four thin wire stems, Tiffany & Co., 1 3/4" (ILLUS.) **$235**

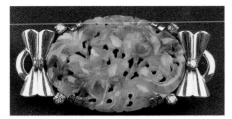

Jadeite, Diamond & Gold Retro Brooch

Brooch, jadeite, diamond & 14k gold, an oval pierced & carved jadeite plaque flanked by gold bow designs highlighted by full-cut diamond mélée, maker's mark of Wordley, Allsopp & Bliss, retailed by Tiffany & Co., boxed, 2" l. (ILLUS.) **$2,938**

Rare Retro Ruby & Diamond Brooch

Brooch, ruby, diamond & platinum, an angled round bar wrapped by three ribbon & buckle-style devices, channel- and bead-set w/64 full-cut & 48 baguette diamonds & channel-set w/step- and calibré-cut rubies, diamonds weighing about 12.05 cts., 2 1/2" l. (ILLUS.) **$24,675**

Gem-set Gold Retro Ballerina Brooch

Brooch, sapphire, diamond & 14k gold, designed as a dancing ballerina w/her hands above her head, a cabochon sapphire face w/three diamonds forming a tiera, the flaring ruffled tutu set w/scattered small prong-set sapphires (ILLUS.) **$881**

Fine Cartier Retro Style Clip

Clip, gem-set 14k gold, a large stylized blossom w/five deep petals w/rolled & pointed tips, centered by a pyramidal double cabochon green tourmaline set en tremblant, long flexible stem w/three long slender gold leaves, signed by Cartier, No. 3497, 4" l. (ILLUS.) **$4,113**

Unusual Retro Aquamarine & Gem Brooch

Clip-brooch, aquamarine, ruby, diamond & 18k gold, an ornate design centering a large emerald-cut aquamarine above a domed base section set w/old European- and full-cut diamonds & a band of small baguette rubies, the top issuing multiple arched & curled leaves in gold & gold set w/old European- and full-cut diamonds, interspersed w/slender stems w/circular-cut ruby blossoms, 2" l. (ILLUS.) **$1,410**

Pair of Gold Retro Style Dress Clips

Dress clips, bicolor 14k gold, two graduated open rings joined by a trefoil ribbon, signed by Tiffany & Co., pr. (ILLUS.) **$940**

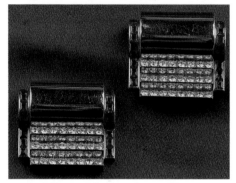

Convertible Retro Dress Clips

Dress clips, diamond, ruby & 18k gold, a rectangular form w/a rounded bar at the top above a rectangular plaque set w/48 full-cut diamonds flanked by rows of 36 step-cut rubies, platinum & 18k gold mount, convertible to a bangle bracelet, French import stamps, each 1 x 1", pr. (ILLUS.).................................... **$10,000-15,000**
Earrings, diamond & 14k rose gold, clip-on type, designed as textured leaves w/bead-set single-cut diamond trim, 2 1/8" l., pr.. **$1,058**

Retro Gold Aquamarine & Diamond Earrings

Earrings, aquamarine, diamond & 14k gold, designed as a tightly looped gold bow centered by a large emerald-cut aquamarine, two loops set w/single-cut diamond mélée, palladium-topped mount, 3/4" l., pr. (ILLUS.)... **$588**

Retro Style Gold Buckle-form Earrings

Earrings, gold (14k), clip-on type, designed as a buckle on a strap, 1 1/4" l., pr. (ILLUS.).. **$529**
Earrings, pearl, sapphire & 14k gold, an abstract flower form w/a curved row of pearls up the center flanked by rows of small round sapphires, all enclosed by stylized gold leaves, signed by Tiffany & Company, late 1940s - early 1950s, pr...... **$441**

Gold Gem-set Retro Earrings

Earrings, tourmaline, diamond & 14k gold, clip-on type, a rounded design composed of stepped gold bands centered by a large pink tourmaline cabochon flanked by two bands of channel-set step-cut green tourmalines & four rows of bead-set diamonds, pr. (ILLUS.)......................... **$823**
Necklace, gold (14k) & citrine, composed of seven stylized blossom links w/four gold petals & a fifth petal formed by a prong-set fancy-cut oval citrine, each link joined by small ring & bar chain links, marked by Wordley, Allsopp & Bliss, No. 1000, 18" l. (ILLUS. of part, top next page).................. **$940**

Retro Gem-set Gold Flower Pin

Retro Blossom-form Gold & Citrine Necklace

Pin, gem-set 14k gold, designed as a single stylized blossom w/four diamond-shaped petals, set in the center w/a full-cut diamond framed by four small sapphires, mark of American firm L.E. Garrigus & Co., ca. 1950 (ILLUS., previous page)....... **$529**

Pin, gold (14k), modeled as bow in pink & yellow gold, signed by Tiffany & Co., late 1940s - early 1950s.................................... **$353**

Retro Ring with Large Citrine

Ring, citrine, 14k gold, ruby & diamond, centering a large prong-set emerald-cut citrine in a mount w/scrolling shoulders w/ruby & diamond mélée highlights, sized, missing one diamond, size 5 1/2 (ILLUS.).. **$470**

Ring, diamond & gold, bow-shaped, bead-set w/full-, old European- and transitional-cut diamonds, diamonds weighing about 1.22 cts., 18k. gold & platinium mount, size 8 3/4....................................... **$823**

Ring, gem-set gold, the oblong top centered by a large prong-set emerald-cut aquamarine flanked by bands of small step-cut rubies & single-cut diamonds w/further diamonds at each end, scrolling gold shoulders w/floret designs, size 4 (ILLUS., top next column).................... **$1,175**

Decorative Gem-set Retro Ring

Ring, gold (18k), diamond & platinum, two old European-cut & six single-cut diamonds vertically set in platinum tiered shoulders, size 6.. **$294**

Retro Scroll-design Diamond Ring

Ring, platinum & diamond, the wide band w/a scroll device at the top prong-set w/a marquise-cut diamond weighing about 1.40 cts., surrounded by baguette & old single-cut diamonds, size 3 3/4 (ILLUS.) **$4,230**

Rare Ruby, Diamond & Gold Ring

Ring, ruby, diamond & 18k white gold, the top centered by a step-cut ruby flanked by emerald-cut & baguette diamonds, diamonds weighing about 1.80 cts., size 7 (ILLUS.)... **$14,100**

Ring, sapphire, diamond & platinum, a central band channel-set w/a graduated line of square step-cut sapphires flanked by triangular section pavé-set w/single-cut diamonds, platinum mount, ca. 1950, size 5 1/2... **$1,998**

Sets

Fine Suite of Retro Style 18k Bicolor Gold Jewelry

Bracelet & earrings, bicolor 18k gold, the bracelet composed of three rows of arched three-band links, the matching clip-on earrings designed as a three-band hoop, bracelet 7 1/16" l., the suite (ILLUS.) **$3,173**

Retro Gem-set Gold Flower-form Brooch and Ribbon Loop Earrings

Brooch & earrings, gem-set 14k bicolor gold; the brooch in the form of a rounded flower blossom w/two tiers of ruffled petals accented w/small calibré-cut rubies, the domed center set w/full-, single- and old single-cut diamonds; the stud-type earrings designed as four gold ribbon loops centered by rubies & diamonds, earrings 7/8" w., brooch 1 7/8" d., the suite (ILLUS.) **$470**

Designer Retro Brooch & Earring Suite

Brooch & earrings, ruby & 14k gold, the brooch designed as a long plume w/a curled tip, the center set w/a thin band of cushion-cut rubies, the matching earrings designed as smaller pointed plumes, designed by Raymond Yard, signed, earrings 1 1/8" l., brooch 2 1/2" l., the suite (ILLUS.) **$2,820**

Feather-form Earrings from Retro Set

Earrings & brooch, gold (14k) & ruby, designed as long curled feathers channel-set down the center w/a band of circular-cut rubies, the clip-on earrings 1 1/4" l., the brooch 2 1/2" l., the set (ILLUS.)......... **$940**

Miscellaneous Pieces

Bar pin, diamond & platinum, the long narrow filigree mount centered by an old European-cut diamond approximately .75 cts., further set w/fourteen bead & bezel-set old European-cut diamonds, millegrain accents, gold pin, ca. 1930 .... **$999**

1940s Diamond & Platinum Bracelet

Bracelet, diamond & platinum, a central narrow oblong entwined band & bar section set w/marquise-, baguette- and full-cut diamond, the narrow bracelet band further set w/diamonds, diamonds weighing about 4.40 cts., ca. 1940, 6 3/4" l. (ILLUS. of part) **$2,350**

Bracelet, enameled 18k gold & jadeite, Art Moderne style, composed of four wide arched gold links each centered by a carved blossom of green jadeite surrounded by black champlevé enamel & joined by triple-bar small links w/further black enamel trim, French guarantee stamps & mark of Gross et Cie, Paris, France, 8" l. (ILLUS., bottom of page)
.... **$4,818**

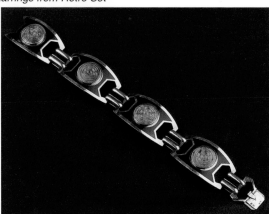

Dramatic French Art Moderne Jadeite & Enameled Gold Bracelet

Wide Gold Woven Strap Bracelet

Bracelet, gold (22k), a very wide band composed of numerous thin woven straps & mounted w/a long rectangular finely engraved closure, stamped "Sezer," tapering from 6 3/4 to 7 1/8" (ILLUS.) **$1,645**

Bracelet, pink spinel, diamond & faux ivory, bangle-type, hinged, a wide faux ivory band centered by a band & fleur-de-lis designs set w/rose-cut diamonds & centering a cushion-shaped pink spinel, narrow border bands also set w/small diamonds in patinated silver, interior circumference 6" **$2,820**

Bold Amethyst & Gold 1950s Brooch

Brooch, amethyst & 14k yellow gold, a large abstract floral form composed of nine large prong-set pear- and oval-cut amethysts w/thin gold extending from the top & base, ca. 1950s (ILLUS.)
.... **$1,116**

Gem-set Flowerpot Brooch

Brooch, amethyst, ruby, sapphire, blue spinel, spessarite, garnet, green beryl, diamond & 14k gold, a large faceted oval amethyst flowerpot overflows w/leafy gem-set stems & blossoms, silver-topped gilt & 14k gold mount, ca. 1940 (ILLUS.).. **$1,058**

Unusual Gem-set Gold Ribbon Brooch

Brooch, diamond, emerald & 18k yellow gold, an abstract openwork design of scrolled & looping ribbons w/a small cluster of stylized flowers, the gold ribbon mount centered by a small ribbon band set w/three round-cut diamonds above a cluster of stems ending in small round-cut emerald blossoms, ca. 1940 (ILLUS.)
.... **$431**

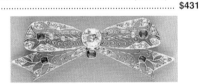

Delicate Diamond & Emerald Bow Brooch

Brooch, diamond, emerald & platinum, the delicate filigree bow-shaped mount centered by a large round old European-cut diamond weighing about 1.50 cts., the lacy frame further set w/34 small old European-cut diamonds weighing about 1.25 cts. & five small cushion-cut emeralds weighing about .85 cts., ca. 1920, 2 1/2" l. (ILLUS.) **$7,475**

Very Fine Tiffany Snowflake Brooch

Brooch, diamond, sapphire & palladium, an openwork snowflake design set w/10 French-cut, five baguette & 39 circular-cut diamonds highlighted by five step-cut blue sapphires, diamonds weighing about 2.51 cts., palladium mount, ca. 1940, signed by Tiffany & Co. w/Tiffany box, 1 3/4" d. (ILLUS.).............................. **$7,638**

Unusual Kunzite, Pearl & Diamond Brooch

Brooch, diamond, seed pearl, kunzite & platinum, an abstract design set at one end w/a large rectangular step-cut kunzite flanked by full-cut diamond accents & suspended from a double row seed pearl chain below a four-ring scroll band accented w/single-cut diamonds, in a fitted box from C. F. Carlman, Stockholm, Sweden, ca. 1940 (ILLUS.)..................... **$4,230**

Gem-set and Enamel Bird Brooch

Brooch, gem-set & enamel, calibré-cut buff-top sapphire, emerald & ruby exotic bird & flowers mounted on meandering black

enamel branch within circular frame bead-set w/seventy-six old European-cut diamonds weighing approx. 1.33 cts., platinum & gold mount, signed "E. Besson," ca. 1920s (ILLUS.)................. **$16,450**
Brooch, gold (18k), lapis lazuli & diamond, spray of three carved lapis flowers, each centering full-cut diamond mélée clusters **$1,763**

Pol Bury Gold Kinetic Brooch

Brooch, gold (18k yellow), kinetic-type, a round shape composed of narrow bars studded w/moveable gold spherules, designed & produced by Pol Bury, French maker & assay marks, signed & numbered "2/30," ca. 1970s (ILLUS.) **$5,875**

Reverse-painted Brooch with Hound Heads

Brooch, reverse-painted crystal & 14k gold, a large rectangular mount w/slightly bowed top & bottom, set w/a reverse-painted crystal depicting two hound heads, 5/8 x 1 3/8" (ILLUS.)................... **$1,880**

Gold Airplane-shaped Cuff Links

Cuff links, gold (18k), each a stylized model of a single-wing airplane joined by trace links to a bar, each set w/three small red stones, English karat stamp, 1 1/4" l., pr. (ILLUS., previous page) **$881**

Ruby & Diamond Dress Clips

Dress clips, platinum, ruby & diamond, five prong-set circular-cut rubies & sixty-one full-cut and baguette diamonds, approx. total wt. 4.48 cts., w/14k gold brooch attachment (ILLUS.) **$5,875**

Fine Citrine & Diamond Earrings

Earrings, citrine, diamond & gold, clip-on type, each set w/a large bezel-set oval fancy-cut citrine framed by a ring of full-cut diamonds, bicolor 14k gold mount, diamonds weighing about 1.00 cts., 1 1/8" l., pr. (ILLUS.) **$1,293**

Earrings, diamond & 18k yellow gold, the asymmetrical form prong-set w/single-cut diamonds suspending two gold tassels, ca. 1940, pr. **$705**

Earrings, gold (14k bi-color) & gem-set earrings, designed as a cluster of yellow & rose gold blossoms, full-cut diamond & garnet accents, 7.4 dwt., pr. **$558**

Cultured Pearl & Diamond Earrings

Earrings, South Sea cultured pearl, diamond & 18k white gold, pendant-type, the top bezel-set w/an old European-cut diamond suspending a large oval white pearl measuring 12.70 x 18.00 mm. & 12.80 x 17.00 mm., 1 1/4" l., pr. (ILLUS.) **$2,233**

Necklace, diamond & platinum, a large slender ring-form w/the thin sides graduating to a wider front section composed of two rows of diamond-set bands flanking a long central looping openwork section, set throughout w/92 transitional-, old European-, baguette- and rectangular step-cut diamonds, weighing 5.20 cts., ca. 1930, 14 3/4" l. **$17,625**

Necklace, gem-set 14k gold, slide-type, composed of 12 slides set w/cabochon green, red & blue stones & prong-set w/seed pearls, strung on a trace-link chain, ca. 1950s, 8" l. **$646**

Unique Emerald & Diamond Pendant

Pendant, emerald, diamond & 18k gold, designed w/a top prong-set square step-cut diamond weighing 3.00 cts. suspending a flexibly-set large pear-shaped emerald framed by twenty graduated old European-cut diamonds, early 20th c. (ILLUS.) **$76,375**

Pendant-necklace, jadeite & 14k gold, the green jadeite plaque carved w/gourd & leaf designs, suspended from a paper clip chain punctuated by four jadeite beads, ca. 1940s, overall 27" l. **$353**

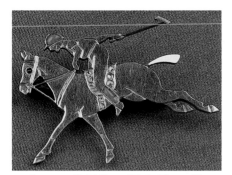

Gem-set Gold Figural Polo Player Pin

Pin, diamond, coral, onyx & 14k white gold, a flat silhouetted design of a mounted polo player, rose-cut diamond & coral accents, onyx eye in horse, Viennese assay mark & mark of the maker, ca. 1920s (ILLUS.) **$823**

Pin, reverse-painted crystal & 14k gold, a slender gold pin centered by a round mount w/a domed crystal painted w/the head of a beagle, 1 7/8" l. **$940**

Retro Ring with Large Citrine

Ring, citrine, ruby, diamond & 14k yellow gold, Retro-style, a large step-cut square citrine flanked by single-cut diamonds & step-cut ruby shoulders, size 5 1/2 (ILLUS.) **$999**

Ring, diamond & 18k white gold, the rounded top w/two back-to-back curved sections & V-form side panels, centered by a large old European-cut diamond flanked by slightly smaller diamonds, the bands bezel- and bead-set w/smaller diamonds, millegrain accents, ca. 1930, total weight 1.56 cts., size 7 3/4 .... **$1,998**

Gold Ring with Large & Small Diamonds

Ring, diamond & yellow gold, the rounded top centered by a bezel-set old European-cut diamond weighing about 1.29 cts. & flanked by small single-cut diamonds & a baguette diamond on each side, size 7 (ILLUS.) **$2,750**

Ring, diamond, yellow radiant-cut solitaire diamond weighing 1.64 cts. framed by ten faceted half-moon shaped diamonds weighing 2.13 cts., shoulders pavé-set w/twenty full-cut diamond mélée weighing 0.31 cts., custom-made 18k white gold mount, size 7 1/2............................. **$9,106**

Ring, platinum & diamond, centered w/European-cut diamond weighing approx. 1.19 cts., w/single-cut diamond highlights, millegrain accents, pierced gallery, size 6 1/2 .... **$2,585**

Very Fine Marquise Diamond Solitaire

Ring, platinum & diamond, solitaire-type, set w/a large old marquise-cut diamond weighing about 4.36 cts., flanked by tapered diamond baguettes, size 5 1/4 (ILLUS.) **$42,300**

Unusual Sapphire & Diamond 1950s Ring

Ring, sapphire & diamond, bead-set w/three pear-cut sapphires in side lobes framed by diamonds & extending from the diamond-set top, w/five full-cut, thirty single-cut & twelve baguette diamonds, platinum mounts, ca. 1950, size 4/3/4 (ILLUS.)... **$8,225**

Sapphire, Diamond & Platinum Ring

Ring, sapphire, diamond & platinum, mounted w/a 5.5 mm round blue sapphire flanked by four old European-cut diamonds in a platinum mount, ca. 1920s, size 6 3/4 (ILLUS.) **$990**

Sapphire & Diamond Ring

Ring, sapphire, diamond & platinum, prong-set w/cushion-cut sapphire weighing 3.01 cts. flanked by old mine-cut diamonds, approx. total diamond wt. 1 ct., open gallery, size 5 (ILLUS.)................... **$4,406**

1920s French Beaded Sautoir

Sautoir (necklace), beaded, the long neck strap composed of loose beaded strands alternating w/rectangular beaded panels decorated w/a stylized green bird on a purple ground, ending in a larger front panel w/a pointed tip edged in beaded fringe & beaded w/a pair of green birds on a purple ground, France, ca. 1920, unsigned, 34" l. (ILLUS.)........................... **$448**

Vintage Wedding Ring Set

Wedding ring set: diamond & platinum; the engagement band centered by a large round old European-cut diamond weighing 1.74 cts. flanked by six round full-cut diamonds; the wedding band mounted w/five round full-cut diamonds alternating w/four baguette-cut diamonds w/a total weight of .86 cts., size 7, early 20th c., the pair (ILLUS.)...................................... **$4,481**

Sets

Cuff Links from Cartier Dress Set

Man's dress set: oval cuff links & two shirt studs; platinum & black diamond, the oval cuff links each bezel-set w/an old European-cut black diamond joined by trace links to an old European-cut black diamond & onyx baguette baton, matching shirt studs, signed by Cartier, New York, w/original fitted box, ca. 1930, the set (ILLUS. of part)................................. **$9,400**

Necklace & two bracelets, composed of rock crystal beads bound by engraved silver bands, ca. 1920, necklace 22 1/2" l., the set (later jump ring closures).. **$881**

Watches

Rare Art Deco Gem-set Ball Watch

Ball watch, Art Deco style, platinum, diamond & demantoid garnet, the ball-shaped case pavé-set overall w/old mine-cut diamonds & channel-set w/step-cut garnets, opening to a white enamel dial w/red & blue Arabic numerals, enclosing a gilt jeweled movement, bezel-set diamond ball (ILLUS.).............. **$4,700**

Art Deco Diamond & Enamel Lapel Watch

Lapel watch, open faced, lady's, Whiteside & Blank, Art Deco style, diamond & enamel case, the case in black enamel w/white enamel stripes alternating w/diamond mélée stripes, the ivorytone dial w/Arabic numerals, cabochon black onyx winding stem, a Cressarow 18-jewel adjusted damascened nickel movement, platinum-topped 18k gold mount, suspended from a long shaped rectangular open watch pin outlined w/rose-cut diamonds & knife edge bar links, retailed by Tiffany & Co., minor edge nick, 2 1/2" l. (ILLUS.).. **$1,293**

Unusual Enameled Art Deco Watch

Pendant watch, lady's, enameled sterling silver, Art Deco style, the domed & paneled case decorated w/alternating panels of black & green enamel, the small top w/alternating yellow & black enameled panels, the metal dial w/abstract numerals, suspended from a tapering enameled baton link chain, dial replaced, overall 19" l. (ILLUS.).. **$353**

Fine Cartier Art Deco Pendant Watch

Pendant watch, open-faced, lady's, Cartier, Paris, Art Deco style, platinum & diamond, the squared diamond-shaped ivorytone dial w/Roman numerals, 18-jewel movement w/eight adjustments, the back of the case edged in tiny rose-cut diamonds, centered by diamond-set geometric monogram on a black enameled ground, suspended from a black cord w/pavé-set rose-cut diamond slide, triple signed, overall 26" l. (ILLUS. of back of case) **$6,463**

Lady's Art Deco Wristwatch. Courtesy of Davida Baron

Agassiz Platinum & Diamond Pocket Watch

Pocket watch, open-faced, man's, Agassiz, platinum & diamond, the goldtone dial w/applied diamond-set Roman & abstract numerals, enclosing a signed 17-jewel unadjusted lever escapement movement, plain polished case (ILLUS.) **$1,175**

Pocket watch, open-faced, man's, American Watch & Clock & Patek Philippe, Art Deco style 18k gold case, goldtone dial w/Arabic numerals, diamond winding stem, enclosing a Patek Philippe movement dated 1891, cased signed by the American Watch & Clock Co..................... **$764**

Pocket watch, open-faced, man's, Meylan for Tiffany & Co., Art Deco style, platinum, the silvertone round dial w/Arabic numerals & a subsidiary seconds dial, enclosing a 19-jewel seven adjustment lever escapement movement, ultra thin plain polished case w/engraved edges, mark of Whiteside & Blank, reverse w/ground initials (ILLUS., top next column) **$1,763**

Fine Art Deco Man's Pocket Watch

Fine Tiffany Art Deco Pocket Watch

Pocket watch, open-faced, man's, Tiffany & Co., Art Deco style, gem-set 18k gold, the hexagonal goldtone dial w/blue Arabic numerals, bezel set w/French-cut diamonds, emeralds, rubies & sapphires, enclosing a signed Touchon 19-jewel movement w/eight adjustments marked "Extra," plain polished back of case w/rose-cut diamond accents, triple signed (ILLUS.) **$4,700**

Wristwatch, lady's, Art Deco style, gold-filled, the octagonal watch case w/etched scrollwork, the white dial w/Arabic numerals & signed "Waltham," dated 1927 inside, on a bracelet composed of rectangular open links (ILLUS., top previous page).. **$150-200**

Wristwatch, lady's, Art Deco style, platinum & diamond, a silvertone dial w/Arabic numerals, 17-jewel Swiss movement, the rectangular case & shaped lugs set w/baguette & single-cut diamonds, completed by a 14k white gold mesh band w/millegrain accents, dial replaced, 6 1/2" l. **$705**

Audiguet Lady's Diamond Wristwatch

Wristwatch, lady's, Audiguet, Art Deco style, platinum & diamond, the rectangular ivorytone metal dial w/Arabic numerals, the bezel & rectangular lugs bead-set w/transitional-cut diamonds, enclosing a manual-wind 17-jewel movement, diamonds weighing about 1.56 cts., case w/engraved accents, completed by a black lizard band w/an additional 18k gold brickwork band (ILLUS.)................. **$1,293**

Modern-style Cartier Lady's Watch

Wristwatch, lady's, Cartier, 18k gold, platinum, enamel & diamond, the round dial framed by bezel-set full-cut diamonds, the blue enamel dial w/baton numerals, diamonds weighing about 1.00 cts., completed by a band composed of ring-shaped blue enamel links, French guarantee stamps, ca.1960-70, 7 3/4" l. (ILLUS.)..... **$7,050**

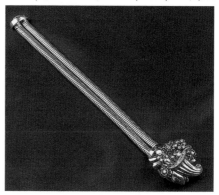

Retro Style Gold, Diamond & Ruby Watch

Wristwatch, lady's, Catena, Retro style, 14k gold, diamond & ruby case in the form of a flower basket w/the blossoms trimmed w/ruby & diamond mélée, the watch w/an ivorytone dial w/Arabic & baton numerals, manual-wind 17-jewel movement, attached to a tubogas gold bracelet, boxed, overall 7" l. (ILLUS.)..... **$1,175**

Wristwatch, lady's, David Webb, 18k gold, the bangle bracelet w/an overall quilted design enclosing the watch w/an ivorytone dial w/Arabic numerals, 14k gold watch case, signed but designer, intercircumference 6 1/4" (ILLUS., top next page)... **$3,290**

Wristwatch, lady's, Doxa, Retro style, 18k gold, the silvertone dial w/abstract numerals, manual-wind movement, completed by a bracelet of arched links, no movement, Swiss assay marks, 7 1/4" l. ... **$588**

Early Lady's Hamilton Diamond Watch

Wristwatch, lady's, Hamilton, 14k white gold & 10% iridium platinum & diamond, the small rectangular watch framed by 62 round single-cut prong-set diamonds & six straight baguette-cut diamonds, the openwork link band mounted w/a total of sixteen round brilliant-cut bezel-set diamonds, along w/four loose bracelet links containing eight round single-cut diamonds, ca. 1930s (ILLUS.) **$1,016**

David Webb-designed Gold Bangle Bracelet Watch

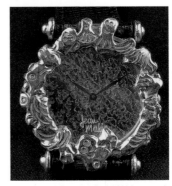

Jean Mahie 18k Gold Wristwatch

Wristwatch, lady's, Jean Mahie, 18k gold, the rounded textured dial & wide scrolled bezel enclosing a quartz movement, joined by cylindrical lugs to a tapered black leather strap completed by a conforming clasp, dial & case signed (ILLUS.) **$3,525**

Fine Lady Elgin Diamond Wristwatch

Wristwatch, lady's, Lady Elgin, platinum & diamond, the rectangular silvertone metal dial w/Arabic & abstract numeral indicators, enclosing a signed 19-jewel movement, the bezel, lugs & loop-link bracelet set w/circular-cut & bagette diamonds weighing about 2.14 cts., 6 3/8" l. (ILLUS.).. **$1,763**

Fine Hamilton Lady's Wristwatch

Wristwatch, lady's, Hamilton, platinum & diamond, square case w/the bezel & lugs set w/baguette & full-cut diamonds, bracelet of box-set full-cut diamonds, square ivorytone dial w/Arabic numerals, 17-jewel movement, diamonds weighing about 3.75 cts., 6 3/4" l. (ILLUS.) **$2,350**

Wristwatch, lady's, Hamilton, Retro style, 14k gold & diamond, the silvertone dial w/Arabic & abstract numerals, joined by arched diamond-set lugs to a brickwork strap, 6 3/8" l. **$353**

Wristwatch, lady's, Omega, 14k gold & diamond, the textured goldtone dial w/abstract numerals within a hinged bangle prong-set w/27 marquise-cut & 13 full-cut diamonds, Omega manual-wind movement, interior circumference 6 1/4" **$1,293**

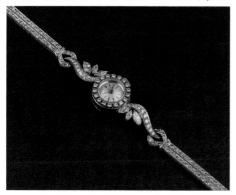

Lady's Patek Philippe Deco Wristwatch

Wristwatch, lady's, Patek Philippe, Art Deco style, platinum & diamond, a silvertone dial w/baton numerals, round platinum case enclosing a 20-jewel movement, the bezel set w/full-cut diamonds & joined to serpentine scroll & leaf links set w/full- and marquise-cut diamonds, the 14k white gold rectangular link strap further set w/diamonds, triple signed, later bracelet, diamonds weighing about 2.60 cts., 6 3/4" l. (ILLUS.) **$2,703**

Fine Lady's Patek Philippe Wristwatch

Wristwatch, lady's, Patek Philippe, the goldtone round dial w/Arabic numerals, enclosing a manual-wind 20-jewel movement, the 18k gold case completed by a flat gold mesh strap adjustable to three sizes, triple signed (ILLUS.) **$2,233**

Wristwatch, lady's, Piaget, gold (18k), jade & gems, the green jade dial within a bezel set w/full-cut diamonds & an emerald at the 12, 3, 6 & 9 positions, enclosing a manual wind movement, completed by a tapering mesh strap, (ILLUS., top next column) **$3,643**

Unusal Piaget Jade & Gem-set Wristwatch

Lady's R. Yard Retro Style Wristwatch

Wristwatch, lady's, Raymond Yard, Retro style, diamond, aquamarine & gold, the oblong silvertone metal dial w/Arabic numerals, enclosing a Movado 17-jewel movement, the platinum case set at each end a large triangular fancy-cut aquamarine accented by diamonds, completed by a later 14k white gold bracelet, 7 3/8" l. (ILLUS.) **$2,938**

Rolex Lady's Oyster Perpetual Watch

Wristwatch, lady's, Rolex, 14k gold, Oyster Perpetual model, the goldtone round dial w/baton numerals, fluted bezel enclosing an automatic movement, completed by a jubilee band w/deployant clasp, w/original box & papers (ILLUS., previous page) **$3,173**

Art Deco Lady's Tiffany Wristwatch

Wristwatch, lady's, Tiffany & Co., Art Deco style, platinum, sapphire & diamond, the rectangular white dial w/Arabic numerals, engraved bezel & edges set w/old single-cut diamonds & calibré-cut sapphires, enclosing a Huguenin 17-jewel three-adjustment manual-wind damascened movement, case w/mark of maker White-

side & Blank, completed by a woven bracelet, signed, 6 1/4" l. (ILLUS.) **$1,880**

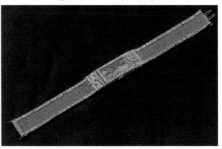

Fine Vacheron & Constantin Art Deco Watch

Wristwatch, lady's, Vacheron & Constantin, Art Deco style, platinum & diamond, the rectangular watch frame, bezel & lugs bead-set w/old single-cut diamond mélée & millegrain accents, foliate-engraved back & sides, the watch integrated into a mesh bracelet framed by box-set old single-cut diamond mélée, the rectangular silvertone dial w/abstract numerals, a manual-wind 18-jewel movement, five adjustments, later dial, closure w/evidence of gold solder, 6 1/4" l. (ILLUS.) **$6,463**

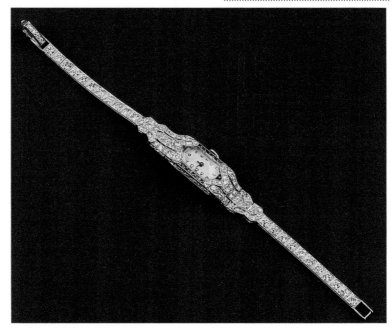

Fine Art Deco Diamond & Sapphire Wristwatch with Waltham Movement

Wristwatch, lady's, Waltham, Art Deco style, diamond & sapphire, the silvertone metal dial w/letter numerals, enclosing the 17-jewel movement, the wide openwork tapering flanking links box & bead-set w/full- and single-cut diamonds w/the dial flanked by thin bands of French- and calibré-cut sapphires, diamond-set bracelet, diamonds weighing about 4.28 cts., millegrain accents, foliate engraved sides (ILLUS.)
.... **$3,995**

Hublot Man's Chronograph Superb

Wristwatch, man's, Hublot, stainless steel, Chronograph Superb model, the round case enclosing the blue dial w/date aperture & three subsidiary dials, bezel w/tachometric scale, a water-resistant automatic movement, w/a rubber band & deployant clasp (ILLUS.).......................... **$2,350**

Fine Patek Philippe Man's Wristwatch

Wristwatch, man's, Patek Philippe, 18k gold, "Calatrava" model, the round silvertone dial w/applied gold Arabic numerals & a subsidiary seconds dial, enclosing a manual-wind 18-jewel five position movement, completed by a leather strap (ILLUS.).. **$6,756**

Patek Philippe Calatrava Wristwatch

Wristwatch, man's, Patek Philippe, "Calatrava" model, the round goldtone dial w/baton indicators, enclosing a jeweled manual-wind movement, 18k gold case joined to a brown leather adjustable strap (ILLUS.).. **$4,700**

Piaget Man's Gold Wristwatch

Wristwatch, man's, Piaget, 18k gold, the squared blue metal dial w/Roman numerals, quartz movement, back-set, completed by a trace link mesh strap (ILLUS.) **$1,293**

CHAPTER 5

Twentieth Century Designer & Fine Estate Jewelry

Designers

Boucheron

Fine Boucheron Gold & Diamond Brooch

Brooch, diamond & 18k gold, a large abstract flower form composed of entwined triple ropetwist rings accented by curved bands of full-cut diamonds, diamonds weighing about 6.06 cts., signed, 2 1/8" d. (ILLUS.) **$9,400**

Boucheron Amethyst & Gold Earrings

Earrings, amethyst & 18k bicolor gold, clip-on type, each half-hoop bezel-set w/a cabochon amethyst above a lower ribbed dome, signed, numbered & w/French guarantee stamp, pr. (ILLUS.)................ **$1,058**

Boucheron Gold & Diamond Earrings

Earrings, diamond & 18k gold, clip-on type, each of oblong form w/a finely ribbed lower panel below thin oval rings enclosing a cluster of pavé-set full-cut diamonds, No. 523 2858, signed, French guarantee stamps, pr. (ILLUS.)............................... **$1,998**

Rare Boucheron Natural Pearl Ring

Ring, natural pearl, diamond & platinum, centering a grey natural pearl measuring 12.80 mm, the shoulders w/channel-set baguette diamonds & bead-set full-cut diamond mélée, signed, France (ILLUS.) **$18,800**

Buccellati (Mario)

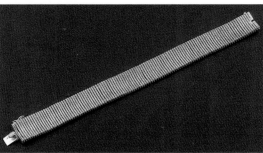

Buccellati Flexible Flat Gold Bracelet

Bracelet, gold (18k), flat flexible straight-line fine rib design, signed, 6 7/8" l. (ILLUS., bottom previous page) **$2,115**

Rare Buccellati Gold & Gem Bracelet

Bracelet, sapphire, emerald & 18k gold, cuff-type, the wide hinged gold band w/a textured surface decorated w/a repeating design of a large oval emerald cabochon encircled by sapphire cabochons alternating w/pairs of sapphire cabochons, signed (ILLUS.) **$12,338**

Buccellati Gem-set Gold Flower Brooch

Brooch, gem-set bicolor 18k gold, designed as a flower sprig, the stem w/two long serrated dark gold leaves flanking the flower w/five rolled petals centered by a circular-cut blue sapphire, signed, w/original presentation pouch, 1 1/2 x 2 1/4" (ILLUS.) **$1,293**

Brooch, turquoise & 18k gold, designed as a gold leafy stem topped by two large blossoms centered by large turquoise cabochons, signed (ILLUS., top next column) **$1,998**

Clip, gem-set 18k gold, designed as a stylized flower & leaf, the tall curved feather-like leaf set w/circular-cut emeralds & enclosing a stylized blossom composed of oval cabochon sapphires, engraved mount, signed, 1 x 1 1/2" (ILLUS., middle next column) **$8,250**

Buccellati Double Flower Brooch

Stylized Leaf & Flower Buccellati Clip

Earrings, diamond, designed as a spray of rose-cut diamond blossoms, silver-topped 18k gold mounts, signed, Italy, in original box **$4,994**

Buccellati Gem-set Floral Earrings

Earrings, gem-set 18k bicolor gold, stud-type, each designed as a ball-form cluster of three large gold blossoms accented w/cabochon rubies & sapphires, signed & dated 1996, pr. (ILLUS.) **$3,525**

Fine Buccellati Braided Gold & Pearl Necklace

Necklace, cultured pearl & bicolor 18k gold, composed of a slender braided gold band set w/30 round white pearls w/rose overtones measuring about 5.80 mm, signed, 15" l. (ILLUS., top of page)..................... **$4,700**

Bold Buccellati Gold Bead Necklace

Necklace, gold (18k), composed of large round gadrooned beads, signed, Italy, ca. 1970, 30" l. (ILLUS.) **$5,405**

Buccellati Gem-set Flower Stem Pin

Pin, diamond & gem-set 18k gold, designed as a leafy stem topped by two round blossoms, one blossom set w/a sapphire & the other a ruby, rose-cut diamond accents, signed (ILLUS.)............................ **$1,880**

Bulgari

Bulgari Bicolor Gold Cuff Bracelet

Bracelet, bicolor 18k gold, cuff-style, "Parentesi" design, a wide band composed of four snake link white gold bands mounted at the top w/two shaped double yellow gold rings, signed, interior circumference 6" (ILLUS.) **$2,703**

Bulgari Gold "Parentesi" Bracelet

Bracelet, bicolor 18k gold, "Parentesi" design, cuff-style, the flat flexible ropetwist band ending in shaped terminals (ILLUS.)
.... **$1,175**

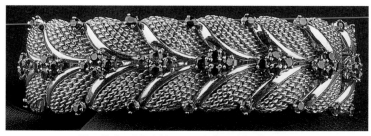

Fine Bulgari Gold Leaves & Sapphire Bracelet

Bracelet, sapphire & 18k gold, designed as links of paired leaf-like devices decorated w/fine ropetwist bands & centered by clusters of small blue sapphires w/a single sapphire at the tip of each leaf, signed, 7" l. (ILLUS., top of page) **$7,638**

Bold Gold & Topaz Bulgari Earrings

Earrings, bicolor 18k gold & blue topaz, clip-on type, each w/a wide square tapering two-color gold frame centered by a pyramidal-cut cabochon blue topaz, signed, pr. (ILLUS.) **$2,703**

Bulgari Diamond & Gold Chevron Earrings

Earrings, diamond & 18k gold, clip-on type, each in the form of a chevron band bead-set w/full-cut diamonds, diamonds weighing about 2.00 cts., signed, pr. (ILLUS.)
.... **$3,173**
Earrings, diamond & 18k gold, "Spiga" design, a wide gold loop w/a bold zigzag design highlighted by a band of pavé-set diamonds, signed, original box, 1" l., pr. (ILLUS., top next column) **$2,938**

Fine Bulgari "Spiga" Design Earrings

Bulgari Pierced Sphere Gold Earrings

Earrings, gold (18k), each designed as a geometrically-pierced sphere, signed, pr. (ILLUS.) **$1,175**

Bulgari "Spiga" Gold Earrings

Earrings, gold (18k), "Spiga" design, each composed of two bands w/a herringbone design, signed, pr. (ILLUS.) **$1,998**

Bulgari Fern Leaf-style Gold Necklace

Necklace, gold (18k), formed of a textured fringe of graduated fern-like leaves strung on a foxtail chain, signed & w/mark of the maker & French export mark, w/original sleeve marked "Bulgari - Roma," w/six additional links, 14" l. (ILLUS.) **$4,113**

Bulgari Gold Chain & Silver Coin Necklace

Necklace, gold (18k) & silver coin, the curb link chain suspending a bezel-set w/a period silver coin w/the portrait of King Ferdinando III of Sicily on one side & dated 1793 on the other, signed, overall 27 1/2" l. (ILLUS.).................................. **$3,819**

Bulgari Signed Gold Heart Pendant

Pendant-necklace, gold (18k) & leather, the black leather cord suspending a thick stylized openwork heart inscribed "BVL-GARI," completed by a hook closure, signed, 14 1/4" l. (ILLUS.) **$588**

Bulgari Wide Gold & Diamond Ring

Ring, diamond & 18k gold, the wide band w/the top decorated w/a squared quatrefoil reserve pavé-set w/40 full-cut diamonds, signed, size 7 1/4 (ILLUS.)......... **$1,763**

Diamond-Set Gold Bulgari Bypass Ring

Ring, diamond-set 18k yellow gold, bypass-style, the two zigzag-decorated bands w/full-cut diamond terminals, signed, size 7 1/2 (ILLUS.)... **$1,116**

Bulgari Gem-set Gold Ring

Ring, gem-set 18k gold, the domed top w/a quatrefoil design w/each loop set w/a cabochon aquamarine, citrine, green tourmaline & pink tourmaline, signed, size 5 1/2 (ILLUS.) **$2,233**

Bulgari White Gold Two-Stone Ring

Ring, gem-set 18k white gold, two-stone style, set w/an oval-cut citrine beside a matching amethyst, a ribbed double-form band, signed, size 6 (ILLUS., previous page) $940
Ring, lapis lazuli & 18k gold, the top centered by a lapis tablet completed by a gold tubogas band, signed $881

Calder (Alexander)

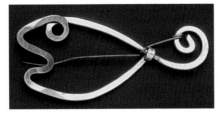

Rare Calder-made Silver Fish Brooch

Brooch, silver, designed as an openwork stylized fish w/a curled tail made from a single strand of planished silver flat wire, unsigned but descended directly from the artist, 1 7/8 x 4 3/8" (ILLUS.) $36,425

Extraordinary Calder Silver Brooch

Brooch, silver, large abstract modernistic design composed single flattened silver wire planished into spiral & scroll designs, designed & produced by Alexander Calder, ca. 1942 (ILLUS.) $88,775

Unusual Calder-made Silver Brooch

Brooch, silver, the flat patinated undulating band ending in a large tight scroll, unsigned, closure added, 1 3/4 x 4 1/4" (ILLUS.) $23,500

Chanel (Coco)

Gold Gem-set Gold Chanel ring

Ring, gem-set 18k gold, a wide gold band mounted w/alternating heavy square & round frames each set w/a fancy-cut amethyst, green beryl, citrine, pyrope & spessartine garnet, No. 9C335, French guarantee mark, size 7 1/4 (ILLUS.) $1,058

Chanel Gem-set White Gold Ring

Ring, gem-set 18k white gold, the large squared top centered by a large cushion-shape faceted amethyst framed by fancy-cut iolites & pink tourmalines, size 7 (ILLUS.) $3,525

Hermès

Hermès Enameled Gold "H" Bracelet

Bracelet, enameled gold, "H" bangle-style, the narrow gold band w/an enameled black inset band joined by a H-shaped clasp, signed, 1/2" w., interior circumference 6 5/8" (ILLUS.) $353

Fine Hermès Gold Cuff Bracelet

Bracelet, gold (18k), cuff-style, "Coriolis" design, the wide band pierced w/bold scrolling designs, signed (ILLUS., previous page) **$3,643**

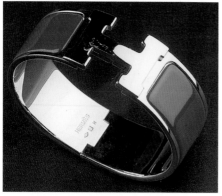

Red Enameled Hermès Bracelet

Bracelet, goldtone & enamel, "H" style bangle-type, the hinged wide band enameled in bright red, swiveling H-form closure, signed (ILLUS.) **$470**

Hermès Sterling & Gold Buckle Bracelet

Bracelet, sterling silver & 18k gold, buckle-style, composed of large flattened curb links completed by an 18k gold buckle clasp, signed, French guarantee stamp, 7 3/4 to 8 3/8" l. (ILLUS.)........................ **$1,293**

Bracelet, sterling silver & 18k gold, composed of silver rectangular links joined by gold H-form links completed by an integral clasp, mark of French maker & guarantee stamp, 7 3/8" l. **$1,116**

Hermès, Paris Snail Brooch

Brooch, lapis lazuli & 18k gold, model of a stylized snail w/a gold body & the shell carved from lapis, signed, Paris, 1 1/2" l. (ILLUS.).. **$999**

Square Studded Gold Hermès Cuff Links

Cuff links, sterling silver & 18k gold, each designed as a square w/studded corners joined to a smaller square, signed, French guarantee stamps, 1/2" l., pr. (ILLUS.)........ **$705**

Hermès Silver and Gold Cuff Links

Cuff links, sterling silver & gold, the silver oblong double links inlaid w/gold, signed, French guarantee stamps, pr. (ILLUS.) **$646**

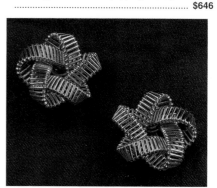

Hermès Gold Ribbon Design Earrings

Earrings, gold (18k), each designed as two entwined ribbons w/ladder-like openwork designs, signed, pr. (ILLUS.) **$2,820**

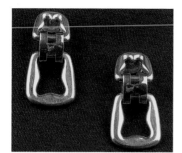

Hermès Sterling & Gold Earrings

Earrings, sterling silver & 18k gold, pendant-type, composed of open tapering rectangular links joined by a gold H-form link, mark of maker, signed & w/French guarantee stamps, 1 1/4" l., pr. (ILLUS.).... **$382**

Hermes Diamond "X" & Gold Ring

Ring, diamond & 18k gold, the tapering gold band w/an opening at the top joined by a diamond-set "X," a gold stitch design along the band edges, No. 32663, signed, French guarantee stamps (ILLUS.).......... **$1,528**

Hermès Gold Pyramidal Ring

Ring, gold (18k), a wide band w/pyramidal design on the top, signed, size 9 3/4 (ILLUS.) **$1,116**
Ring, gold (18k), designed as a bold gold knot, marked & signed, in original fitted box, size 6 .... **$940**

Hermès Sterling & Gold Ring

Ring, sterling silver & 18k gold, designed as a ropetwist strap w/buckle, signed, No. 51, size 4 1/4 (ILLUS.) **$470**

Hermès Silver & Gold Ring

Ring, sterling silver & 18k gold, the wide silver band inset w/a wide band of gold, the top centered by a silver "H," No. 51, signed, size 5 1/2 (ILLUS.)........................ **$235**

Heyman (Oscar)

Rare Heyman Sapphire, Diamond & Platinum Bracelet

Bracelet, platinum, sapphire & diamond, composed of square cut-corner & trapezoidal step-cut light blue sapphires joined by full-cut diamond bars & shaped links, signed, No. 64699, 7" l. (ILLUS., bottom previous page) **$21,150**

Rare Heyman Gem-set Floral Brooch

Brooch-pendant, emerald, diamond & platinum, the rounded design composed of tightly packed flowers w/the petals prongset w/oval & marquise-cut diamonds & centered & accented by oval, round & marquise-cut emeralds, diamonds weighing about 16.00 cts., the emeralds weighing about 3.00 cts., unsigned, No. 70111 (ILLUS.)..................................... **$21,150**

Necklace, diamond & 18k white gold, composed of wide & narrow alternating links forming a scalloped efffect, set overall w/208 princess-cut diamonds weighing about 15.00 cts., unsigned, No. 504057, 15 1/2" l. (ILLUS., bottom of page) **$12,338**

Fine Oscar Heyman Diamond Necklace

Kieselstein-Cord (B.)

Grouping of B. Kieselstein-Cord Gold & Gem Bat Pattern Jewelry

Bracelet, gold (18k), diamond & ruby, "Bat" patt., the flexible links each designed as a stylized bat set w/princess-cut diamonds & circular-cut rubies, diamonds weighing about 1.74 cts., signed (ILLUS. far left with other Kieselstein-Cord Bat pieces, top of page)................................ **$5,523**

Brooch, gold (18k), diamond & ruby, "Bat" patt., composed of two facing bats separated by a panel of channel-set diamond baguettes & pavé-set full-cut diamond mélée highlights, ruby eyes, the back designed as a spider's web, signed, 2" l. (ILLUS. far right with other Kieselstein-Cord Bat pieces, top of page).. **$3,525**

Cuff links, bloodstone & 18k gold, each bezel-set w/a bloodstone intaglio w/a Greek inscription, joining a bar link, signed & dated, pr... **$588**

Earrings, gold (18k), diamond & ruby, "Bat" patt., composed of two flexible bat-form links w/circular cut rubies & princess-cut diamonds, signed, pr. (ILLUS. third from left with other Kieselstein-Cord Bat pieces, top of page) **$2,233**

Gem-set Heart & Crown Earrings

Earrings, sapphire, diamond & 18k gold, each designed as a crowned heart w/ the heart set overall w/circular-cut sapphires, full-cut diamond highlights, signed, pr. (ILLUS.)... **$1,880**

Kieselstein-Cord Sapphire Ring

Ring, blue & yellow sapphire & 18k gold, the top centered by a prong-set oval-cut blue sapphire flanked by circular-cut yellow sapphires, gold mount, size 4 1/2, together w/a gold band, both signed (ILLUS.) **$1,998**

Ring, gold (18k), diamond & ruby, "Bat" patt., composed of a bat gripping a frame enclosing a step-cut tourmaline, circular-cut ruby eyes, signed, size 6 3/4 (ILLUS. second from left with other Kieselstein-Cord Bat pieces, top of page) **$2,115**

La Nouvelle Bague

La Nouvelle Bague Heart-form Earrings

Earrings, bicolor 18k gold, enamel & diamond, clip-on type, a stylized heart composed of yellow gold & deep red enamel enclosing a pavé-set diamond circle above a small inset white gold bead, the top composed of two white gold rings suspended from a yellow gold bead, signed, each 7/8" l., pr. (ILLUS.) **$940**

Diamond & Gold La Nouvelle Bague Pendant

Pendant-necklace, bicolor 18k gold & diamond, the white gold spade-shaped banded pendant centered at the top by a round dome pavé-set overall w/full-cut diamond, two upper yellow gold bars also set w/diamonds, suspended from a high heavy white gold arch enclosing a diamond-set circle, suspended from a fine ropetwist chain, signed, pendant 2" l., overall 32" l. (ILLUS.) **$2,820**

La Nouvelle Bague Heart-form Pendant

Pendant-necklace, bicolor 18k gold, enamel & diamond, stylized heart shape pendant decorated w/wavy navy blue enamel bands alternating w/wavy white gold bands, a large & small round pavé-set diamond reserve, the top mounted w/a yellow gold band & high white gold loop enclosing a yellow gold ball, suspended from a slender gold ropetwist chain, signed, overall 33 1/2" l. (ILLUS. of pendant) **$999**

Ring, bicolor 18k gold, enamel & diamond, composed of a navy blue enameled band & a gold band overlaid by an angled pavé-set diamond band, signed, size 7 (ILLUS., top next column) **$940**

Three-band La Nouvelle Bague Ring

Four Band La Nouvelle Bague Ring

Ring, tricolor 18k gold, enamel & diamond, composed of four bands joined by a pavé-set diamond X, red enamel accents, signed, size 7 (ILLUS.) **$1,175**

La Nouvelle Bague Bracelet & Earrings in Gem-set Gold & Enamel

Set: bangle bracelet & earrings, enamel & gem-set 18k bicolor gold; the bracelet half in gold & half enameled in marbleized blue w/bands of green enamel further accented w/a section of gold rings & a spearhead device set w/diamonds, the matching clip-on earrings formed by a wide gold band applied w/a spearhead device set w/diamonds & a thin blue enamel band along one side, signed, the suite (ILLUS.) **$3,290**

Unusual Suite of La Nouvelle Bague Jewelry in Gold & Diamond-set Enamel

Set: bangle bracelet, earrings, ring & pendant-necklace; diamond-set bicolor 18k gold & enamel, the bracelet in gold w/four sections of teal blue enamel, the ring composed of a narrow teal blue enameled band & a wide gold band centered by a thin diamond-set band, the pendant-earrings w/a white gold ball w/a white gold link to a flat round disk enameled in navy blue & teal blue w/dots & a central square enclosing small diamonds, the pendant-necklace designed as a flat square enameled in teal blue centered by diamonds, ring size 7, bracelet w/7" interior circumference, pendant necklace overall 15 1/2" l., the suite (ILLUS.)
.... **$2,350**

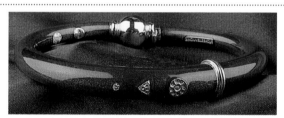

Green Enamel & Diamond-set Gold Bangle Bracelet & Ring

Set: bracelet & ring; enamel, diamond & 18k gold, the hinged narrow band decorated w/dark green enamel, the top w/a thin gold band & a small round & triangular reserve set w/diamonds, matching multi-band ring w/an X design on top, signed, ring size 7, the set (ILLUS.) **$823**

La Nouvelle Bague Gem-set Gold & Enamel Bracelet & Ring

Set: bracelet & ring; gem-set 18k bicolor gold & enamel, the hinged bangle w/marbleized blue enamel w/a top ringed gold band set w/a thin ring of channel-set green garnets & an angled band set w/diamonds, matching ring size 7 1/4", the set (ILLUS.) **$2,938**

Lalaounis (Ilias)

Lalaounis Round Cabochon Ruby Brooch

Brooch, cabochon ruby & 18k gold, round
slightly scalloped gold mount set overall
w/tightly packed cabochon rubies, Athens, Greece, marked & w/original pouch,
1 5/8" d. (ILLUS.) **$705**

Brooch, gold (18k), modeled as a serpent,
signed, w/original pouch, 2 1/4 x 2 1/4" **$940**

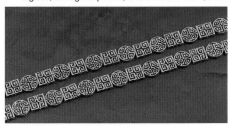

Lalaounis Gold Geometric Necklaace

Necklace, gold (18k), composed of alternating pierced square & round geometric
links, marked, Athens, Greece, 14 1/2" l.
(ILLUS. of part) **$2,703**

La Nouvelle Bague Earring & Ring Set

Set: earrings & ring; enamel & diamond-set
18k gold, the ring w/a squared top w/an
undulating border band of red enamel
centering a circle set w/small diamonds,
the pendant-style earrings w/a gold &
blue enameled loop suspending a small
square of black enamel centered by a circle set w/small diamonds, ring size 6 1/2,
the suite (ILLUS.) **$705**

Bold Lalaounis Gold Disk Necklace

Necklace, gold (18k), designed as hammered disks interspersed w/beaded rondels strung on a herringbone chain, boxed, 16 1/4" l. (ILLUS., bottom previous page) **$6,463**

Necklace, gold (18k), torque-style, hinged & centering a knot, unsigned but in Lalaounis box, No. R. 12, interior circumference 12" **$529**

Gem-set Gold Lalaounis Pendant

Pendant, gem-set 18k gold, a flat round disk centered by a bezel-set cabochon ruby surrounded by alternating cabochon emeralds & seed pearls, unsigned but in Lalaounis pouch, Athens, Greece, 1" d. (ILLUS.).. **$558**

Marina B.

Marina B. Bicolor Gold Bangle Bracelet

Bracelet, bicolor 18k gold, bangle-type, composed of abstract rounded links alternating w/abstract spade-form links, signed, interior circumference 5 3/4" (ILLUS.) **$1,175**

Simple Citrine & Gold Ring

Ring, citrine & 18k bicolor gold, a large oval facet-cut citrine in a simple gold mount, signed, size 7 (ILLUS.)............................ **$1,410**

Marina B. Gold & Diamond Ring

Ring, diamond & 18k gold, designed as a band of three curved gold teardrop devices each pavé-set w/diamonds, signed, size 6 1/2 (ILLUS.) **$1,293**

Marina B. Pink Tourmaline Ring

Ring, pink tourmaline, diamond & 18k gold, the top set w/an oval cabochon pink tourmaline, the gallery w/diamond mélée heart designs, signed, size 6 1/2 (ILLUS.) **$1,175**

Mexican Designers

Unusual Sterling Silver Mask-shaped Belt Buckle

Belt buckle, sterling silver, designed as a long narrow face mask w/pointed ends, round black cabochon stone eyes, signed by Hubert Harmon, Taxco, 5 1/2" l. (ILLUS.) **$2,468**

Aquilar Silver Bracelet with Abstract Links

"Georgia O'Keefe" Silver & Suede Bracelet

Bracelet, silver & black suede, "Georgia
O'Keefe" model, the wide band of suede
decorated w/large line-engraved "X" designs, marked by Hector Aquilar, 6 3/4" l.
(ILLUS.).. **$3,525**

Silver Hinged Bracelet by Los Castillo

Bracelet, silver, composed of hinged plaques
w/ geometric designs, No. 117, signed by
Los Castillo, Taxco, 7" l. (ILLUS.)................. **$470**
Bracelet, silver, composed of narrow links
w/engraved designs, bordered by double
circular links, applied bead accents,
signed by Emma, Taxco, 7 1/2" l. **$705**

Bracelet, silver, composed of oblong
domed links w/abstract engraved scrolls,
mounted at each side by a heavy link
chain, mark of Hector Aquilar, Taxco,
7" l. (ILLUS., top of page) **$764**

Aquilar Loop Link Silver Bracelet

Bracelet, silver, composed of open links
formed by joined rounded arches each
w/a ball-form tip, mark of Hector Aquilar,
Taxco, 8" l. (ILLUS.).................................... **$999**

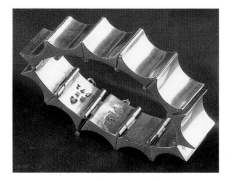

Taxco, Mexico Silver Bracelet

Bracelet, silver, composed of wide, con-
cave links, No. ZZ 571, mark of maker
Antonio, Taxco, 6" l. (ILLUS.) **$1,116**

Sterling Bracelet with Four-petaled Links

Spratling Silver & Wood Cuff Bracelet

Bracelet, silver & wood, cuff-style, wide band composed of alternating silver & wood scallops w/bead accents, maker's mark of Spratling, Taxco (ILLUS.).............. **$999**

Bracelet, sterling silver, composed of large four-petal links deeply incised w/scrolls & a center button in each petal, signed by Los Castillo, Taxco, wear to signature, 7" l. (ILLUS., top of page)......................... **$529**

Bracelet, sterling silver, composed of stylized geometric links w/engraved accents, marked by Spratling, Taxco, 7" l. **$705**

Bracelets, silver, cuff-style bangles, each w/engraved ropetwist design, marked by Spratling, Taxco, ca. 1940s, interior circumference 5 1/2", pr............................ **$1,410**

Silver & Amethyst Bow Brooch by Spratling

Brooch, silver and amethyst, designed as a large stylized bow suspending a large

amethyst cabochon, signed by Spratling, Taxco, 4 1/2" w. (ILLUS.)......................... **$470**

Silver Ribbon Brooch by Spratling

Brooch, silver & bronze, designed as two curled silver ribbons suspended from a bronze disk, mark of Spratling, Taxco, 3 1/8" l. (ILLUS.) **$470**

Brooch, silver & coral, designed as a ribbed sea horse w/a coral cabochon eye, signed by Matl, Taxco, 2 1/2" l. (ILLUS. left with two other figural Mexican silver brooches, top next page) **$264**

Brooch, silver & turquoise, designed as a stylized bulbous blowfish w/bead trim & a turquoise cabochon at the top & bottom, signed by Matl, Taxco, 2" l. (ILLUS. center with two other figural Mexican silver brooches, top next page) **$235**

Brooch, sterling silver, copper & turquoise, model of a leaping swordfish w/detailed fins, copper fin & head inlaid w/a turquoise cabochon eye, signed by Matl, Taxco, 4 1/4" l. (ILLUS. right with two other figural Mexcian silver brooches, top next page) **$294**

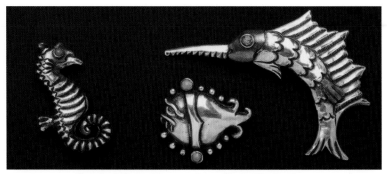

Group of Three Mexican Silver Figural Brooches

Brooch, sterling silver & hardstone, the hammered surface centered by a cabochon brown & white stone, signed by Matl, Taxco, 1 3/4" d. **$323**

Gem-set Silver Key-shaped Brooch

Brooch, sterling silver, turquoise, coral & amethyst, in the shape of a large stylized door key w/bold open scrolls at the top, set w/rows of small turquoise cabochons, oblong coral beads & a circular-cut amethyst in the central section, signed by Matl, Taxco, ca. 1945, 2 1/2" l. (ILLUS.) **$382**

Spratling Clasped Hands Silver Clip

Clip, silver, a rectangular plaque decorated w/raised clasping hands over a map of North & South America, registration No. 12778, mark of Spratling, 1 1/2" l. (ILLUS.) **$353**

Brass Foot-shaped Cuff Links

Cuff links, brass, each modeled as a foot w/applied bead accents, signed by Hubert Harmon, ca. 1940s, 1 1/4" l., pr. (ILLUS.) **$411**

Pair of Bird-shaped Silver Dress Clips

Dress clips, silver, each designed as a curled long-tailed parrot-like bird, engraved details, signed by Los Castillo, Taxco, 1 3/4" l., pr. (ILLUS.) **$294**

Necklace, sterling silver, a narrow band comprised of interlocked paper clip links forming a chain accented along the sides by balls, mark of Spratling, Taxco, 17 1/2" l. (ILLUS. bottom with other Spratling sterling silver necklace, top next page) **$646**

Two Spratling, Taxco Sterling Silver Necklaces

Necklace, sterling silver, a slender band composed of closely woven interlocking links, marked by Spratling, Taxco, 19" l. (ILLUS. top with other Spratling silver necklace, top of page)............................. **$1,880**

Pin, 980 grade silver & malachite, an ornate design centered by an oval malachite stone, Taxco, Mexico, 1 1/2 x 2 1/2" **$75-95**

Pin-pendant, sterling silver & hardstone, the silver mount designed as a circle inlaid w/a greenish brown stone forming the background for a silver inlay design, suspending five silver teardrops inlaid w/the same stone, signed "B   Taxco," 1 1/8" w., 2" l. **$165-185**

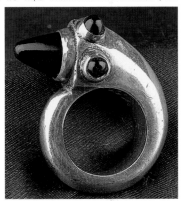

Harmon-designed Silver & Onyx Ring

Mexican Silver & Abalone Shell Butterfly Pin. Courtesy of Marion Cohen

Pin, sterling silver & abalone shell, designed as a stylized butterfly w/three large scalloped leaf-shaped wings set w/abalone shell, Taxco, Mexico, 2 1/4 x 2 3/4" (ILLUS.)........................ **$165-195**

Ring, sterling silver & black onyx, a spiral form set around the top w/a band of small onyx cabochons & w/a large pointed onyx cabochon at the tip, signed by Hubert Harmon, size 4 (ILLUS.) **$764**

Spratling Silver & Copper Sun & Moon Brooch & Earring Suite

Silver & Blue Glass Jewelry Suite by Margot de Taxco

Set: brooch & earrings; silver & copper, each piece designed as a round copper sun face overlapping a silver disk w/a crescent man-in-the-moon & star design, marked by Spratling, Taxco, ca. 1942, clip-on earrings 1 1/4" l., brooch 3 3/8" l., the suite (ILLUS., bottom previous page) **$1,293**

Set: necklace, bracelet & earrings; sterling silver, the necklace composed of open-work scrolling heart-form links bezel-set w/an oval blue glass cabochon, matching bracelet & clip-on earrings, signed by Margot de Taxco, necklace 14 3/4" l. (ILLUS. of the group, top of page) **$1,058**

Set: necklace, bracelet & ring; enameled silver, the necklace designed as an articulated polychrome enamel snake grasping its tail, highlighted by bezel-set green pastes, other pieces match, designed by Margot de Taxco, signed, No. 5554, ring size 4, necklace 15" l., the set **$1,293**

Silver & Onyx Set

Set: necklace & earrings; silver & onyx, necklace composed of bar links suspending a pendant w/ inlaid abstract designs,

clip-on oval earrings w/matching inlaid design, Los Castillo, Taxco, necklace 15 1/2" l., the set (ILLUS.) **$441**

Pablo Picasso

Picasso-designed Bull Head Pendant

Pendant, gold (23k), a flat gold medallion w/a design of a stylized bull head, designed by Picasso, mark of French maker Ste. M.H., signed, No. 1413, No. 6 of 20, original fitted wood box (ILLUS.) **$9,400**

Picasso-designed Pendant with Head

Pendant, gold (23k), the rounded flat medallion w/a low-relief design of a stylized head, designed by Picasso w/the mark of the maker "Ste. MH," No. 6 of 20, No. 1409, w/original fitted box (ILLUS., previous page) **$9,988**

Pablo Picasso Gold Face Pendant

Pendant, gold (23k yellow), flattened rounded shape decorated as a stylized human face, designed & signed by Pablo Picasso, No. 6/20 & 1434, French maker's mark "Ste MH," w/original box (ILLUS.)............. **$9,988**

Picasso-designed Gold Fish Pendant

Pendant, gold of high karat, a flat disk decorated in low-relief w/an abstract fish design, designed by Picasso w/maker's mark of Francis Hugo, No. 1411, No. 6 of 20, original numbered velvet-lined wood box (ILLUS.)... **$10,575**

Pablo Picasso-designed Gold Pendant

Pendant, high-karat gold, a rounded flattened disk decorated w/a low-relief abstract figural design, guarantee stamp & marker's mark for Francois Hugo, No. 6 of 20, signed, w/original velvet-lined wood box, 2" d. (ILLUS.)........................ **$9,400**

Ruser (William)

Bracelet, cultured pearl & 14k gold, composed of realistic oyster shell links w/each sell concealing a pearl on the underside, signed, 7" l. (ILLUS., bottom of page)... **$1,175**

Ruser Gold Oyster Shell & Pearl Bracelet

Ruser Angel on Cloud Pearl & Gold Brooch

Brooch, freshwater pearl, diamond & 14k gold, designed as a child angel w/pearl wings & flexible seed pearl halo seated on a heart-shaped quilted pearl cloud highlighted by ten full-cut diamonds, 14k gold & platinum mount, signed, 2 1/2" l. (ILLUS.)... **$2,468**

Brooch, pearl & 14k gold, designed as an angel w/freshwater pearl wings sitting on a cloud of three freshwater pearls, seed pearl halo, sapphire eyes, signed **$529**

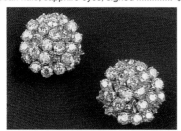

Fine Ruser Diamond & Gold Earrings

Earrings, diamond & 14k gold, clip-on type, rounded shape prong-set w/full-cut diamonds scattered among gold bead clusters, diamonds weighing about 4.56 cts., signed, pr. (ILLUS.)................................. **$4,406**

Pendant, gold (14k), modeled as cherubs among stars, signed, Beverly Hills, California, 1 1/2" l. **$294**

Ruser Pearl & Diamond Butterfly Pin

Pin, freshwater pearl, diamond & 14k gold, designed as a butterfly w/the four-part wings composed of freshwater pearls,

the five-segment gold body set w/full-cut diamonds & diamonds at the tip of the antennae, signed, 1 x 1 1/4" (ILLUS.)......... **$1,763**

Ruser Pearl & Diamond Duck Pin

Pin, freshwater pearl, diamond & yellow diamond, designed as a very stylized flying duck, the head, wings & body each made of a pearl, the center of the body pavé-set w/diamonds & two yellow diamond eyes, 18k gold & platinum mount, signed (ILLUS.) **$1,175**

William Ruser Gem-set Gold Monkey

Pin, gem-set 14k gold, modeled as a monkey perched on a branch & reaching for a coral strawberry, ruby mélée eyes, signed, Beverly Hills, California, 1 1/2" l. (ILLUS.)... **$1,175**

Ruser 14k Gold Poodle Pin

Pin, gold (14k), modeled as a seated poodle w/a bow & blue stone eyes, signed (ILLUS.) **$264**

Rare Jeweled Seaman Schepps Gold Link Bracelet

Pair of Ruser Bumblebee Pins

Pins, freshwater pearl & 14k gold, each designed as a gold bumblebee w/freshwater pearl wings, blue stone eyes, signed, 3/4" l. & 1/2" l., pr. (ILLUS.) **$705**

Seaman Schepps
Bracelet, sapphire bead, cultured pearl & 18k white gold, composed of oval gold links alternatively set w/bands of pearls & blue sapphire beads, signed, No. 11814, 9" l. (ILLUS., top of page)....................... **$7,638**

Bracelet, sapphire, emerald, diamond, platinum & 14k yellow gold, designed as graduating lines of prong-set cabochon blue sapphires & emeralds joined by curving yellow gold links, two links w/bead-set diamond mélée, w/original box, 7 1/4" l. (ILLUS., top of next page)
.... **$18,800**

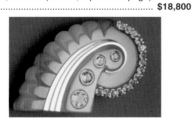

Unusual Seaman Schepps Carved Brooch

Brooch, chalcedony, citrine & 18k gold, chalcedony piece carved as a stylized scrolling shell design w/an inlaid center band of gold below a row of four inset circular-cut citrines & w/an arched band of citrines set across the top, signed, 2" l. (ILLUS.).. **$3,525**

Diamond-set Stylized Floral Brooch

Brooch, diamond & platinum, designed as a stylized floral spray w/the long stem set w/baguette diamonds, the cluster of flowers featuring squared-off petals, set w/a circular-cut old European-cut diamonds weighing about 1.69 cts. below the flower cluster, further set overall w/old European-, old single-, full-, marquise-, triangular- and calibré-cut diamonds weighing about 7.50 cts., signed, 14k white gold pin stem, 1 7/8" l. (ILLUS.)...................... **$7,344**

Rare Seaman Schepps Sapphire, Emerald & Gold Bracelet

Seaman Schepps Gold & Gem Brooch

Brooch, gem-set 18k gold & chalcedony, designed as a carved white chalcedony carp w/the body bezel-set w/carnelian & coral speckles & blue sapphire eyes, No. 8391, 2 3/8" l. (ILLUS.)............................ **$4,465**

Schepps Large Gem-set Shell Brooch

Brooch, gem-set seashell, designed as a large turbo shell mounted w/a gold sprig of seaweed & set w/two green chalcedony cabochons, 14k gold mount, signed, 1 1/2 x 1 5/8" (ILLUS.).............................. **$2,703**

Seaman Schepps "Shrimp" Earrings

Earrings, blue chalcedony & 18k white gold, clip-on type, shrimp design, the wide domed milky white stone resembling the back of a shrimp wrapped w/white gold wiretwist bands, No. 9155, signed, 3/4 x 1 1/4", pr. (ILLUS.)............ **$1,645**

Schepps Gem-set Crystal Shell Earrings

Earrings, carved crystal, turquoise, cultured pearl & 18k gold, clip-on type, each designed as a carved crystal spiraling quilted shell backed by turquoise & surmounted by a white button pearl, No. 13620, signed, 7/8" l., pr. (ILLUS.).......... **$2,350**

Schepps Earrings of Gem-set Shell

Earrings, gem-set shell & 14k gold, clip-on type, designed as a white turbo shell set at the ends w/a cabochon coral & turquoise, wrapped w/gold wire, partially worn signatures, 1" l., pr. (ILLUS.)......... **$1,410**

Sapphire-set Schepps Shell Earrings

Earrings, gem-set shell & 14k gold, clip-on type, each designed as a turbo shell near

the top w/a cabochon sapphire, wrapped w/gold wire, signed, 1 1/2" l., pr. (ILLUS.)
.... **$1,998**

Seaman Schepps Rosewood & Gold Earrings

Earrings, rosewood & 18k gold, clip-on type, a rounded rectangular piece of dark rosewood crisscrossed w/18k gold ropetwist wires, signed, 7/8 x 1", pr. (ILLUS.) **$1,645**

Seaman Schepps Shell & Coral Earrings

Earrings, shell, coral & gold, clip-on type, a spiraling white shell bezel-set at the top & bottom w/coral cabochons & wrapped w/14k gold wire & gold mounts, signed, pr. (ILLUS.)... **$1,410**

Seaman Schepps Shell & Lapis Earrings

Earrings, shell, lapis lazuli & 14k gold, a white spiral shell wrapped in gold wire & bezel-set at the tip w/a lapis cabochon, signed, 1 1/4" l., pr. (ILLUS.).................... **$1,293**

Schepps Shell & Ruby Earrings

Earrings, turbo shell, ruby & 14k gold, each designed as a white shell capped by a small cabochon ruby & wrapped w/a band of gold wire, signed, 1" l., pr. (ILLUS.)...... **$1,880**

Schepps Gem-set White Stone Ring

Ring, kocholong, citrine, sapphire & 18k gold, a wide rounded white stone bezel-set at the top center by a cushioin-cut citrine flanked by circular-cut sapphires, No. 12757, signed, size 6 (ILLUS.)......... **$2,468**

Smith (Art)
Choker, brass, "Half & Half" design, a tripartite form composed of long undulating & looping bands curving around & into a flattened tapering band, signed, ca. 1952, 14" l. (ILLUS., top next page)
.... **$9,988**

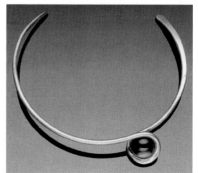

Simple Art Smith-signed Chocker

Choker, silver & glass, a slender silver curved band w/a loop enclosed a grey glass marble, stamped mark, late 20th c., interior width 4" (ILLUS.)........................... **$227**

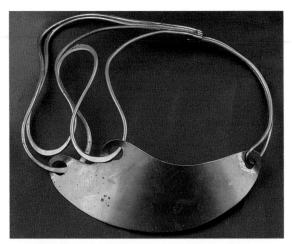

Rare Early Art Smith "Half & Half" Brass Choker

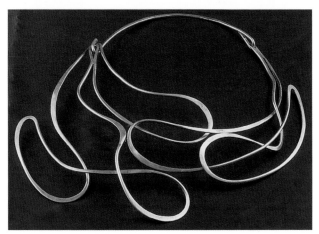

Rare Art Smith Sterling Silver Collar from 1971

Collar, sterling silver, an ornate design of abstract looping planished silver wire, 1971, 15 1/2" l. (ILLUS., above) **$15,275**

Art Smith Triple-ring Earrings

Earrings, brass, a flattened wire vertical bar suspending three graduated rings, signed, ca. 1952, 3 1/8" l., pr. (ILLUS.) ... **$1,645**

Vock (Donna)

Earrings, Keshi pearl, diamond & gem-set 18k white gold, clip-on type, a large pearl capped w/an arched cluster composed of a prong-set oval green tourmaline, pale green chrysoberyl & four diamonds, signed, 3/4" d., pr. **$8,813**

Donna Vock Tourmaline & Pearl Earrings

Earrings, pink tourmaline, South Sea Keshi pearl & 18k white gold, clip-on type, each prong-set at the top w/an oval-cut pink tourmaline above a large white pearl, signed, pr. (ILLUS.) **$1,880**

Fine Vock Pearl & Gem-set Earrings

Earrings, South Sea Keshi pearl & gem-set 18k gold, clip-on type, a large white pearl topped by a cluster of gems including oval-cut mandarin garnets, a large step-cut Madeira citrine & full-cut diamonds weighing about .80 cts., signed, 3/4" l., pr. (ILLUS.) **$7,638**

Donna Vock Pearl & Citrine Earrings

Earrings, South Sea pearl, citrine & 18k gold, clip-on type, each designed as a stylized flower w/each petal formed by a white semi-baroque pearl centering a fancy-cut orange citrine, marked, pr. (ILLUS.) **$2,703**

Fine Donna Vock Pearl & Diamond Earrings

Earrings, Tahitian Keshi pearl & diamond, clip-on type, each set w/four silvery grey pearls centered by a cluster of full-cut diamonds weighing about 1.31 cts., 18k white gold mount, signed, 7/8" l., pr. (ILLUS.) **$4,700**

Webb (David)

Bracelet, enameled 18k yellow gold, designed w/alternating white enamel links accented w/tiny gold diamond-shaped devices & gold textured links, w/original presentation pouch, signed, 7 1/8" l. (ILLUS., bottom of page) **$9,400**

Large David Webb Gold Cuff Bracelet

Bracelet, gold (18k), cuff-style, the wide hinged band w/a finely hammered surface & decorated w/a raised band of large diamond-shaped devices, signed (ILLUS.) **$5,581**

Fine David Webb White Enamel & 18k Yellow Gold Bracelet

*David Webb Ivory, Ruby & Gold Bangle
Bracelet*

Bracelet, ivory, ruby & 18k gold, bangle-type, the simple carved ivory band set around the top w/spaced-out cabochon rubies alternating w/gold diamond-shaped ropetwist mounts, signed, interior circumference 7 3/4" (ILLUS.) **$3,055**

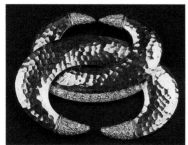

David Webb "Crab" Design Brooch

Brooch, platinum, 18k gold & diamond, "Crab" design, two large interlocked wide C-forms w/a hammered surface, each ending in pointed tips set w/full-cut diamonds & w/an edge band set w/diamonds, signed, 2 5/8" l. (ILLUS.) **$4,348**

Earrings, platinum, 18k gold & diamond, clip-on type, a wide half-hoop of gold w/a bold diamond lattice design, the central band of diamonds set w/diamond mélée highlights, signed, 1" l., pr. **$3,290**

Simple Round David Webb Earrings

Earrings, platinum, diamond & 18k gold, clip-on type, a small simple round disk pavé-set w/full-cut diamonds, signed, pr. (ILLUS.) **$2,233**

David Webb Gold & Citrine Ring

Ring, citrine & 18k gold, set w/a large rectangular fancy-cut citrine, signed, w/ring guard, size 3 (ILLUS.) **$823**

Fine Enameled Gold & Diamond Webb Ring

Ring, enameled 18k gold & diamond, designed as domed overlapping petals enameled in white & centered by a bezel-set marquise-cut diamond weighing about 3.00 cts., signed, size 5 1/4 (ILLUS.) **$7,638**

Rare Webb Yellow Sapphire Ring

Ring, yellow sapphire, diamond & 18k gold, large oval top centered by a large oval fancy-cut yellow sapphire framed by two narrow gold bands each set w/groupings of full-cut diamonds, signed, size 6 (ILLUS.) **$11,750**

Rare David Webb Suite in Enamel & Diamonds

Set: bracelet & earrings; enameled 18k gold & diamond, the hinged cuff-style bracelet decorated w/a ropetwist design in cream-colored enamel, interwoven w/bands of full-cut diamonds, clip-on earrings of matching design, diamonds weighing about 2.94 cts., signed, earrings 1 1/8" l., bracelet interior circumference 6 1/4", the suite (ILLUS., top of page) **$12,925**

David Webb Frog Cuff Links & Tie Tack

Set: cuff links & tie tack; enameled 18k gold & garnet, each piece designed as a green enameled crouching frog w/cabochon garnet eyes, signed, w/original suede pouch, cuff links 3/8" l., tie tack 1/2" l., the suite (ILLUS.) **$1,645**

David Webb Tiger Head Shirt Studs

Shirt studs, enameled 18k gold & ruby, designed as a tiger head w/cabochon ruby eyes, signed, set of 3 (ILLUS.)............... **$1,175**

Yurman (David)

David Yurman Gold Bangle Bracelet

Bracelet, diamond & 14k gold, bangle-type, a narrow ropetwist band decorated w/two X designs set w/bands of full-cut diamonds, signed (ILLUS.) **$881**

Bracelet, sterling silver, 14k gold & onyx, the wiretwist cuff design w/cabochon onyx terminals, signed & w/original presentation pouch.. **$353**

Choker, tanzanite & 14k gold, the braided torque suspending a fancy-cut tanzanite pendant, w/Yurman pouch & box from Saks Fifth Avenue, interior circumference 14 1/2"... **$823**

Yurman Chalcedony & Diamond Earrings

Earrings, blue chalcedony & diamond, clip-on type, each ribbed gold half-hoop w/a pavé-set diamond center band topped by a cabochon chalcedony, sterling silver & 14k gold mounts, original presentation pouch, pr. (ILLUS.)...................................... **$764**

David Yurman Sterling & Gold Trace Link Necklace

Earrings, diamond & 18k gold, the ga-drooned shell design w/bead-set full-cut diamonds, signed, 1" l., pr...................... **$1,763**

Yurman Pearl & Diamond Pendant Earrings

Earrings, sterling silver, 18k gold, diamond & pearl, pendant-style, each ropetwist band top suspending a mother-of-pearl cabochon capped by full-cut diamond mélée, signed, 1 1/4" l., pr. (ILLUS.) **$823**

Earrings, sterling silver & gem-set 14k gold, clip-on type, each designed as a ropetwist coil w/cabochon amethyst terminal, bezel-set cabochon amethyst highlights, signed, pr. **$441**

Necklace, sterling silver & 18k yellow gold, designs as circular & ropetwist trace links, w/signature medallion marked "D.Y.," w/original presentation box, 16 1/2" l. (ILLUS., top of page).................. **$705**

David Yurman Aquamarine Ring

Ring, sterling silver, 18k gold & aquamarine, the top set w/a squared fancy-cut aquamarine w/a plain gold border, ropetwist design on shoulders, signed, size 5 1/4 (ILLUS.) **$353**

Two David Yurman Rings

Ring, sterling silver, 18k gold & diamond, squared gold top pavé-set w/full-cut diamond mélée, silver shank, signed & w/presentation pouch, size 6 (ILLUS. top with other Yurman ring, previous page) **$705**

Ring, sterling silver, 18k gold & diamond, the oblong gold top frame enclosing pavé-set full-cut diamond mélée, silver shank, signed in presentation pouch, size 7 (ILLUS. bottom other Yurman ring, previous page) **$999**

David Yurman Gold & Sterling Ring

Ring, sterling silver & 18k yellow gold, a wide yellow gold band inset w/two thin silver ropetwist bands, signed, w/original presentation pouch, size 6 (ILLUS.).......... **$470**

Set: necklace & earrings; sterling silver & cultured pearl, the necklace composed of a trace link chain suspending a white pearl in a ropetwist frame & 14k gold bezel, matching stud-type earrings, signed, necklace 16 1/2" l. **$353**

Miscellaneous Designers

Bracelet, amethyst & enameled 18k gold, composed of five round ring-form links centered by bezel-set round fancy-cut amethysts framed by a ring of green enamel, alternating w/shaped ribbed gold links, signed by de Vroomen, 7" l. (ILLUS., below) **$3,173**

Bracelet, bicolor 18k gold, designed as four bangles on a pierced frame, by Mauboussin, marked, French guarantee stamps, No. C4754, interior circumference 7 1/2" **$1,763**

de Vroomen Amethyst & Enameled Gold Bracelet

Paloma Picasso Gold Figure-eight Link Bracelet

Bracelet, bicolor 18k gold & diamond, composed of large openwork figure-eight links w/the central link bead-set w/full-cut diamond mélée, designed by Paloma Picasso for Tiffany & Co., signed, 7 1/4" l. (ILLUS.)
.... **$1,293**

Fine Gioia-Designed Diamond Bracelet

Bracelet, diamond & gold, bangle-type, hinged form set w/full-cut diamond mélée, diamonds weighing about 5.84 cts., mark of French maker & Gioia Designs, guarantee stamp, boxed (ILLUS.) **$5,581**

Modern Ugo Bellini Gem-set Bracelet

Bracelet, gem-set & enameled 18k gold, bangle-type, the wide hinged bangle decorated at the top w/an abstract design w/six scattered prong-set step-cut citrines surrounded by scattered full-cut diamonds against a ground w/black enameled geometric blocks w/the black enamel continuing around the gold band, by Ugo Bellini, Florence, Italy, contemporary, boxed, interior circumference 6 1/2" (ILLUS.) **$1,880**

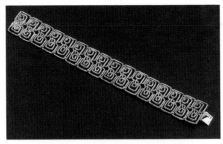

Zolotas-designed Gold Greek Key Bracelet

Bracelet, gold (18k), composed of a double row of openwork abstract Greek key designs, designed & marked by Zolotas, Greece, 7 1/8" l. (ILLUS.) **$881**

Rare Martinazzi Gold Hand Bracelet

Bracelet, gold (20k & 18k), cuff-style, designed as a 20k gold human hand w/four fingers opposing the thumb, completed by an 18k white gold cuff, designed by Bruno Martinazzi, signed "Martinazzi X/XII" (ILLUS.) **$16,450**

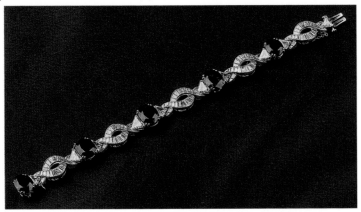

Extraordinary Harry Winston Sapphire & Diamond Bracelet

Bracelet, sapphire, diamond & platinum, composed of entwined openwork links channel-set w/ten trillion and 120 tapered baguette diamonds alternating w/five large cushion-cut blue sapphires, diamonds weighing about 9.30 cts., signed by House of Harry Winston, 6 1/2" l. (ILLUS.) **$27,025**

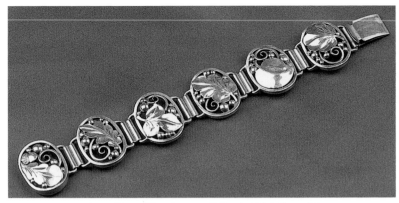

Larry Foss Silver Leaves & Berries Link Bracelet

Bracelet, silver, composed of oval open-work links each decorated w/a different leaf & berries & scrolled tendril, joined by a bar link, designed by Larry Foss, signed, 6 7/8" l. (ILLUS., top of page) **$1,763**

Mauboussin Stylized Snake Bracelet

Bracelet, turquoise, diamond & 18k gold, bangle-type, hinged, a stylized design of a looping snake w/a textured b,ody, the looped top surrounds a pear-shaped turquoise cabochon, the pointed head set w/full-cut diamonds, signed by Mauboussin, interior circumference 6 1/2" (ILLUS.) **$1,410**

Mikimoto Pearl & Gold Brooch

Brooch, cultured pearl & 14k gold, designed as a gold tree branch set w/13 white pearls w/rose overtones, signed by Mikimoto, 1 1/4" l. (ILLUS.) **$470**

Brooch, diamond & gem-set, cascade of flexibly set cabochon ruby, faceted emerald, sapphire, aquamarine & old mine-cut diamond & champagne diamond blossoms, approx. total wt. 3.05 cts., interspersed w/engraved vines & leaves, 18k gold & platinum mount, made by Anna Bachelli **$14,100**

Hammerman Gem-set Gold Flower Brooch

Brooch, gem-set 18k gold, designed as an asymmetrical chrysanthemum-like flower w/textured gold petals centered by a full-cut diamond surrounded by scattered small cabochon lapis lazuli & turquoise, Hammerman Bros., New York, New York, marked, 2" w. (ILLUS.) **$646**

Brooch, gem-set tricolor 18k gold, designed as a large beetle-like winged insect, the back centered by a large cabochon emerald surrounded by a ring of small cabochon blue sapphires, two of the wings & the lower body set w/small single- and full-cut diamonds, the neck set w/two

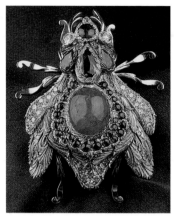

Cazzaniga Gem-set Insect Brooch

pear-shaped rubies flanking a pear-shaped andalusite, the head mounted w/large circular-cut diamond eyes flanking a cabochon blue sapphire, signed by Cazzaniga, Rome, 2 1/8" l. (ILLUS.) **$3,055**

Abstract Eric deKolb Gold Brooch

Brooch, gold (14k), an abstract rounded outer frame enclosing three openwork panels, one framing a fish, one framing a row of standing figures & the third framing a running unicorn, designed by Eric deKolb,   signed, ca.   1960s-1970s, 1 1/2 x 1 3/4" (ILLUS.)................................ **$353**

Carved Ivory Brooch with Chinese Scene

Brooch, ivory & 18k gold, the rounded rectangular ivory plaque pierced & carved overall w/a scene depicting the god of Longevity offering a peach to another Immortal at a temple in the forest, by Janiyé, signed (ILLUS.) **$382**

Delicate Abstract Designer Brooch

Brooch, platinum & diamond, the delicate openwork mount of abstract design w/a cluster of round blossoms at one end each prong-set w/full-cut diamonds, the other end w/fanned wire clusters w/each mounted w/full-cut diamonds, signed by Retzignac, diamonds weighing about 4.60 cts., 2 1/2" l. (ILLUS.)..................... **$3,055**

Unique Dali-designed Gem-set Lips Brooch

Brooch, ruby, cultured pearl & 18k gold, designed as large smiling lips bead-set w/about 212 circular-cut rubies, the mouth set w/ten white pearl teeth, designed by Dali, unsigned but made by Henryk Kaston (ILLUS.)........................ **$16,450**

Brooch, sterling silver, in the shape of a stylized cornucopia, designed by Peer Smed, Denmark, No. 1934, signed, 3" l..... **$323**

Lona Schaeffer Silver Floral Brooch

Brooch, sterling silver, modeled as a large lily-like blossom enclosed by wide curled leaves w/curling tendrils, designed by Lona Schaeffer, signed "LPS," ca. 1930s, 2 3/4" l. (ILLUS., previous page) **$382**

Parenti Sisters Silver & Gemstone Brooch

Brooch, sterling silver, moonstone & sapphire, designed as a flower w/five long oval moonstone petals centered by a circular-cut sapphire, long thin silver stem & leaves, signed by the Parenti Sisters, Boston, first half 20th c., 3 1/4" l. (ILLUS.)......... **$441**

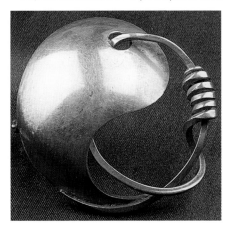

Paul Lobel Abstract Silver Brooch

Brooch, sterling silver, tapering curled abstract leaf-like design joined to wire bands, signed by Paul Lobel, modern, 1 1/2" d. (ILLUS.) **$1,116**

Luis Sanz Blackamoor Head Brooch

Brooch, sunstone feldspar & 18k gold, designed as the head of a turbanned blackamoor w/a curved petal-form necklace, signed by Luis Sanz, Madrid, Spain, 1 1/2" l. (ILLUS.) **$705**

Fine Bojesen Silver & Hardstone Brooch

Brooch-pendant, sterling silver, malachite & lapis lazuli, the top composed of arched stylized silver leaves & blossoms centered by lapis cabochons above a large open-set round malachite cabochon above another pair of stylized blossoms centered by lapis cabochons above a forked vine joined to a beaded silver openwork link suspending a large oval malachite cabochon, mark of Kay Bojesen (ILLUS.)..................................... **$3,055**

Choker, gold (18k) & diamond, 'Pavé Twig' design, the flexible grosgrain band suspending a drop bead-set w/full-cut diamond mélée, mark of Jordan Schlanger, in original Saks Fifth Avenue pouch, 2 1/4" l. **$294**

Ventrella Gold & Agate Cuff Links

Cuff links, landscape agate & 18k gold, each double-link set w/a plain gold oval frame enclosing an oval agate tablet, unsigned Davide Ventrella, Rome, Italy, in fitted signed box, the set (ILLUS.) **$1,880**

Earpendants, platinum, ruby & diamond, chandelier designed as cascade of flexibly set circular-cut rubies & full, marquise- and pear-cut diamonds, platinum mount, signed "HW" for Harry Winston, pendants detachable............................ **$11,750**

Intaglio Carnelian & Gold Earrings

Earrings, carnelian & 18k gold, clip-on type, the center w/a flat oval carnelian plaque intaglio-carved w/the head of a Greek warrior, mounted in a wide ringed gold frame decorated w/four bars, signed by Vahe Naltch & dated 1987, pr. (ILLUS.) **$646**

Citrine & 14k Gold Squared Earrings

Earrings, citrine & 14k gold, clip-on type, each w/a squared stepped gold frame surrounded a cushion-shaped fancy-cut citrine, MAZ, 7/8" l., pr. (ILLUS.) **$411**

Citrine & Blue Topaz Designer Earrings

Earrings, citrine, blue topaz & pearl, pendant-type, the top w/a heart-shaped large citrine beside a matching topaz above a central pearl suspending a detachable fancy-cut citrine drop, diamond accents, signed by Pelegrin, 2 3/8" l., pr. (ILLUS.)... **$940**

Heart-form Hess Gold & Diamond Earrings

Earrings, diamond & 18k gold, clip-on type, each designed as a scrolled gold heart enclosing pavé-set diamonds, diamonds weighing about 4.45 cts., designed by Jose Hess, signed, missing one diamond, pr. (ILLUS.) **$3,760**

Earrings, diamond & 18k gold, each fan-shaped & prong-set w/25 full-cut diamonds weighing about 3.37 cts., designed by Kurt Wayne, signed, pr. **$2,585**

Sterlé Paris Gold & Diamond Earrings

Earrings, diamond, 18k gold & platinum, clip-on type, a rounded shape composed of groups of rounded gold wirework bands alternating w/scattered full-cut diamonds & w/two bottom bands pavé-set w/small diamonds, diamonds weighing about 1.85 cts., signed "Modele Sterlé, Paris," pr. (ILLUS.) **$4,700**

Elizabeth Locke Glass & Gold Earrings

Earrings, glass intaglio & 18k gold, clip-on type, each set w/an oblong flat glass plaque engraved w/a crest design w/an animal, gold frame & applied gold beads & a glass cabochon accent, marked by Elizabeth Locke, pr. (ILLUS.) **$1,880**

Unusual Zolotas Gold Pendant Earrings

Earrings, gold (18k), pendant-type, the top composed of a cluster of flame-like leaves issuing from three open arches & suspending a triangular arrangment of open arches above a row of five leaf-form

drops, mark of Zolotas, original presentation pouch, 2 1/4" l., pr. (ILLUS.) **$823**

Angela Cummings Gold Knot Earrings

Earrings, gold (18k), stud-type, each designed as a four-sided ribbed knot w/an open center, signed by Angela Cummings, 1/2" w., pr. (ILLUS.) **$470**

Glass Intaglio & Gold Earrings by Locke

Earrings, pearl, glass intaglio & 18k gold, clip-on type, each set w/an oval glass intaglio plaque engraved w/the image of a rider on a rearing steed fighting a serpent, an arched band of gold beads across the top, a gold bar w/ropetwist ends & seed pearl accents below, signed by Elizabeth Locke, pr. (ILLUS.) **$1,528**

Masriera Pendant Flower Vine Earrings

Earrings, plique-a-jour enamel, diamond & 18k gold, pendant-type, each designed as a trailing vine w/green enameled leaves & two multi-petaled flowers w/blue enameled petals alternating w/diamond-set petals, 18k gold & platinum mount, signed by Masriera, pr. (ILLUS.) **$4,113**

Annabel Jones Crystal Earrings

Earrings, rock crystal, cultured pearl & sapphire, pendant-style, the round gold top w/a ropetwist border & four spearpoint devices centered by a pearl flanked by four small bezel-set cabochon sapphires, suspending a detachable rock crystal sphere, Annabel Jones, boxed, 14k gold mounts, pr. (ILLUS.).................................. **$499**

Gem-set Orchid Fred Leighton Earrings

Earrings, ruby, diamond & 18k gold, clip-on type, each designed to resemble an orchid blossom, large side & base petals bead-set w/oval-cut rubies, alternating w/three smaller diamond-set petals & a diamond cluster centered in the bottom petal, unsigned but purchased from designer Fred Leighton & boxed, pr. (ILLUS.) **$7,050**

Paul Lobel Modern Style Silver Earrings

Earrings, sterling silver, pendant-style, simple modernistic design w/a trapezoidal top suspending a long trapezoidal plaque flanked by straight wires, signed by Paul Lobel, 2 1/2" l., pr. (ILLUS.) **$558**

Kramer Abstract Silver Earrings

Earrings, sterling silver, pendant-type, composed of flat abstract geometeric forms w/engraved designs, designed by Sam Kramer, New York, New York, 2" l., pr. (ILLUS.) **$353**

Morelli Gold & Diamond Slide Necklace

Necklace, diamond & 18k gold, slide-type, pair of delicate ball chains joined by a rounded disk slide decorated on the front & back w/moon, star & sunburst designs accented w/diamonds, the chains w/small ball terminals accented w/tiny diamonds, designed by Morelli (ILLUS.)....... **$793**

Gold Maple Leaf & Diamond Necklace

Fine H. Winston Emerald Bead Necklace

Necklace, emerald bead, diamond & platinum, composed of three strands of tumbled emerald beads graduating in size from 4.85 to 6.48 mm, completed by an arched band platinum clasp set w/baguette, full- and oval-cut diamonds weighing about 1.77 cts., clasp signed w/the initials of Harry Winston, No. 79744 (ILLUS.).. **$17,625**

Necklace, gem-set sterling silver, the large plaque bezel-set w/a faceted amethyst, smoky quartz, hematite & rhodolite garnet, further set w/cabochon jadeite, lapis lazuli, pink tourmaline & emeralds, suspended from a jointed torque, artist-designed & hallmarked, ca. 1965, 16 1/2" l
.... **$441**

Necklace, gold (14k) & diamond, designed as nine graduated gold maple leaves each accented w/tiny scattered single-cut diamonds, completed by a snake chain, signed by Forstner, 15 1/2" l. (ILLUS., top of page)... **$1,880**

Necklace, gold (18k) & diamond, open abstract-form links, each bezel-set w/full-cut diamonds, signed "C. Deneuve" for Catherine Deneuve, approx. total wt. 0.82 cts., 15" l. **$1,410**

Unique Sapphire & Diamond Necklace

Necklace, platinum, sapphire, diamond & 18k gold, composed of bezel-set cushion-shaped sapphires alternating w/cabochon sapphires, spaced by diamond mélée rondels, suspended from a sapphire bead necklace w/additional diamond rondels, signed by Memmerle, Munich, Germany, 15" l. (ILLUS.) **$7,050**

Elizabeth Gage Red Jasper Bead Necklace

Necklace, red jasper & gold, composed of 35 red jasper beads completed by an 18k gold spherical engraved clasp w/applied scrolls, by Elizabeth Gage, unsigned but w/original burgundy suede presentation pouch, 16" l. (ILLUS., top of page) **$499**

Arman-designed Violin Necklaces

Necklaces, gold (18k), each designed as an openwork violin-form pendant suspended from a curb link chain, designed by Fernandez Arman, ca. 1973, French guarantee stamps & partial hallmarks of Gennari, Paris, unsigned but designer, 19" & 23" l., pr. (ILLUS.) **$1,998**

Pendant, diamond, ruby & 18k gold, designed as a heart w/a flat monogrammed center framed by ribs & diamond-set diamonds, a ruby cabochon highlight, signed by Judith Ripka (ILLUS., top next column) **$294**

Gem-set Gold Heart by Judith Ripka

Rebus-style Gem-set Gold Pendant

Pendant, gem-set 18k gold, the flat gold disk bordered by a ring of rose- and single-cut diamonds w/further diamonds on the pin, decorated w/a rebus-type design of a small "plus" sign set w/diamonds above the French phrase "Qu'Hier" above a "minus" signed channel-set w/rubies above the phrase "Que Demain," translates to "More than Yesterday - Less than Tomorrow," signed by A. Augis (ILLUS.) **$558**

Small Max Ernst-designed Pendant

Pendant, gold (23k), a large flattened disk deeply incised w/an abstract design, Marseilles, France guarantee stamps & maker's mark of Francois Hugo, Aix en Provence, designed by Max Ernst, signed & dated January 1975, No. 4 of 6, original numbered wood velvet-lined box, 1 3/4" d. (ILLUS.) **$7,344**

Rare Max Ernst-designed 23k Gold Round Pendant

Pendant, gold (23k), a large flattened disk deeply incised w/an abstract design, Marseilles, France guarantee stamps & maker's mark of Francois Hugo, Aix en Provence, designed by Max Ernst, signed & dated 1975, No. 4 of 6, original numbered wood velvet-lined box, 4 1/2" d. (ILLUS.) **$18,800**

Pendant-brooch, gold (18k), designed as a large octopus w/wide curled arms & engraved body & bezel-set cabochon opal eyes, by Ugo Bellini, Florence, Italy, ca. 1973, unsigned, 3 1/4 x 3 1/2" (ILLUS., top next column)..................................... **$3,055**

Bellini Gold Octopus Pendant-Brooch

Fancy Dunay Kunzite, Diamond & Gold Pendant-Brooch

Pendant-brooch, kunzite, diamond & 18k gold, set w/a very large rectangular step-cut pinkish kunzite within an openwork delicate scrolling gold mount w/a top & bottom center wedge set w/full-cut diamonds, designed by Henry Dunay, 1 3/4 x 2 1/4" (ILLUS.) **$4,700**

Pendant-necklace, diamond & 18k gold, the round trace link chain suspending a full cut pavé-set diamond sphere & heart, signed by Gerard, 27" l. **$1,528**

Kurt Wayne Gold Heart Pendant-Necklace

Pendant-necklace, gold (18k), designed as a stylized gold heart suspended on a black silk cord w/a gold ring above the heart, mark of Kurt Wayne, No. 111343, overall 22" l. (ILLUS.)................................. **$441**

Pin, enameled 18k bicolor gold & diamond, in the form of a flower w/shaded blue basse taille enamel & full-cut diamond mélée highlights, signed by Leo Pizzo **$588**

Abstract Gem-set Gold Ed Weiner Pin

Pin, gem-set 18k gold, the abstract mount composed of randomly set straw-like gold strips centering a large rectangular rough-cut purplish blue rock crystal, signed by Ed Weiner, 2 3/4" l. (ILLUS.) .. **$1,410**

Two J. Cooper Gold Fish Pins

Pins, diamond & 18k gold, each designed as a stylized gold koi-type fish, each w/a bezel-set full-cut diamond eye & one blowing a pearl bubble, signed by J. Cooper, the two (ILLUS.) **$1,058**

Maria Cassetti Gem-set Gold Ring

Ring, amethyst, citrine & 18k gold, a wide gold band channel-set w/baguette amethyst & citrine, signed by Maria Cassetti, size 8 1/2 (ILLUS.) **$411**

Schlumberger Coral & Gold Ring

Ring, coral & 18k gold, the wide domed top set w/a cluster of coral cabochons among gold beads within a wide ropetwist mount, signed by Schlumberger, coral not original to mount, size 6 1/2 (ILLUS.) **$1,880**

Fine Helen Woodhall Diamond Ring

Ring, diamond & 22k gold, solitaire-type, the top centered by a large emerald-cut diamond weighing about 2.00 cts. flanked by full-cut diamond mélée, thick scrolling gold shoulders, mark of Helen Woodhall, size 5 3/4 (ILLUS.) **$8,225**

Erté-designed Natutilus Shell Ring

Ring, diamond, ruby & 14k gold, "L'Argonaute" design, in the form of a stylized nautilis shell bead-set w/small diamonds & centering a circular-cut ruby, designed by Erté for Circle Fine Art, No. 3 of 500, signed, w/original presentation boxes & certificate, size 5 (ILLUS.) **$940**

Unusual Paul Flato Fire Opal Ring

Ring, fire opal & gem-set 18k gold, the large cabochon opal weighing about 50.00 cts. framed by gold leaf designs set w/marquise-cut sapphire & diamond mélée, designed by Paul Flato, probably Mexico City, 1940s, size 7 1/2 (ILLUS.) **$8,225**

Reversible Garnet & Gold Flip Ring

Ring, garnet & 18k gold, flip-type, one side of the top bezel-set w/a cabochon rhodolite garnet in a simple gold mount, the reverse w/a classical figure w/cabochon green stone accents, signed by Seiden-Gang, w/box & receipt from Saks, size 6 (ILLUS.)... **$1,175**

Modern Bellini Gem-set Abstract Ring

Ring, gem-set & enameled 18k gold, the abstract teardrop-form top prong-set w/a step-cut citrine flanked by bands of full-cut diamonds & a background enameled w/black geometric panels, by Ugo Bellini,

Florence, Italy, contemporary, boxed, size 6 (ILLUS.) **$764**

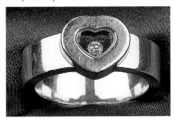

Chopard Gold & Diamond Heart Ring

Ring, gold (18k) & diamond, a simple gold band centered by a small heart-shaped crystal locket centered by a small bezel-set diamond, signed by Chopard, size 7 (ILLUS.)... **$411**

Large Yellow Beryl & Gold Ring

Ring, heliodor & 18k gold, the wide top bead-set w/a large cushion-shaped fancy-cut yellow beryl, heavy gold mount, signed by G. Vollrath, size 7 (ILLUS.)..... **$1,058**

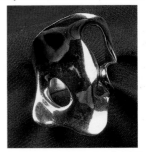

Artist-designed Abstract Gold Ring

Ring, high-karat gold, the top w/an oblong dished abstract organic form, signed by Fireshine, No. 3 of a series, ca. 1970s (ILLUS.)... **$1,058**

H. Stern Rubellite & Diamond Ring

Ring, rubellite & diamond, the top prong-set w/a large oval-cut rubellite flanked by an openwork shank set w/full-cut and baguette diamond mélée, marked by H. Stern, size 6 3/4 (ILLUS.)........................ **$3,055**

Craig Drake Ruby & Diamond Ring

Ring, ruby, diamond & 18k gold, designed as two wide entwined bands, one bead-set overall w/rubies & the other bead-set overall w/full-cut diamonds, diamonds weighing about 1.20 cts., mark of Craig Drake, size 7 3/4 (ILLUS.)...................... **$1,293**

Sally Weckstein Rutilated Quartz Ring

Ring, rutilated quartz, silver & 18k gold, the top bezel-set w/a large oval quartz cabochon, hand-inscribed by Sally Weckstein & dated 1993, size 7 3/4 (ILLUS.) **$499**

Kurt Wayne Sapphire & Diamond Ring

Ring, sapphire, diamond & 18k gold, the top centered by an oval-cut sapphire framed by ten full-cut diamonds weighing about 1.06 cts., signed by Kurt Wayne, size 6 1/4 (ILLUS.).. **$1,763**

Pair of Elan Diamond Rings

Rings, diamond & pink diamond, 18k gold & platinum, each half pavé-set w/full-cut diamond mélée, signed by Elan Collection, size 6, pr. (ILLUS.) **$2,350**

French Designer Bracelet & Earrings

Set: bangle-type bracklet & earrings; diamond, emerald & 18k yellow gold, each piece in a stylized leaf form in gold, the hinged bracelet set w/six round full-cut diamonds & 18 round faceted emeralds; the clip-on earrings each w/two round full-cut diamonds & four round faceted emeralds, designed by Réné Borien, France, the set (ILLUS.)......................... **$4,481**

Michael Good Bracelet & Ring Suite

Set: bracelet & ring, 18k gold, the bracelet formed by an undulating serpentine narrow band, the ring of similar design, designed by Michael Good, ring size 8 1/2, necklace interior circumference 4 7/8", the suite (ILLUS.) **$1,410**

Arthur King Gold & Pearl Bracelet

Set: bracelet & ring, cultured baroque pearl & 18k gold, bangle-type, the hinged serpentine rustic-style gold band set w/four cultured baroque silver pearls, signed by Arthur King, together w/a similar ring, ring size 5 1/2, bracelet interior circumference 6 1/2", the set (ILLUS. of bracelet).... **$705**

Fireworks Design Brooch & Earrings by Michael Walkin

Set: brooch & earrings; 18k gold, sapphire, diamond & ruby, the brooch designed as a fireworks burst centered by an oval sapphire w/the long arched rays bead-set w/circular-cut rubies or full-cut diamonds, matching clip-on earrings, diamonds weighing about 5.00 cts., signed by Michael Walkin, the set (ILLUS., top of page) **$6,169**

Gem-set Gold Snake Jewelry Suite

Set: earrings & ring; gem-set 18k gold, each in the shaped of a coiled gold snake centered by a foil-backed faceted cabochon green rock crystal, signed by Stephen Dweck, clip-on earrings 1" d., ring size 6 1/2, the suite (ILLUS.) **$470**

Set: necklace, bracelet & earrings; sterling silver & marcasite; each composed of abstract links w/marcasite highlights, stamped "Original Fahrner TF 925," Theodore Fahrner, ca. 1940s, the suite **$264**

Set: necklace & bracelet; gold (18k), "Connections" necklace & bracelet designed as interlocking circles, signed "Paloma Picasso & Tiffany & Co.," w/original suede sleeve, necklace 16 1/2" l., bracelet 7 1/2" l., the set **$2,233**

Modern Tiffany & Co. Petal-form Necklace & Earrings

Set: necklace & earrings; gold (18k yellow), the necklace composed of overlapping leaf-form rose petals, matching petal-shaped earrings, designed by Angela Cummings, Tiffany & Co., ca. 1979-80, necklace 15 1/2" l., the set (ILLUS.) **$6,463**

Set: ring & earrings, pink tourmaline, diamond & 18k gold, the ring bezel-set w/an oblong emerald-cut tourmaline, the shoulders set w/full-cut diamond highlights, the mount w/scale designs, matching clip-on earrings, signed by Angela Cummings, ring size 6 1/2, the set **$3,525**

Famous Retailers

Cartier
Belts, silver & gilt, composed of ropetwist rings alternating w/gilt figural plaques, one w/parrots, the other w/donkeys, signed by Cartier & Janna, Mexico, each 40" l., the two **$323**

Cartier Gold Bracelet with Diamond Clasp

Bracelet, diamond & 18k gold, composed of flattened rectangular links w/the closure made of a narrow loop joined to a ring, both bead-set w/full-cut diamonds, diamonds weighing about 1.02 cts., No. 864619, mark of French maker & guarantee stamp, signed, 7 1/2" l. (ILLUS.) **$2,938**

Very Rare Cartier Gold & Diamond Scarab Bracelet

Bracelet, diamond & 18k gold, cuff-style, the wide flexible band composed of long rectangular links each set w/a long oval ring of full-cut diamonds, the top cast w/a large stylized scarab, diamonds weighing about 12.32 cts., French guarantee stamps & mark of the maker, signed Cartier, Paris, expands from 5 3/4 x 6 1/4" (ILLUS.).......................... **$12,925**

Cartier Gold Screwhead "Love" Bracelet

Bracelet, gold (18k), bangle-type, "Love" design, the narrow flat band engraved w/a design resembling screwheads & a screwdriver, No. 746504, signed, interior circumference 6" (ILLUS.)...................... **$1,645**

Cartier, Italy Gold Cylinders Bracelet

Bracelet, gold (18k), composed of small plain & textured cylinders edged by spheres, signed by Cartier, Italy, 7 1/2" l. (ILLUS.)... **$1,293**

Bracelet, tricolor 18k gold, rolling bangle-type, composed of seven interlocking bangles in yellow, rose & white gold, signed, interior circumference 7" **$3,173**

Rare Diamond & Gold Cartier Brooch

Brooch, diamond, platinum & 18k yellow gold, designed as a wide entwined ribbon pavé-set w/187 full-cut diamonds weighing about 13.92 cts., accented w/tiny gold ball accents, No. 10991, signed, ca. 1960s (ILLUS.).................................... **$43,475**

Cartier Gold Bunny Brooch

Brooch, gem-set 18k gold, designed as a comical seated bunny rabbit w/an oversized head, cabochon ruby eyes, Cartier, France (ILLUS.) **$1,528**

Cartier 18k Gold Woodpecker Pin

Brooch, gem-set 18k gold, model of a woodpecker, the body w/engraved feathers & a crest of cabochon turquoise highlights, full-cut diamond mélée eye, signed & boxed, 2" l. (ILLUS.) **$3,055**

Gold & Ruby Rope Bow Brooch

Brooch, gold (18k) & ruby, designed as a long rope-tied bow centered by three circular-cut rubies, signed, Cartier, France (ILLUS.).. **$705**

Cartier Gold & Opal Bumblebee Pin

Brooch, opal & 18k gold, designed as a large flying bumblebee, the wings, legs & head in gold, the body set w/opal cabochons, signed "Cartier Paris - No. 130," 1 x 1 3/8" (ILLUS.).................................... **$2,233**

Very Rare Cartier 1930s Gem-set Brooch

Brooch, topaz, citrine, diamond & gold, modeled as a large stylized flower on a leafy stem, five large rectangular petals set w/rectangular fancy-cut citrines alternating w/small marquise-cut citrines, the center composed of circular-cut topaz & nine old European- and mine-cut diamonds weighing about 1.16 cts., signed by Cartier, London, No. 1510, evidence of minor solder, 1930s (ILLUS.)............ **$17,625**

Gold Ingot Cartier Charm

Charm, gold (18k), in the shape of a gold ingot w/the Cartier name stamped on the side, ring link at one end, 1" l. (ILLUS.) **$646**

Cartier Gold & Enamel Charm Bracelet

Charm bracelet, gold (18k) & enamel, the long oblong gold links suspending three polychrome enameled flat animal-form charms, one a white seated elephant, one a white, black & yellow standing stork & the third a white circus pony w/two riders signed by Van Cleef & Arpels, the rest signed by Cartier, minor loss to elephant trunk enamel, 7 3/8" l. (ILLUS.).. **$940**

Cartier Reverse-painted Crystal Dress Clip

Dress clip, reverse-painted crystal & 14k gold, the round domed crystal reverse-painted w/a scene of a fox hunter on horseback & hound jumping a hedge, framed by a gold model of a snaffle bit, signed (ILLUS.) **$1,116**

Cartier Gold Double-Loop Earrings

Earrings, gold (14k), composed of two entwined gold oval loops, partial signatures, pr. (ILLUS.)... **$588**

Cartier Hoop Gold & Diamond Earrings

Earrings, gold (18k) & diamond, the wide ribbed hoops trimmed w/full-cut diamond mélée in a "C" design, signed, 5/8" l., pr. (ILLUS.).. **$588**

Triple Hoop Gold Earrings

Earrings, tricolor 18k gold, designed as three interlocking hoops each of a different color of gold, No. J 46774, w/original presentation box, pr. (ILLUS.)................ **$1,116**

Cartier White Gold Double-C Earrings

Earrings, white gold (18k), clip-on type, designed as back-to-back entwined "Cs," No. 774752, signed, 3/4" l., pr. (ILLUS.) **$881**

Cartier Diamond Heart & Gold Necklace

Necklace, diamond & 18k gold, the flat herringbone links centered by a pavé-set diamond heart, diamonds weighing about 2.75 cts., 14 3/4" l. (ILLUS.)................... **$4,700**

Fine Cartier Gold & Diamond Necklace

Necklace, diamond & 18k gold, the wide fancy link chain centered by pavé-set diamond double "C" design, 15 3/4" l. (ILLUS. of part, previous page) **$7,050**

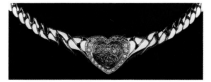

Cartier Gold & Diamond Heart Necklace

Necklace, diamond, yellow diamond & 18k gold, the flattened ropetwist designed links centering a heart pavé-set w/full-cut yellow diamonds surrounded by a band of full-cut colorless diamonds, diamonds weighing about 2.00 cts., signed, 15" l. (ILLUS.).. **$2,703**

Very Fine Signed Cartier, Paris Ruby & Diamond Necklace

Necklace, ruby, diamond & platinum, composed of clusters of ruby mélée interspersed w/diamond baguettes, signed, Paris, French hallmarks, No. 05037, 16" l. (ILLUS.).. **$27,025**

Cartier Gold Open Heart Pendnat

Pendant, gold (18k), the heart form designed like an open book with four "pages" open, each incised w/crossed "Cs," French hallmark & guarantee stamps, signed, No. 824041, together w/a 14k gold chain (ILLUS.) **$646**

Cartier Heart & Bee Gold Pin

Pin, enameled 14k gold, designed as an open heart w/flat curving sides, mounted near the bottom w/a model of a bee w/blue-enameled wings, signed, 1 1/4" l. (ILLUS.).. **$411**

Cartier Enameled Gold Fish Pin

Pin, enameled 18k gold, designed as a bulbous fish, the face enameled in green w/a ruby eye, green enamel body stripes, 1 1/4" l. (ILLUS.) **$1,293**

Gem-set Gold Snail Pin by Cartier

Pin, gem-set 18k gold, model of a realistic snail w/sapphire & diamond mélée accents, signed, 1 1/2" l. (ILLUS.) **$1,763**

Ring, gem-set 18k gold, "Panthere" model, designed as the stylized head & front paws of a panther w/emerald eyes & an onyx nose, signed, No. C47067-62, size 6 .... **$1,645**

Cartier-retailed Ruby & Diamond Ring

Ring, ruby, diamond & platinum, the three-stone top centered by an oval-cut ruby flanked by full-cut round diamonds, No. 5145, obliterated maker's mark, signed by Cartier (ILLUS.) **$2,350**

Cartier White Gold & Diamond Ring

Ring, white gold (18k) & diamond, the pen-annular form edge w/bead-set full-cut diamonds, signed & dated 2001, size 5 1/4 (ILLUS.) **$1,175**

Cartier Gold, Diamond & Sapphire Ring

Ring, white gold (18k), sapphire & diamond, the wide gold band prong-set across the top w/three old European-cut diamonds separated by pairs of cabochon sapphires, diamonds weighing about 1.75 cts., signed, No. 81128, size 7 (ILLUS.) **$3,173**

Cartier Gold & Enamel Ladybug Set

Set: bracelet & earrings; 18k gold & enamel, the bracelet composed of sections of small circular links joined by four inlaid enamel ladybugs, the earrings in the form of a ladybug, No. C7870 & 99781, signed, the set (ILLUS.) **$2,938**

Set of Gold Cartier Earrings & Brooch

Set: brooch & clip-on earrings; 14k gold, each piece designed as pairs of wide interlocking swirls, brooch w/partial Cartier signature & numbers, the set (ILLUS.).... **$1,763**

Stylized Leaf-form Brooch & Earrings

Set: brooch & earrings; diamond & 14k gold, the brooch designed to resemble a pair of joined curled & ribbed oblong leaves centered by a row of three full-cut diamonds, the clip-on earrings of the same design, mark of American maker & Cartier mark, in original fitted box, earrings 3/4" l., brooch 1 3/4" l., the suite (ILLUS.) **$1,645**

Cartier "Trinity" Earring & Ring Suite

Set: earrings & ring; tricolor 18k gold, "Trinity" design, the earrings composed of three entwined gold rings, the ring also composed of three rings, signed, ring size 7, the suite (ILLUS.)......................... **$1,175**

Georg Jensen

Georg Jensen Fine Gold Navette-link Bracelet

Bracelet, gold (18k), composed of tightly woven navette-shaped links w/tiny bead edge accents, signed, No. 350, 7 1/2" l. (ILLUS.).. **$5,581**

Bracelet, sterling silver & agate, composed of silver stylized leaves & bud links, completed by a carved carnelian agate clasp, No. 11, signed, 7 1/2" l. **$470**

Bracelet, sterling silver, composed of foliate links joined by blossoms, No. 18, signed, 6 3/4" l. **$646**

Georg Jensen Designer Bracelet with Abstract Links

Bracelet, sterling silver, composed of interlocking abstract amoeba-like open links,

designed by Henning Koppel, No. 88A, signed, 7 1/2" l. (ILLUS.)........................ **$2,115**

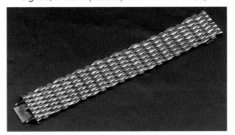

Tightly Arranged Jensen Link Bracelet

Bracelet, sterling silver, composed of tightly arranged navette-form links w/bead accents, signed, No. 86, 7 1/2" l. (ILLUS.).. **$1,880**

Bracelet, sterling silver & green onyx, composed of double-leaf links set w/a green onyx cabochon alternating w/rounded berry cluster links centered by a round green onyx cabochon, No. 3, signed, 7 3/8" l. **$1,293**

Jensen Single Leaf & Berries Brooch

Brooch, sterling silver, designed as a large spade-shaped leaf on a curled looping stem also mounted w/four berries, Georg Jensen, USA, signed, 2" l. (ILLUS.)........... **$118**

Georg Jensen Silver Grape Cluster Brooch

Brooch, sterling silver, designed as a pair of large leaves suspending a large grape cluster, designed by Harald Nielsen, No. 217B, mark of maker & company mark, 2 3/4" l. (ILLUS.)... **$470**

Silver & Onyx Leaf & Berry Brooch

Brooch, sterling silver & green onyx, designed as three wide swirled leaves trimmed w/berries & centered by a round green onyx cabochon, No. 71, signed, 1 1/4" w. (ILLUS.).. **$705**

Jensen Silver & Green Onyx Brooch

Brooch, sterling silver & green onyx, pair of stylized blossoms arranged in a diamond form w/small green onyx cabochons at each tip, signed, No. 54 (ILLUS.)............... **$588**

Jensen Sterling & Lapis Lazuli Brooch

Brooch, sterling silver & lapis lazuli, designed as a stylized petaled blossom centered by a small lapis cabochon & flanked by pairs of long oval leaves, suspending a large bezel-set lapis oval cabochon, signed, No. 193, 1 3/4" l. (ILLUS.)............ **$1,998**

Jensen Designer Silver Freeform Brooch

Brooch, sterling silver, large curled leaf-like freeform design by Torun Buelow-Huebe, signed by Jensen & designer, No. 374, 2 1/4 x 2 1/2" (ILLUS.)................ **$499**

Quatrefoil Georg Jenson Silver Brooch

Brooch, sterling silver, oblong openwork quatrefoil design w/stylized florals, No. 305, signed, 1 3/4" l. (ILLUS.)................... **$235**

Freeform Spooned Jensen Silver Brooch

Brooch, sterling silver, oblong spooned freeform design, signed, initial "NJ," No. 328, 1 1/2 x 2" (ILLUS.) **$176**

Jensen Abstract Star-form Brooch

Brooch, sterling silver, openwork four-point abstract star-like design, No. 339, 2 1/4" w. (ILLUS.)....................................... **$294**

Jensen Silver Dove & Leaf Brooch

Brooch, sterling silver, round openwork designs w/a stylized dove framed w/scrolling leaves, No. 165, signed, possible repair to pin stem, 1 1/2" d. (ILLUS.)............. **$253**

Scalloped Leafy Jensen Brooch

Brooch, sterling silver, rounded slightly scalloped form w/an openwork center composed of entwined leaves, No. 20, signed (ILLUS.) **$823**

Jensen Rounded Abstract Brooch

Brooch, sterling silver, rounded square abstract openwork ring w/folded sides, No. 368, signed, w/original box, 1 3/4" w. (ILLUS.) **$294**

Pairs of Georg Jensen Sterling Silver Cuff Links

Cuff links, sterling silver, two pairs, one w/a simple flat oval top w/a thin incised band, the other w/a round head decorated w/a nautilus-type shell, each marked "Sterling - Denmark," the pair (ILLUS.)............. **$538**

Jensen Abstract Silver Loop Earrings

Earrings, sterling silver, clip-on type, designed as an abstract wide tapering hoop, signed, No. 126B, pr. (ILLUS.)......... **$206**

Nanna Ditzel Earrings by Jensen

Earrings, sterling silver, pendant-style, long tapering abstract teardrop design by Nanna Ditzel, No. 128, signed by Jensen, 3 1/4" l., pr. (ILLUS.) **$499**

Necklace, gem-set sterling silver, composed of openwork links w/a pair of stylized leaves enclosing a bezel-set cabochon almandite garnet & alternating w/openwork stylized blossom links centered by a cabochon garnet or w/links formed by pairs of silver bars & beads, No. 1, signed, 13 5/8" l. **$2,938**

Jensen Silver, Green Onyx and Carnelian Floral Necklace

Necklace, silver & hardstone, composed of silver leaf & blossom-form links alternately set w/small cabochon green onyx & carnelian, completed by a T-clasp, signed, carnelian added, 18" l. (ILLUS.) . **$3,173**

Fine Georg Jensen Silver & Moonstone Necklace

Necklace, silver & moonstone, composed of stylized leaf links bezel-set w/small moonstone cabochons alternating with berry-like clusters also centered by a moonstone cabochon, signed, 16 3/4" l. (ILLUS.)... **$4,230**

Georg Jensen Necklace with Abstract Links

Necklace, sterling silver, composed of abstract amoeba-like open links, designed by Henning Koppel, No. 88A, signed, 18 1/4" l. (ILLUS.).................................... **$4,406**

Jensen Leaf-and-Bar Link Silver Necklace

Necklace, sterling silver, composed of scrolled leaf links alternating w/bar & double bead links, completed by a circular box clasp, designed by Harald Nielsen, marked, No. 96A, 16 5/8" l. (ILLUS.) ... **$999**

Jensen Silver & Green Onyx Necklace

Necklace, sterling silver & green onyx, composed of double-leaf links set w/a green onyx cabochon connected by pairs of double-bar & bead links & alternating w/rounded berry cluster links centered by a round green onyx cabochon, No. 1, signed, 16 1/2" l. (ILLUS.)...................... **$3,173**

Georg Jensen Onyx & Silver Pendant

Pendant-necklace, silver & green onyx, the oval pendant centered by an oval onyx plaque framed by openwork silver mount decorated w/leaves, suspended from a silver chain, No. 54, signed, overall 35" l. (ILLUS., previous page) **$2,938**

Jensen Silver Openwork Ring Pin

Pin, sterling silver, openwork ring w/finely petaled sides w/a grooved crossbar, No. 310, signed, 1 1/8" d. (ILLUS.) **$235**

Georg Jensen Round Leaf & Berry Pin

Pin, sterling silver, round shape composed of three curled leaves separated by lines of bead-like berries, No. 82A, signed (ILLUS.) **$235**

Pair of Georg Jensen Oval Silver Pins

Pins, sterling silver, both designed as a narrow open oval ring w/a feathered design fitted at the top by a pair of simple stylized leaves centered by a small blossom, No. 227, signed, 1 1/4" l., pr. (ILLUS.) .. **$264**

Jensen Lapis Lazuli & Gold Ring

Ring, lapis lazuli & 18k gold, bezel-set w/a large oval lapis cabochon framed by a gold band, signed, No. 1046A, 7/8" l., size 6 3/4 (ILLUS.) **$999**

Ring, sterling silver & moonstone, bezel-set cabochon moonstone framed by floral devices, No. 1C, signed, size 7 1/2............ **$382**

Georg Jensen Moonstone Ring

Ring, sterling silver & moonstone, the top fitted w/a large oval moonstone cabochon in a silver mount, No. 51, signed, size 6 (ILLUS.) **$764**

Jensen Silver & Moonstone Brooch

Set: brooch & earrings: brooch in sterling silver & moonstone, a thin four-lobed openwork framed enclosing two back-to-back curled-petal blossoms centered by a long oval silver cabochon w/a single small moonstone cabochon at the top & bottom, signed, No. 236B, w/similar clip-on earrings by Laurence Foss, brooch 1 1/2" l., the set (ILLUS.)........................... **$470**

Fine Jensen Silver Bracelet & Earring Set

Set: necklace & earrings; sterling silver, the necklace composed of small flexible navette-form links accented by tiny bud designs, the clip-on earrings w/a leaf & bud design, necklace No. 86, earrings No. 106, signed, earrings 3/4" l., necklace 15 1/2" l., the suite (ILLUS.) **$3,760**

Set: pair of earrings & brooch; sterling silver, designed as stylized tulip blossoms, No. 100, signed, earrings 3/4" l., brooch 1 3/4" l., the set **$323**

Heyman (Oscar) & Brothers

Fine Sapphire & Diamond Heyman Earrings

Earrings, sapphire, diamond & platinum, clip-on type, each w/an openwork spiraling starburst design, the arms prong-set w/circular-cut blue sapphires alternating w/tapering baguette & full-cut diamonds, all centered by a large cushion-cut blue sapphire, No. 49205, marks, 1" d., pr. (ILLUS.) **$7,050**

Heyman & Bros. Emerald & Diamond Ring

Ring, emerald & diamond, the top set w/alternating step-cut emeralds & diamonds, 18k gold & platinum mount, signed, No. 36728, size 5 1/2 (ILLUS.) **$2,703**

Tiffany & Company

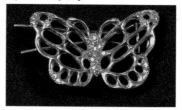

Tiffany Gem-set Butterfly Barrette

Barrette, diamond & 18k gold, designed as an openwork gold butterfly bead-set w/full- and single-cut diamond mélée, designed by Angela Cummings for Tiffany, signed (ILLUS.) **$940**

Tiffany Gem-set Gold Link Bracelet

Bracelet, bicolor 14k gold, sapphire & diamond, composed of six large open slightly arched rectangular links joined by small gold band links centered by a cabochon sapphire flanked by bands of small diamonds, mark of an American maker, signed, 7 3/4" l. (ILLUS.) **$2,468**

Tiffany Cultured Pearl & Sapphire Bracelet

Bracelet, cultured pearl & sapphire, composed of four strands w/a total of 144 white pearls divided into segments by narrow gold spacers set w/circular-cut sapphires, completed by a heart-shaped clasp pavé-set w/sapphires, signed, 7" l. (ILLUS.) **$1,763**

Tiffany 1960s Gold & Diamond Bracelet

Bracelet, diamond & 18k gold, bangle-type, hinged, designed as two bands decorated w/spaced double gold rings flanking clusters of four full-cut diamonds, diamonds weighing about .96 cts., marked, ca. 1967, interior circumference (ILLUS.)... **$2,233**

1970s Tiffany Diamond & Gold Bracelet

Bracelet, diamond & 18k gold, bangle-type, hinged, the wide band w/an open center band ending in bead-set diamond points flanking a large central "X" bead-set w/full-cut diamonds, diamonds weighing about 1.40 cts., ca.1970, signed, interior circumference 6 1/2" (ILLUS.)................ **$2,938**

Delicate Tiffany Gold Three-Band Bracelet

Bracelet, gold (18k), bangle-type, designed as two very thin ropetwist bands flanking a smooth center band, signed, interior circumference 7 3/4" (ILLUS.).................... **$999**

Gold Serpent Bracelet from Tiffany

Bracelet, gold (18k), bangle-type, hinged, in the form a serpent biting its tail, engraved scales, made in Italy, retailed by Tiffany & Co., signed (ILLUS.)................................. **$2,350**

Tiffany Gold Bracelet with Ring & Textured Links

Bracelet, gold (18k), composed of plain round links joined by pairs of flat banded oval links centered by a bar, signed "Tiffany Italy," partial signature plaque missing, boxed (ILLUS.)................................. **$1,528**

Tiffany Decorative Link Gold Bracelet

Bracelet, gold (18k), composed of wide oblong ribbed links alternating w/plain ring links, signed, 7 3/4" l. (ILLUS.)................ **$2,585**

Bracelet, gold (18k) & diamond, designed as three joined bracelets w/tapering ribbed links, each w/bead-set full-cut diamonds, diamonds weighing about 4.35 cts., signed, 7" l. (ILLUS., bottom of page).. **$6,169**

Gold Diamond Link & Sapphire Bracelet

Bracelet, gold (18k) & sapphire, designed as a double band of small open diamond links alternating w/a smooth or textured surface, accented along the sides w/small blue sapphires, 6 3/4" l. (ILLUS.) **$1,880**

Bracelet, sterling silver, composed of floral plaques, signed, ca.1950s, 7" l. **$441**

Tiffany Three-band Gold & Diamond Bracelet

Stone-set 18k Gold Tiffany Bracelet

Bracelet, turquoise, lapis lazuli & 18k gold, composed of large spiral-designed links alternating w/smaller ring loops topped by a band of alternating small lapis & turquoise cabochons, signed, 7" l. (ILLUS.) **$4,348**

Domed Gold & Gem-set Tiffany Brooch

Brooch, cultured pearl, emerald & 18k gold, a rounded & domed openwork gold design resembling small swirling leaves set w/scattered small emeralds & centered at the top w/a cluster of white pearls w/rose overtones & further emerald accents, signed, 1 1/2" d. (ILLUS.) **$1,645**

Unique Jeweled Stuart Little Brooch

Brooch, diamond, enamel & 18k gold, modeled as the children's character Stuart Little the mouse, the body pavé-set w/smaller-cut diamond mélée, wearing a sailor cap & jacket decorated in basse taille & en plein blue & white enamel, yellow diamond eye, seed pearl snout, platinum & gold mount, designed by Donald Calflin, signed, 3 1/8" l. (ILLUS.) **$17,625**

Tiffany Diamond Butterfly Brooch

Brooch, diamond & platinum, designed as a stylized butterfly w/the four-part wings composed of bands bead-set w/full-cut diamonds weighing about 1.07 cts., signed, 1 1/8" l. (ILLUS.) **$2,115**

Tiffany 14k Gold Flowerhead Brooch

Brooch, gold (14k), designed as a rounded flowerhead w/graduated pointed tiers of petals, 1 1/4" d. (ILLUS.) **$294**

Tiffany Gold & Diamond Feather Brooch

Brooch, gold (14k), platinum & diamond, designed as a long, realisitc yellow gold feather w/the center band set w/full- and single-cut diamond mélée accents, signed, ca. 1940s, 3" l. (ILLUS.) **$1,410**

Tiffany Gold & Tanzanite Flower Brooch

Brooch, tanzanite & 18k gold, designed as a stylized flower w/eight arched & tapering open gold petals centered by a large oval-cut tanzanite, signed, 1 5/8" l. (ILLUS.) **$3,819**

Tiffany Gold Three-leaf Sprig Brooches with Gem Accents

Brooches, gem-set 18k gold, each designed as a sprig of three shaped & pointed textured leaves, one accented w/three small sapphires & the other w/three small rubies, signed, 2" l., pr. (ILLUS.) **$1,293**

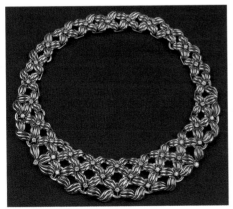

Rare Schlumberger-designed Gold & Diamond Collar

Collar, gold (18k) & diamond, composed of interlocking flexible stylized blossoms each centering a full-cut diamond, dia-

monds weighing 2.95 cts., designed by Jean Schlumberger & marked by Tiffany, mark of French maker Boazzachi, Paris & guarantee stamps, 1957, 12" l. (ILLUS.) **$23,500**

Tiffany Tiger Head Gold Cuff Links

Cuff links, enameled & gem-set 18k gold, each modeled as a tiger head w/black enamel stripes, diamond highlights & emerald eyes, each signed, boxed pr. (ILLUS.) **$2,115**

Tiffany Aquamarine Flower Earrings

Earrings, aquamarine, diamond & platinum, clip-on type, each designed as a large four-petal flower w/each petal set w/a pear-cut aquamarine, full-cut diamond center & single-cut diamonds down the stem, signed, 14k gold clips, 1" w., pr. (ILLUS.) **$8,225**

Earrings, citrine & 18k yellow gold, each w/a mounting fashioned as leafy cluster centered by a pear-cut citrine, total weight approx. 26.81 cts., ca. 1940 .... **$1,380**

Gold & Coral Fan-shaped Earrings

Earrings, coral & 18k gold, clip-on type, each designed as a coral fan w/a gold stem, signed, w/original presentation box, pr. (ILLUS.) **$1,410**

Tiffany Gold & Diamond Earrings

Earrings, gold (18k) & diamond, oval form composed of tapering basketweave-style bands highlighted w/prong-set full-cut diamonds, diamonds weighing about 2.40 cts., signed, pr. (ILLUS.) **$2,350**

Tiffany "Etoile" Gold & Diamond Earrings

Earrings, platinum, 18k gold & diamond, "Etoile" design, simple gold loop set w/four diamond mélée, signed, pr. (ILLUS.)........ **$1,645**

Modern Tiffany Pendant Earrings

Earrings, platinum, diamond & aquamarine, "Legacy Collection," pendant-type, the top designed as a stylized flower w/the petals set w/full-cut diamonds surrounding a circular-cut aquamarine, suspending a cascade of diamond-set leaf links alternating

w/two circular-cut aquamarines, signed & w/original presentation box & receipt, contemporary, pr. (ILLUS.) **$3,408**

Earrings, ruby, diamond & platinum, stud-type, square top centered by a bezel-set square step-cut ruby framed by a ring of full-cut diamonds, signed, w/original presentation boxes & receipt, contemporary, pr. **$3,290**

Tiffany Designer Turquoise & Gold Earrings

Earrings, turquoise & 18k gold, clip-on type, a central oval turquoise cabochon framed by a wide rounded gold band decorated w/a swirled ropework stripes, designed by Schlumberger, signed, 1/2" l., pr. (ILLUS.) **$1,880**

Tiffany Gold Gadrooned Bead Triple-strand Necklace

Necklace, gold (14k), composed of a triple strand of gold swirled gadrooned beads, signed, 18" l. (ILLUS.)............................. **$2,115**

Tiffany Signature Collection Gold Necklace

Necklace, gold (18k), triple-strand w/each strand composed of oblong ribbed beads spaced by small beads, Signature Collection, signed, w/original presentation pouch, 16 1/4" l. (ILLUS. of part)............. **$6,463**

Tiffany Ruby & Gold Necklace

Necklace, ruby & 18k gold, composed of stepped, ribbed half-round openwork links set w/ruby mélée, w/Tiffany & Co. sleeve, 14 1/4" l. (ILLUS.) **$1,645**

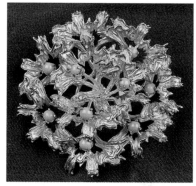

Tiffany Stylized Flower Pendant-Brooch

Pendant-brooch, turquoise & 18k gold, designed as a large openwork stylized flowerhead prong-set w/small turquoise cabochons, signed, 2" d. (ILLUS.) **$1,058**

Delicate Gold Chain & Heart Tiffany Pendant-Necklace

Pendant-necklace, gold (18k), composed of multiple strands of very fine trace link chains connected to an open heart pendant, signed, original presentation sleeve, 16 1/2" l. (ILLUS.) **$940**

Italian Fish Pin Sold by Tiffany

Pin, enameled 18k gold, designed as a tropical fish w/a red, yellow & blue basse taille enameled body, single-cut diamond eye, made in Italy, signed (ILLUS.)........ **$2,115**
Pin, gold (14k), designed as an abstract wing, signed... **$499**

Tiffany Amethyst & Gold Ring

Ring, amethyst & 18k gold, centered by a square-cut amethyst flanked by faceted half-oval amethysts, size 5 (ILLUS.) **$999**

Tiffany Aquamarine & Diamond Ring

Ring, aquamarine, diamond & platinum, prong-set w/a large rectangular cut-cornered aquamarine, the shoulders set w/trillion & full-cut diamonds, signed, boxed, w/ring guard, size 7 1/2 (ILLUS.) **$5,875**

Tiffany Gold & Enamel Basketweave Ring

Ring, enameled 18k gold, wide domed basketweave design w/green enamel high-

lights, signed, minor enamel loss, size 6
(ILLUS.)... **$259**

Tiffany Ribbed & Domed Gold Ring

Ring, gold (18k), a wide domed & ribbed design, signed, size 6 1/2 (ILLUS.) **$353**

Green Tourmaline & Gold Ring

Ring, green tourmaline & 18k gold, the top
set w/a rectangular step-cut tourmaline
flanked by graduating "X" designs, designed by Schlumberger, retailed by Tif-
fany, signed, size 4 3/4 (ILLUS.) **$2,115**

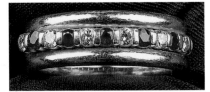

Tiffany Lapis & Gold Ring

Ring, lapis lazuli & 18k gold, the top set
w/an oval cabochon lapis within a ringed
mount, signed, size 4 1/2 (ILLUS.)............. **$646**

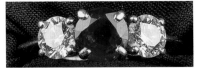

Tiffany Ruby, Diamond & Gold Ring

Ring, ruby, diamond & 18k gold, the simple
gold band centered by a narrow row of
alternating full-cut diamonds & circular-
cut rubies, signed, size 5 1/2 (ILLUS.) **$823**

Fine Tiffany Ruby & Diamond Ring

Ring, ruby, diamond & 18k gold, the top
centered by a prong-set circular-cut

ruby flanked by full-cut diamonds, platinum & 18k gold mount, signed, size
5 1/4 (ILLUS.) **$7,050**

Miscellaneous Estate Pieces

Cultured Pearl & Diamond Bracelet

Bracelet, cultured pearl & diamond, the
wide band of 80 pearls w/silver overtones spaced by bead-set single-cut diamonds, completed by a round wheel-
form clasp set overall w/full- and single-
cut diamonds, diamonds weighing about
2.25 cts., 14k white gold mount, 7 1/4" l.
(ILLUS.) **$2,350**

Gold Mesh and Diamond Bracelet

Bracelet, diamond & 14k gold, a fine gold
mesh band widening at the center where
it is mounted w/11 full-cut round diamonds, total diamond weight about 1.75
cts, 6" l. (ILLUS.) **$999**
Bracelet, diamond & 14k gold, composed of
three lines of 144 flexibly-set full-cut diamonds weighing about 10.08 cts., 7" l.
(ILLUS., top next page).......................... **$4,406**

Three-Line Diamond & Gold Bracelet

Rare Thin Diamond & Platinum Bracelet

Ribbed Gold & Diamond Bracelet

Bracelet, diamond & 18k gold, bangle-type, hinged, a wide ribbed gold mount centered by a band bead-set w/113 diamonds weighing about 4.21 cts., one diamond missing, interior circumference 6 3/4" (ILLUS.) **$3,055**

Diamond Bracelet with Oblong & Ringed Links

Bracelet, diamond & 18k white gold, composed of large oblong links channel-set w/rows of full-cut diamonds alternating w/triple-ring links prong-set w/diamonds, diamonds weighing about 19.34 cts., 7" l. (ILLUS.).. **$7,638**

Rare Diamond & Emerald Bangle Bracelet

Bracelet, diamond & emerald, bangle-type, the wide tapering openwork band de-

signed w/long scrolls & leaves prong- and bead-set w/170 square-, step-, full- and single-cut diamonds all centered by a single slightly curved band centered by a large emerald-cut emerald flanked by eight smaller step-cut emeralds, diamonds weighing about 13.38 cts., interior circumference 6 1/2" (ILLUS.).............. **$12,925**

Green Lion Head Gold Bangle Bracelet

Bracelet, diamond & gem-set 18k gold, bypass bangle-type, the sides textured & trimmed w/bead-set single-cut diamonds & ending in a figural lion heads w/collars also trimmed w/diamonds & set w/ruby eyes, Greek hallmarks (ILLUS.)............. **$1,645**

Bracelet, diamond & platinum, composed of sixteen emerald-cut diamonds & 32 diamond baguettes, total weight about 9.60 cts., 6 1/2" l. (ILLUS., second from top) **$12,925**

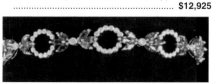

Diamond & Sapphire Link Bracelet

Bracelet, diamond, sapphire & white gold, composed of seven round links each w/12 diamonds & a single diamond flanked by six baguette-cut blue sapphires, marked "Nl3212 18K," 7" l. (ILLUS.) **$345**

Two Emerald, Diamond & Gold Bracelets

Bracelet, emerald, diamond & 18k gold, the flexible fancy links set w/36 full-cut diamonds & 72 circular-cut emeralds, 7" l. (ILLUS. top with other emerald, diamond & gold bracelet) **$3,055**

Bracelet, emerald, diamond & 18k gold, the flexible band composed of small overlapping fishscale links prong-set w/alternating groups of four full-cut diamonds & circular-cut emeralds, 7 1/2" l. (ILLUS. bottom with other emerald, diamond & gold bracelet) **$1,880**

Enameled Gold Ladybug Bracelet

Bracelet, enameled 18k gold, designed as links in the shape of ladybugs enameled in dark red, joined by curb links & w/a toggle end & ring clasp, 7 1/2" l. (ILLUS.) **$999**

Gold & Diamond Flower Blossom Bracelet

Bracelet, gold (18k & 22k) & diamond, each link designed as a four-petal blossom centered by a full-cut diamond, 7 1/4" l. (ILLUS.) **$1,763**

18k Gold Woven Mesh Bracelet

Bracelet, gold (18k), a wide woven mesh band w/a subtle herringbone design edged w/thin ropetwist border bands, the clasp w/bezel-set rubies, 8" l. (ILLUS.) **$823**

Bracelet, gold (18k) & diamond, composed of layered small gold flower petals, some w/a bead-set single-cut diamond, 7" l. (ILLUS., second from bottom of page).... **$5,875**

Bracelet, gold (18k) & diamond, composed of tightly woven stylized four-petal floral links highlighted by 75 diamond mélée, diamonds weighing about 5.25 cts., 7 1/8" l. (ILLUS. top with gold & enamel bracelet, bottom of page) **$5,288**

Fine Gold Floral Petal & Diamond Bracelet

Unusual Gold Bracelet

Fancy Diamond-set Floral Brooch

Brooch, diamond & platinum, designed as a cluster of three five-petal blossoms amid long undulating diamond-set leaves, diamonds weighing about 3.90 cts., 2 1/2" l. (ILLUS.).. **$2,585**

Serpentine & Scroll Diamond Brooch

Brooch, diamond & platinum, designed w/two long serpentine bands & one C-scroll band joined in the center by three-section bar set w/three large full-cut diamonds, set overall w/smaller prong- and bead-set old European-, old single- and single-cut diamonds w/fanned accents each ending in a small diamond, millegrain accents, diamonds weighing 3.57 cts., 2 5/8" l. (ILLUS.) **$1,528**

Emerald, Diamond & Gold Spiral Brooch

Brooch, emerald, diamond & 18k gold, designed as a tight spiral w/two tiers prong- and bead-set w/98 single-cut diamond mélée, highlighted w/ an inner band of 21

circular-cut emeralds, diamonds weighing about 1.00 cts., 1 1/2" l. (ILLUS.) **$2,703**

Enameled & Gem-set Octopus Brooch

Brooch, enameled & gem-set gold, designed as a comical octopus decorated w/basse taille enamel in shades of dark & light blue, the ends of the tentacles set w/full-cut diamonds, ruby eyes, 18k bicolor gold mount, 1 3/4 x 2" (ILLUS.) **$940**

Fine Enamel & Diamond Sailfish Brooch

Brooch, enameled gold & diamond, designed as a realistic sailfish, the fins & head enameled in shades of green & dark blue, the body pavé-set w/51 full-cut diamonds, 18k gold & platinum mount, 3" l. (ILLUS.) **$4,348**

Pearl, Diamond & Gold Flower Brooch

Brooch, freshwater pearl, diamond & 14k gold, designed as a stylized flower w/the flaring pointed petals made from freshwater pearls centering a cluster of three single-cut diamonds, on a gold leafy stem (ILLUS.).. **$235**

Gem-Set Grotesque Mask Brooch

Brooch, gem-set 18k bicolor gold, designed as a round grotesque mask w/flame-like beard & hair, bead-set w/26 circular-cut rubies & 125 full-cut diamonds, two circular-cut emeralds in the eyes, signed "R. W.," 2" d. (ILLUS.).................................. **$4,113**

Gem-set Gold Comical Cat Brooch

Brooch, gem-set 18k gold, designed as a comical upright grinning cat holding a bone, the bone & his buck teeth set w/single-cut diamonds, emerald eyes & a ruby nose, mark of maker, 2" l. (ILLUS.).... **$823**

Gem-set 18k Gold Clown Brooch

Brooch, gem-set 18k gold, modeled as a clown w/a long tassel on his pointed cap, articulated hands & arms, ruby mélée

nose, diamond, sapphire & ruby mélée buttons, 2 1/4" l. (ILLUS.).......................... **$294**

Gem-set Gold & Rock Crystal Flower Brooch

Brooch, gem-set gold, carved rock crystal & emerald, designed as a flower on a leafy stem, the large blossom w/the five petals carved from frosted clear rock crystal centered by small diamonds surrounded by small round emeralds, the long curved gold stem w/one gold leaf & two other oblong leaves carved from emeralds, the stem also w/a tiny flower w/blue sapphire petals around a diamond center, 14k gold mount, 2" h. (ILLUS.) **$764**

French Shaggy Dog Gold Brooch

Brooch, gold (18k), designed as a short shaggy terrier-like dog w/the hair composed of flexible foxtail fringe, sapphire eye, mark of French maker & guarantee stamp, 2" l. (ILLUS.)................................ **$1,998**

Gold Two Kitten Brooch

Brooch, gold (18k) & emerald, designed as the upper bodies of two kittens w/emerald eyes, stamped "KN" (ILLUS.).............. **$999**

Danish Silver & Rhodochrosite Brooch

Brooch, silver & rhodochrosite, designed as a large open oval leaf ring decorated w/four 4-petal blossoms each centered by a rhodochrosite cabochon, the center w/a large oval cabochon rhodochrosite, Denmark, signed w/assay marks (ILLUS.)......... **$206**

Fine Turquoise, Diamond & Gold Brooch

Brooch, turquoise, diamond & 18k gold, an oblong abstract flower design set w/nine turquoise cabochons interspersed w/full-cut diamonds & framed by delicate gold leaves, diamonds weighing about 2.00 cts., 2 1/2" l. (ILLUS.) **$2,468**

Floral Spray Diamond & Sapphire Brooch

Brooch-pendant, diamond, sapphire & platinum, designed as a stylized floral spray w/long curved stems supporting two large flowers w/three long openwork petals all set w/bead- and channel-set baguette & full-cut diamonds & centered by three clusters of circular-cut blue sapphires, 2 3/8" l. (ILLUS.)......................... **$2,350**

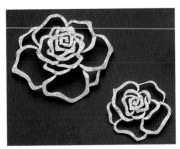

Fine Openwork Rose Diamond Brooches

Brooches, diamond & 14k white gold, set of two each in the form of an openwork rose bead-set overall w/single-cut diamonds, the set (ILLUS.)..................................... **$3,643**

Cameo habillé (gem-set) pin, carved shell & diamond, the cameo carved w/a bust portrait of a woman w/upswept hair, bezel-set w/an old European-cut diamonds weighing about 2.25 cts., 14k gold frame inscribed & dated 1947 .... **$5,875**

Gold & Enamel Nantucket Basket Charm

Charm, enameled 14k gold, designed in the shape of a Nantucket basket w/a small green-enameled map of Nantucket in the center of the lid, enclosing a miniature penny, signed & dated 1977, 1" w. (ILLUS.) **$294**

Group of Three Gold Charm Bracelets

Charm bracelet, gold (14k), composed of fancy baton links, suspending 13 charms including an artist's palette, bicycle, boater hat, rose-cut diamond & enamel car, diamond lantern & a sapphire & diamond fly, marked "14kt Landin 1922," 7 1/4" l. (ILLUS. top with two other charm bracelets, previous page) **$940**

Charm bracelet, gold (14k), composed of fancy links suspending 25 charms, including Romeo & Juliet letter, lighter w/flame, Jonah & the whale, Ferris wheel & devil w/cocktail shaker, 6 3/4" l. (ILLUS. bottom with two other charm bracelets, previous page) **$764**

Charm bracelet, gold (14k), composed of fancy twisted links suspending 21 charms including "I Love You" spinner, pram, baby shoes, enameled American flag, articulated skeleton, enameled Santa Claus, egg timer, Airedale, Boxer, Scottie & Cocker Spaniel, 6 3/4" l. (ILLUS. center with two other charm bracelets, previous page) **$881**

Charm bracelet, gold (14k), the trace link bracelet w/green tourmaline beads & freshwater pearls suspending 15 charms including a movable lobster, abacus & Irish harp, one charm in silver, 1950s **$382**

Cross pendant, emerald & 18k gold, set w/12 rectangular-, step- and emerald-cut emeralds, engraved mount, suspended from a 14k gold fancy link chain, pendant 2 3/4" l., overall 18" l. **$940**

Gold, Amethyst & Diamond Earrings

Earrings, amethyst, diamond & 18k gold, clip-on type, a simple rounded gold frame surrounding a large bezel-set amethyst cabochon, a bottom bar channel-set w/baguette diamonds & cabochon amethyst highlights, pr. (ILLUS.) **$940**

Amethyst & Diamond Pendant Earrings

Earrings, amethyst, diamond & 18k white gold, pendant-type, a top floret of single-cut diamonds suspending a large oval fancy-cut amethyst framed by a band of small diamonds, gold mount, pr. (ILLUS.) **$588**

Aquamarine & Diamond Earrings

Earrings, aquamarine, diamond & platinum, clip-on type, prong-set w/a large rectangular step-cut aquamarine flanked along one side w/a spray of diamonds, 14k white gold findings, pr. (ILLUS.) **$3,643**

Pair of Oval Gold & Diamond Earrings

Earrings, bicolor 18k gold & diamond, clip-on type, oval domed shape w/a criss-cross band design, bead-set w/full-cut diamonds weighing about 6.70 cts., 1" l., pr. (ILLUS.) **$7,050**

Citrine Teardrop & Gold Earrings

Earrings, citrine & 14k gold, designed w/a large faceted bead suspending a gold link w/a small bead about a large faceted teardrop citrine, pr. (ILLUS.) **$999**

18k Gold Clip-on Knot Earrings

Earrings, gold (18k), clip-on type, each designed as a two-band rounded knot, 1" d., pr. (ILLUS.) **$823**

Gold Fish-shaped Earrings

Earrings, gold (18k) & diamond, clip-on type, designed as angel fish w/long flowing ribbed fins, each w/a small diamond eye, 1 3/8 x 1 3/4", pr. (ILLUS.)................. **$940**

Long Jadeite, Diamond & Onyx Earrings

Earrings, green jadeite, diamond & 18k white gold, pendant-type, each w/the long top mount designed as a diamond-set bellflower above & below an onyx disk, suspending a long teardrop of green jadeite, 2 3/4" l., pr. (ILLUS.).................. **$1,528**

Pair of Kunzite & Gold Earrings

Earrings, kunzite & 18k gold, clip-on type, each set w/a large oval-cut lavender kunzite, pr. (ILLUS.)... **$999**

Earrings, lapis lazuli, coral & 18k gold, octagonal form centering a reddish orange coral cabochon framed by lapis lazuli, signed by Adioro, 1/2" l., pr........................ **$646**

Rare Yellow Diamond Earrings

Earrings, light yellow diamond, platinum & 18k gold, stud-type, the square top centered by a faceted cushion-style yellow diamond weighing about 1.60 cts., framed by small full-cut diamonds weighing about 3.67 cts., pr. (ILLUS.)............ **$12,925**

Pair of Purple Pansy Earrings

Earrings, patinated 18k gold, omega clip-on type, designed as a stylized pansy blossom w/a purple finish, signed by JAR, Paris, w/original presentation pouch, pr. (ILLUS.)... **$1,528**

Mikimoto Cultured Pearl Necklace

Necklace, cultured pearl, composed of 54 white pearls w/rose overtones measuring about 7.50 to 7.80 mm, 18k gold clasp, mark of Mikimoto, w/original presentation box, 18" l. (ILLUS.) **$1,998**

Gold & Diamond Chevron Necklace

Necklace, diamond & 14k gold, a heavy herringbone design chain centered by a chevron-shaped section pavé-set w/full-cut diamonds, 16 1/4" l. (ILLUS.) **$1,175**

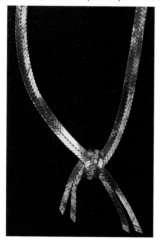

Gold & Diamond Lariat Necklace

Necklace, diamond & 18k gold, lariat-style, composed of a flat herringbone design chain w/a wrapped loop trimmed w/ten full-cut diamonds, 18" l. (ILLUS.) **$999**

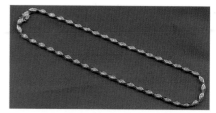

Diamond Necklace with Navette-shaped Links

Necklace, diamond & platinum, composed of navette-form links each bead-set w/a full-cut diamond, diamonds weighing about 4.06 cts., 15 1/2" l. (ILLUS.) **$3,995**

Extremely Fine Diamond & Platinum Necklace

Necklace, diamond & platinum, the single band link band channel-set w/diamonds, centered by a long C-scroll-ended band w/a bottom rim sprig, prong- and bead-set overall w/marquise- and full-cut and baguette diamonds, diamonds weighing about 14.16 cts., 14 1/2" l. (ILLUS.) **$12,925**

Gold & Diamond Heart Necklace

Necklace, gold (14k) & diamond, the smooth necklace suspending an open stylized heart w/a glossy border & matte front gyp-sy-set w/ten full-cut diamonds, diamonds weighing about .70 cts., 15 1/2" l. (ILLUS.)... **$558**

Four-diamond & Gold Pendant

Pendant, diamond & 14k gold, composed of a cluster of four prong-set full-cut diamonds, total weight about 1.10 cts., 3/4" l. (ILLUS., previous page) **$1,116**

Diamond & Gold Flower Pendant

Pendant, diamond & 14k white gold, modeled as a five-petal flower, each petal paved w/small diamonds, the center w/three yellow gold-mounted diamonds, marked "14k BH," w/a 16" l. white gold chain marked "585 BH" pendant 3/4" w. (ILLUS.)............... **$690**

Whimsical Gold Purse Pendant

Pendant, diamond & 18k gold, made in the shape of a rectangular purse w/a basketweave design & the edge of the pointed flap set w/a line of tiny full-cut diamonds, suspended on a delicate curb-link chain, 7/8 x 1 1/4" (ILLUS.).................. **$646**
Pendant, enameled silver, "Red Grooms" design, designed as a pair of polychrome enameled dancers, signed front & back, No. 007.. **$999**

Opal, Diamond & Sapphire Pendant

Pendant, opal, diamond, sapphire & 18k gold, the large prong-set oval white opal framed by a mixed band of circular-cut sapphires & full-cut diamonds (ILLUS.)...... **$646**

Fine Reverse-painted Crystal Pendant

Pendant, reverse-painted crystal & 14k gold, large round domed crystal reverse-painted w/a terrier puppy, the gold frame designed as a collar & crop, suspended from a later rope link chain completed by a barrel clasp, overall 24" l., pendant 1 1/2" d. (ILLUS.) **$2,350**
Pendant-brooch, cultured pearl & 18k gold, centering a cluster of white pearls w/rose overtones, within a shaped frame, suspended from a trace link chain, mark of Mikimoto, pendant 2 1/4" d., overall 23 3/4" l.. **$823**

Pendant with Large Aquamarine

Pendant-pin, aquamarine, diamond & platinum, centered by a large rectangular cut-cornered aquamarine suspended from a decorative band of full-cut diamonds, on a silver trace link chain (ILLUS.) **$3,173**
Pin, amethyst & 14k gold, the gold rosette prong-set w/circular-cut amethysts, signed by J.E. Caldwell & Co., 2 3/4" d. **$206**

Carved Coral & Gold Blossom Pin

Pin, coral & 14k gold, designed as a carved peony-like blossom w/engraved gold leaves wrapping up the side, 1 1/2 x 1 3/4" (ILLUS.) **$558**

Gold & Diamond Crab-shaped Pin

Pin, diamond & 18k bicolor gold, designed as a realistic gold crab w/the back pavé-set w/35 single-cut diamonds, 1 1/4" w. (ILLUS.).................................... **$940**

Gold Knotted Ribbon Pin with Diamonds

Pin, diamond & 18k gold, designed as an openwork knotted feathered gold ribbon prong-set down the center w/a band of full-cut diamonds, diamonds weighing about 1.89 cts., 2" l. (ILLUS.) **$1,528**

Enameled Gold Puppy Pin

Pin, enameled 18k gold, designed as a puppy walking w/one front paw raised, red enamel on his head w/black & white eyes, 1 1/8" l. (ILLUS.) **$382**

Pin, freshwater pearl & 14k gold, figure of an angel w/freshwater pearl wings & cloud, blue stone eyes **$264**

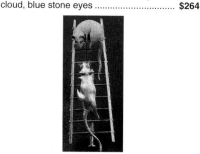

Gold Mice on Ladder Pin

Pin, gem-set 18k bicolor gold, designed as two mice w/ruby eyes climbing a ladder (ILLUS.)... **$2,703**

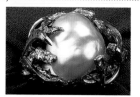

Baroque Pearl & Gold Ring

Ring, baroque pearl & 18k gold, a large silvery grey pearl grasped by gold leaf prongs, size 5 3/4 (ILLUS.) **$294**

Fine Black Opal & Diamond Ring

Ring, black opal, diamond & gold, prong-set w/a long oval cabochon black opal framed by 28 full-cut diamonds weighing about 1.12 cts., 14k white gold mount, size 6 (ILLUS.) **$2,938**

Carved Moonstone & Textured Gold Ring

Ring, carved moonstone & 18k gold, a rectangular gold textured mount w/rounded corners, dished gold top centered by a moonstone carved as the head of a woman w/swirling hair, w/ring guard, size 5 1/2 (ILLUS.)... **$1,175**

Unusual Citrine & Orange Garnet Ring

Ring, citrine, orange garnet & 18k white gold, the top centered by an oval-cut citrine framed by a narrow ring of orange garnets, patinated gallery & shoulders

pavé-set w/orange garnets, size 6 1/2
(ILLUS.)... **$1,293**

Cultured Pearl and Diamond Ring

Ring, cultured pearl, diamond & 14k gold, the top centered by a large white pearl measuring about 11.00 mm, flanked by a mount w/pointed sides set w/32 marquise- and full-cut diamonds, size 6 1/2 (ILLUS.)... **$646**

Dramatic Diamond & Gold Ring

Ring, diamond & 14k gold, the wide band w/gold ribs alternating w/three rows of small diamonds, centered at the top by a large prong-set full-cut diamond weighing about 2.07 cts., size 7 (ILLUS.)......... **$7,638**

Gold Ribbon Band & Diamond Ring

Ring, diamond & 18k gold, a rounded ribbon band w/loops at each side & centering ten prong-set full-cut diamonds, diamonds weighing about 1.15 cts., size 4 1/2 (ILLUS.)... **$940**

Diamond Ring Converted from Old Pin

Ring, diamond & 18k gold, the long oblong gold mount w/ornate pierced floral & foliate designs centered by a row of three bezel-set old mine-cut diamonds weighing about 3 cts., antique pin converted to a ring, size 6 3/4 (ILLUS.) **$3,878**

Gold & Diamond "I Love You" Ring

Ring, diamond & bicolor 14k gold, a simple band w/a pierced design spelling out "I Love You," each letter set w/single-cut diamonds, size 7 1/2 (ILLUS.) **$264**

Cognac Diamond Ring

Ring, diamond, colored diamond & platinum, the top centered by a large navette-shaped cognac diamond weighing about 3.09 cts., flanked on the sides by a graduating row of four full-cut diamonds weighing about .94 cts., size 8 3/4 (ILLUS.) **$5,500**

Fine Pear-cut Diamond Solitaire Ring

Ring, diamond & gold, solitaire-type, prong-set w/a large pear-cut diamond weighing about 4.20 cts., flanked by small diamond baguettes weighing about .21 cts., 14k white gold mount, two laser-drilled holes, size 5 (ILLUS.) **$14,100**

Eternity Band with Marquise Diamonds

Ring, diamond & platinum, eternity band-style, the wide band composed of 18 prong-set marquise-cut diamonds weighing about 5.85 cts., size 5 1/2 (ILLUS.)... **$4,113**

Rare & Unique Rectangular Diamond Ring

Ring, diamond & platinum, prong-set w/a very large emerald-cut diamond weighing about 7.90 cts. flanked by tapered baguette diamonds, size 7 1/2 (ILLUS., previous page)... **$56,400**

Diamond & Platinum Bypass Ring

Ring, diamond & platinum, twin-stone bypass-style, the overlapping bands each set w/a pear-cut diamond weighing about .99 & 1.99 cts., flanked by narrow bands of diamond baguettes, total diamond weight about 2.68 cts., size 7 (ILLUS.) ... **$6,463**

Dramatic Diamond & Sapphire Ring

Ring, diamond, sapphire & platinum, set w/a large marquise-cut diamond weighing about 1.68 cts. beside an oval-cut blue sapphire, flanked by tension-set small diamonds, w/laser-inscribed girdle, size 6 1/4 (ILLUS.) **$7,050**

Extremely Rare Diamond Solitaire Ring

Ring, diamond solitaire, the prong-set round brilliant-cut diamond weighing about 11.55 cts., accompanied by an 18k gold mounting, size 5 1/2 (ILLUS.).............. **$113,800**

Fine Italian Gem-set Gold Ring

Ring, emerald, diamond & 18k gold, the wide band centered by a rosette of full-cut diamonds, the sides prong-set w/outer bands composed of 20 circular-cut emeralds flanking two bands of full-cut diamonds, diamonds weighing about 2.80 cts., Italy, size 6 3/4 (ILLUS.) **$1,175**

Unusual Enameled & Diamond Tiger Ring

Ring, enameled 18k gold & diamond, designed as a snarling tiger head w/black & white enameled stripes & a red & black-enameled nose & a red tongue, the upper lips & side of the head set w/single-cut diamonds, the black & white-striped tail curls up at one side, size 5 (ILLUS.).......... **$499**

Dramatic Tourmaline & Diamond Ring

Ring, green tourmaline, diamond & 18k white gold, the top prong-set w/a long rectangular step-cut tourmaline flanked by curved clusters of full-cut diamonds, diamonds weighing about 3.30 cts., size 7 1/2 (ILLUS.)... **$5,581**

Rare Lady's Alexandrite & Diamond Ring

Ring, lady's fashion-type, diamond, natural Alexandrite & 18k gold, the round top centered by a large 4.32 ct. Alexandrite set in gold prongs & flanked by two .35 ct square diamonds & ten round diamonds set in platinum, ring stamped "PT950" (ILLUS.).. **$13,800**

Lady's Ring with Large Ruby & Diamonds

Ring, lady's fashion-type, ruby, diamond & platinum, the top centered by a single oval faceted ruby weighing 2.24 cts. flanked by two oval diamonds w/a total weight of .74 cts., slender band, size 6 (ILLUS.).. **$3,107**

Fine Lady's Star Ruby & Diamond Ring

Ring, lady's fashion-type, star ruby, diamond, platinum & yellow gold, the top centered by a large round 9 ct. cabochon star ruby within a hexagonal band decorated w/a mélée of round-cut & rectangular diamonds set in platinum w/a yellow gold backing, diamond-set panels at the sides of the top, stamped "PT950" (ILLUS.) **$4,600**

Lovely Lavender Jadeite & Diamond Ring

Ring, lavender jadeite, diamond & platinum, the oblong top centered by a large lavender jadeite cabochon framed by full-cut round & baguette diamonds, diamonds weighing about 1.52 cts., hinged shank, size 6 3/4 (ILLUS.) **$2,703**

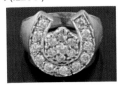

Horseshoe-shaped Man's Diamond Ring

Ring, man's fashion-type, diamond & 14k yellow & white gold, the top in the shape of a large horseshoe set w/a band of round cut diamonds & enclosing a clusters of diamonds, diamond mélées 1.50 cts. (ILLUS.) **$960**

Fine Man's Diamond & Gold Ring

Ring, man's fashion-type, diamond & 18k yellow gold, a 1 ct. round brilliant cut diamond set in a square of white gold, the shank in yellow gold w/accent machining down the sides, stamped "18k Jabel," Jabel Ring Manufacturing Company, Newark., New Jersey (ILLUS.) **$2,520**

Man's Sapphire, Diamond & Gold Ring

Ring, man's, sapphire, diamond, platinum & 18k gold, the wide stippled gold band bezel-set at the top w/a round faceted blue sapphire weighing 2.57 cts., flanked by mélée bands of 10 round full-cut diamonds down the sides (ILLUS.) **$598**

Ring, opal & 14k gold, the bezel-set white opal carved w/leaves & berries, shoulders w/applied bead & wirework designs, size 6 .. **$411**

Opal, Diamond & Emerald Ring

Ring, opal, diamond, emerald & 18k gold, the top centered by a large oval cabochon white opal framed by a mixed band of marquise-cut emeralds & full-cut diamonds, size 5 1/2 (ILLUS.) **$529**

Rare Orange Sapphire & Diamond Ring

Ring, orange sapphire, diamond & 18k gold, the top centered by an oval-cut orange sapphire w/pink tones framed by 36 full-cut diamonds weighing about 2.52 cts., size 6 3/4 (ILLUS.) **$11,750**

Extraordinary Pink & Clear Diamond Ring

Ring, pink & colorless diamond & 18k rose gold, the top centered by a square step-cut fancy deep pink diamond weighing about .90 cts., gold side bands flank panels pavé-set w/full-cut colorless diamonds weighing about 1.38 cts., size 5 1/2 (ILLUS.) **$44,650**

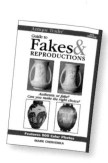